D0680578

After Apartheid

After Apartheid
Renewal of the
South African Economy

EDITED BY

John Suckling & Landeg White

Centre for Southern African Studies
University of York

CENTRE FOR SOUTHERN AFRICAN STUDIES
UNIVERSITY OF YORK
In association with
JAMES CURREY
AFRICA WORLD PRESS

The Centre for Southern African Studies
University of York, Heslington, York YO1 5DD

in association with

James Currey Ltd
54b Thornhill Square, Islington, London N1 1BE

Africa World Press
PO Box 1892
Trenton, New Jersey 08608

British Library Cataloguing in Publication Data
After apartheid : political renewal of the
    South African economy.
    1. south Africa. Economic development
    I. Suckling, John
330.968

ISBN 0-85255-109-X
ISBN 0-85255-110-X Pbk

Library of Congress Catalog Card Number: 88-71830

ISBN: 0-86543-112-4 Cloth
        0-86543-113-2 Paper

Typeset by Opus 43
Printed in Great Britain by Villiers Publications London N6

Contents

	List of Tables & Diagrams	vii
	Introduction	ix
	Contributors	xv
1	Fuad Cassim *Growth, Crisis and Change in the* *South African Economy*	1
2	Terence Moll *'The Limits of the Possible': Macro-economic Policy* *and Income Redistribution in Latin America and* *South Africa*	19
3	Colin Murray *The Political Economy of Forced Relocation:* *A Study of Two Households Through Time*	36
4	David Cooper *Ownership and Control of Agriculture* *in South Africa*	47
5	A Rural Community Worker *Land Use and the Community: A Case Study*	66
6	Daryl Glaser *Regional Development in South Africa:* *Towards an Alternative?*	76
7	Georgina Jaffee & Collette Caine *The incorporation of African Women into the* *Industrial Workforce: Its Implications for the* *Women's Question in South Africa*	90

8 Jesmond Blumenfeld
*Investment, Savings and the Capital Market
in South Africa* 109

Colin Stoneman
A Rejoinder to Blumenfeld 126

9 C. M. Rogerson
Late Apartheid and the Urban Sector 132

10 James Cobbe
Economic Policy Issues in the Education Sector 146

11 Peter Robbins
The South African Mining Industry After Apartheid 163

12 Rob Davies
*Nationalisation, Socialisation and
the Freedom Charter* 173

13 Vishnu Padayachee
*The Politics of International Economic Relations:
South Africa and the International Monetary Fund,
1975 and Beyond* 191

Appendix A 205
Appendix B 208
Index 211

List of Tables and Diagrams

TABLES

1.1 Composition and growth of GDP in South Africa 16
1.2 Unemployment rates in South Africa, 1960−82 16
1.3 Average capital:labour and capital:output ratios for the economy
as a whole and for manufacturing industry (constant 1970 prices) 16
1.4 Balance of payments − current account summary 17
1.5 Terms of trade (1975 = 100) 17
1.6 South Africa's foreign liabilities at the end of 1981 18
1.7 Government foreign issues and foreign holdings of domestic
non-marketable stock (R million) 18
4.1 Private ownership of land in South Africa outside bantustans,
according to race 47
4.2 Number and area of white owned farms, according to
type of ownership 48
4.3 Value and index of volume growth of agriculture by sector 1950−85 48
4.4 Number of farm units 1950−85 49
4.5 Subsidies to agriculture (R million) 49
4.6 Expenditure on short-term requisites (R million) 1950−85 51
4.7 Gross capital formation − investment in fixed improvements,
tractors and machinery, and numbers of tractors imported 51
4.8 Gross land values in South Africa 51
4.9 Index of values of land in recent years in different sectors,
compared with index of producer prices 52
4.10 Agricultural debt 52
4.11 Value of imports and exports into agriculture (R million) 52
4.12 Rural population, level of employment and remuneration on
white farms, 1980 55
7.1 Percentage of economically active women aged 15-59 in the South
African labour force by racial group 93
7.2 Women as a percentage of the labour force by industrial sector 94
7.3 Percentage of African female workforce in selected occupations 94
7.4 Percentage of women by racial group in food, textiles and clothing,
1980, and average monthly wage 95
8.1 Financial balances, 1970−84 (R Million) 121
8.2 Private corporate enterprises: uses of funds (1970−84) (R million) 122

10.1 African pupil enrolment by standard, 1983   155
10.2 Pupil progression rates by race, Std 1 to Std 10   156
10.3 Pupil progression rates by race, Std 6 to Std 10   156
10.4 Pupil:teacher ratios   156
10.5 Total education expenditures, 1984/5   156
10.6 Per pupil recurrent expenditure, 1983/4   157
10.7 Projections of matriculation results   157
10.8 Projections of relative probabilities of persons aged 15 to 19 years
      old of passing matriculation   158
10.9 Qualifications of African teachers, 1983 (Excluding TBVC)   158
10.10 Enrolments, 1977−84   159
10.11 Teachers, 1979−83   160
10.12 Apparent pupil progression rates   160
10.13 Portions of 1985 Zimbabwe education salary scales   161
10.14 Education expenditures   161
10.15 Number of schools of different types   161

DIAGRAMS

Figure 3.1   Household MM Onverwacht   40
Figure 3.2   Household MT Onverwacht   41

Introduction

The contributors to this volume are concerned with the range of problems which a South African government responsive to the demands of its people will have to confront in the period following national liberation.

Since Soweto 1976, the deepening crisis in South Africa has spawned a vast number of books. Some have been documentary, a necessary exercise given the ferocity of censorship within South Africa and the international dimension of the struggle. Some have been historical, South African historiography coming of age in major reassessments of the roles of capital, labour and black resistance from the mid-nineteenth century to the present day. Among the most influential and harrowing have been investigations into the social affairs of apartheid — notably the encyclopaedic report of the Surplus People's Project (1983; Platzky and Walker, 1985) and the papers tabled at the Second Carnegie Inquiry into Poverty and Development in Southern Africa in 1984 (see Wilson, 1986 and Wilson and Ramphele, 1987). Finally, as with all countries in crisis, South Africa has attracted the political futurologists. From R.W. Johnson's *How Long Will South Africa Survive?* (1977) to Robin Cohen's *Endgame in South Africa?* (1986), there has been a steady flow of monographs projecting political, constitutional and diplomatic scenarios for a surrender of power by the present regime.

To these debates, economists have so far made little contribution. With honourable exceptions, including most notably those associated with the Second Carnegie Inquiry, they have by and large been preoccupied more with the current slump than with economic growth, with crisis management than with radical reconstruction. Those venturing into political arenas have been concerned with the intricacies of the sanctions debate, or with the question of whether apartheid does or does not serve as an effective instrument of capital. In this latter area, the most recent study has been Merle Lipton's *Capitalism and Apartheid: South Africa 1910-84* (1985) which from an avowedly liberal-capitalist perspective attempts to persuade business that apartheid has always been a dubious ally and that it is time capital cemented an alliance with black nationalism. The book has been immensely influential in British business circles but it was notable that no contributor to the York conference found it useful to refer to it. Nor did the current Economist Intelligence Unit report *South Africa to 1990: Growing to Survive* (March 1986) feature in discussions. More urgent matters were at stake than the need to secure British capital.

It is one of the tragedies of independent Africa that the trajectory of liberation struggles in the context of colonial capitalism has compelled a shelving of debates about future economic policies. All too often, the result has been to leave newly installed governments helplessly dependent on 'expert' advice and non-African models — whether derived from London or Washington or Moscow or Sofia! By the time local economists have begun to research local issues, they have found themselves outmanoeuvred, their role reduced to radical critiques of already entrenched policies (see, for example, Mandeza, 1987). In country after country, governments and university departments of economics have ceased to be on speaking terms within two years of independence.

It is not, of course, for academics meeting at a British university to devise policies for a liberated South Africa. Delegates to the conference where some of these chapters were first tabled were forcibly and repeatedly reminded that the ANC draws its legitimacy from popular struggle within South Africa and that economic policy is adequately laid out for present purposes in the relevant clauses of the Freedom Charter (see Appendix A).

What economists can do, and it is their job to do it, is to indicate the fundamental economic problem which the post-apartheid government will face, namely, that popular demands on that government will exceed the resources available to it. In making immediate decisions under extreme pressure to alleviate equally immediate needs, the government will be setting precedents and establishing institutions perhaps contradictory to its long-term aims. The reputation of economics as 'the dismal science' (or in Marx's terms 'that load of shit') may stem in part from its gloomy insistence that hard political decisions often have to be made, decisions which popularly elected politicians would rather avoid.

In the selection which follows, no attempt is made to predict the course of the struggle over the immediate future. Our starting point is the assumption that the South African economy has survived the transfer of power relatively undamaged and that the options a government responsive to popular demands will face in the future are largely those it would face the day after tomorrow. The disadvantages of such an approach are manifest. But it does have one supreme advantage, that of focussing minds on the formidable and unprecedented problems of dismantling the structures and abolishing the consequences of apartheid.

The case for redistribution is overwhelming, most starkly symbolised by the 87%-13% division of the land with its well-known consequences of poverty and deprivation. The Carnegie Commission found that of all those families living below the measure of poverty, 80% were in the reserves and a further 13-14% on the platteland. But even for those in urban wage employment, the gap between black and white incomes remains at a ratio of one to four, and even this contrast understates the true division of income. White wages are supplemented in a variety of ways — from fringe benefits of employment, from state expenditure on education and health, from unequal ownership of assets such as land, property, shares and pensions as well as human capital. Whites dominate government and parastatal employment and gain from firm-employee agreements and the general framework of racial discrimination. In all these areas, blacks are disadvantaged while black wage rates are further affected by much higher dependency ratios and by the removal of subsidies on basic foodstuffs, commuter transport and housing which have hit black purchasing power.

Moll's paper draws on the examples of Argentina under Peron, Chile under

Frei and Allende and Peru between 1948 and 1975 to discuss the most efficient means of achieving a degree of redistribution without undermining macro-economic objectives. The experience of Latin America suggests that redistributive measures have a highly selective impact on the poor, partly because the poor are precisely those excluded from the 'modern' sector of the economy and hence difficult to reach by economic measures, and partly because such benefits as were distributed were rapidly overtaken by inflation and balance of payment crises. Even the most efficient means of alleviating poverty, through increasing social spending on housing, education, health and pensions, ran the risk of extreme urban bias and of being appropriated by the politically active middle classes. Moll's conclusions are too well-considered to be summarised here but they contain a warning, that 'it seems preferable to view the Freedom Charter as a statement of long-run policy goals while recognising that trade-offs and compromises are inevitable in the short run'.

The remaining papers represent attempts at just such an investigation and it is striking how much less formidable many of the problems appear when considered separately. This is particularly evident in those areas (for example, the implications of rural protest over 'betterment' schemes or of women's increasing voice in trade unions) where writers feel able to put trust in the good sense of popular demand. As Cassim remarks, the 'task cannot be separated from the people, for it is in their strength and potential that the future lies'.

Similarly, Colin Murray's paper of the complexities of removing what Cosmas Desmond calls 'the cornerstone of the whole edifice of apartheid' (1985, xviii), namely the forced relocation of three and a half million people, is informed throughout by an awareness of real people living real lives behind and within the language of analysis. He presents two case studies from the Onverwacht relocation slum in the eastern Orange Free State. Together, they illustrate not only the extremes of economic deprivation, the 'desperate struggle for jobs and housing' suffered by apartheid's worst victims, but demonstrate more profoundly the 'fundamental interconnectedness of all sectors of the economy — "white" farming, mining and manufacturing industry, domestic and other services, and poverty in the bantustans'.

Three papers, by David Cooper, Daryl Glaser and by a black community worker (who significantly prefers to remain anonymous), deal with current ownership of land and the need for radical land reforms to increase both productivity and employment, with the prospects for regional development in the context of the need for a regional policy, and with the importance of community organisation coupled with a spirit of self-reliance. The same emphasis informs the paper by Georgina Jaffee and Collette Caine on the incorporation of African women into the industrial workforce. Acknowledging the continuing role of the trade unions in manoeuvring the South African economy towards a system of industrial democracy, they demonstrate, with a wealth of data, the degree to which women's rights are still underrepresented on the trade union agenda.

Implicit in the papers covering aspects of redistribution of land and income is the need to create conditions for future growth. Jesmond Blumenfeld (with a rejoinder by Colin Stoneman) examines the capacity of the capital market to generate, mobilise and allocate savings on the scale required, focussing in particular on savings in the private corporate, public corporate, general government and housing sectors and arguing that without an annual growth rate in the region of 5.5% and without access to international capital markets, redistribution policies will not be viable. Chris Rogerson explores issues relating to the capacity of the urban informal sector to generate employment opportunities. With current unemployment estimated at anything between 600,000 and 3 million and with further estimates that the number of new job seekers will be in the region of 300,000 *per annum* to the year 2000, the problem is among the most urgent the new government will confront. Rogerson argues that whether officially encouraged or not the informal sector *will* exist and that under a wise government unleashing 'the inherent economic dynamism of urban small-scale enterprise' it could contribute significantly both to employment and to low-cost training.

Training is the subject of James Cobbe's survey of economic policy issues in the education sector. Recognising the inherent conservatism of most educational systems and the dangers involved in making radical changes — the danger, for instance, that the rich and powerful will simply opt out, undermining resources — Cobbe maps out in considerable detail a possible future system: eight years free compulsory primary education, four years free selective secondary education, and two years compulsory but paid National Service. The costs of post-primary education, including those of university and teaching training, would be recovered through a tax on subsequent earnings. Drastic as this scheme sounds, it 'may be the only way in which a continuing crisis of conscience and policy choice over issues of equity, finance and access in the education system in post-apartheid South Africa can be avoided'. (It should be noted that his paper does not consider the content of education, debate about which has begun under the head of the 'people's education' and which might have different economic implications (see Adler, 1986).)

Peter Robbins and Rob Davies are equally forthright on the subject of the ownership and control of South African industries. Pointing out that the mining sector has as much to do with banking and fiscal policy-making as it does with industrial strategy. Robbins shows that the structures of interlocking directorships means that general mining policy 'is almost certainly made by less than 100 men'. Public ownership in a future South Africa will be easier to accomplish due to this high degree of centralised control. The main problems will arise from controlling corruption ('endemic in the mining industry') especially in the marketing of minerals, and in improving technical skills. Meanwhile, it is important to get the record straight: a new government 'should be ready with a complete dossier of the mismanagement by mining companies and its anti-worker record together with its failure to take advantage of market movements'. Rob Davies, in a closely parallel paper, examines the prospects for 'nationalisation' or 'socialisation' across a broad range of the South African economy including banks, insurance and agriculture as well as mining and other industries. He charts the increasing concentration of capital in South Africa since 1973, and draws some conclusions from Mozambique after 1975 about the relative success of workers' production councils. Like Robbins, he sees the central structure of monopoly control as facilitating public ownership. State action, however, will have to be complemented by the actions of workers organised at the point of production if a socialist transformation is to be achieved.

Finally, Vishnu Padayachee examines the politics of international economic relations, discussing in particular the likely future role of the IMF. Behind its cloak of neutrality, Padayachee argues, the IMF in recent years has acted as an instrument of western industrial capitalist interests. No future South African government, especially not one committed to a two-stage model of the transformation from apartheid to socialism, could afford to ignore the IMF's capacity 'both to subvert the goals of a mixed economy form of development and to break this transition from a mixed economy to socialism'. If there is a solution to this problem, it will lie in developing a future regional market in southern Africa and 'in the use of physical controls and planning — in foreign exchange allocation, foreign trade policy, import budgeting and credit and investment budgeting'.

As will be clear from these summaries, the contributors to this book sometimes differ in their vision of the southern African economy after apartheid, and given that the economic debate is in its earliest stage we have not attempted to impose an editorial consensus. From the radical liberals to the scientific socialists, however, all have three things in common. First and foremost, all writers accept that the parameters of debate about the southern African economy after apartheid are laid out in the economic clauses of the Freedom Charter. Secondly, all writers show a willingness to learn from the experience of other developing countries — in Latin America, Asia and Europe — and for the first time in recent years this includes a willingness to learn from independent Africa. Radical opinion in South Africa has not always been noted for taking the 'front-line' states as seriously as they deserve. Yet despite obvious contrasts in the scale of industrialisation and proletarianisation, independent African states have now accumulated up to three decades of experience of dealing with international capital and of managing nationalist or multi-ethnic coalitions, and South Africans will neglect this experience at their peril. Thirdly, all contributors recognise the urgent need for further research with several writers identifying specific projects.

Five specific areas require urgent attention. A strategy for job creation in both formal and informal sectors, catering for present unemployment and future population growth, would go far to resolve many of the difficulties discussed in this book. There is a need to investigate further the present structure of capital in South Africa, with implications for the future control of capital, the role of foreign investment, access to technology, and the objectives of nationalisation/socialisation. A future industrial strategy, identifying vertical and horizontal linkages together with the tariff policies needed where protection will be appropriate, needs to be spelt out given the critical connections between industrialisation, growth and employment. A foreign exchange regime should be developed which facilitates foreign trade and investment without sacrificing economic autonomy. Lastly, a social accounting matrix (SAM) analysis, if constantly updated, would be useful in pointing out the links between income distribution, the structure of output and production, and factor prices in the economy.

There is a need to coordinate research of the various bodies interested in the problem; for example the Southern African Economic Research and Training Project in Amsterdam, the Scandinavian Institute of African Studies in Uppsala, and of course the Centre here in York. More generally, there is a need to monitor and update information on economic change in South Africa, together with a need to identify skill shortages and to set up training programmes to meet these shortages. To these tasks, effort should now be directed.

REFERENCES

ADLER, D., 1986, 'Education and training for and in South Africa beyond apartheid'. Paper presented to the Conference on 'The Southern African Economy After Apartheid', York, September 1986.

ANONYMOUS, 1986. 'Broadening the agenda: COSATU Resolution on Women'. *Southern African Report 2* (1), pp.9-13.

CARNEGIE INQUIRY INTO POVERTY AND DEVELOPMENT IN SOUTHERN AFRICA, 1986. *Second Carnegie Inquiry . . . Conference Papers.* Rondebosch, University of Cape Town, Southern Africa Labour and Development Research Unit.

COHEN, R., 1986. *Endgame in South Africa?.* London, James Currey.

DESMOND, C., 1986. 'Foreword'. pp.xvii-xix in L. Platzky and C. Walker, *The Surplus People: Forced Removals in South Africa.* Johannesburg, Ravan Press.

DEWAR, D., TODES, A. and WATSON, V., 1983. 'Development from below? Basic needs, rural service centers and the South African Bantustans, with particular reference to the Transkei'. *African Urban Studies 15* (Winter), pp.59-75.

ECONOMIST INTELLIGENCE UNIT, 1986. *South Africa to 1990: Growing to Survive.* London, The Unit.

HORRELL, M., 1978. *Laws Affecting Race Relations in South Afica, to the End of 1976.* Johannesburg, South African Institute of Race Relations.

JOHNSON, R.W., 1977. *How Long Will South Africa Survive?* London, Macmillan.

LIPTON, M. 1986. *Capitalism and Apartheid: South Africa, 1910-1986.* Aldershot, Wildwood House, Inc. (First published Gower, 1985).

MANDAZA, I. (ed.), 1987. *Zimbabwe: the Political Economy of Transition, 1980-1986.* Dakar, CODESRIA Book Service.

MACMILLAN, H., 1986. 'Economists, separate development and the "common society" '. Paper presented to the Conference on 'The Southern African Economy After Apartheid'. York, September 1986.

PLATZKY, L. 1986. In Southern African Research Service (ed.), *South Africa Review: Three.* Johannesburg, Ravan Press.

PLATZKY, L. and WALKER, C., 1985. *The Surplus People: Forced Removals in South Africa.* Johannesburg, Ravan Press.

SAIRR, 1954-55. *A Survey of Race Relations in South Africa, 1954-55.* Johannesburg, South African Institute of Race Relations.

SIMKINS, C., 1983. *Four Essays on the Past, Present and Possible Future of the Black Population of South Africa.* Rondebosch, University of Cape Town, Southern Africa Labour and Development Research Unit.

SURPLUS PEOPLES' PROJECT, 1983. *The SPP Reports: Forced Removals in South Africa.* 5 vols. Cape Town, The Project.

WILSON, F. (ed.), 1986. *South Africa: The Cordoned Heart.* New York, London, W.W. Norton and Co. Inc.; Newlands, S.A., The Gallery Press.

WILSON, F and RAMPHELE, M., 1987. *Towards Reconstruction in South Africa.* Cape Town, David Philip.

Contributors

Jesmond Blumenfeld, Department of Economics, Brunel University, London, U.K.

Collette Caine, Department of Sociology, University of the Witwatersrand, Johannesburg, R.S.A.

Fuad Cassim, Department of Economics, University of the Witwatersrand, Johannesburg, R.S.A.

James Cobbe, Department of Economics, The Florida State University, Tallahassee, Florida, U.S.A.

David Cooper, Environmental and Development Agency, Johannesburg, R.S.A.

Rob Davies, Centro de Estados Africanos, Universidade Eduardo Mondlane, Maputo, Mozambique.

Daryl Glaser, Department of Sociology, University of the Witwatersrand, Johannesburg, R.S.A.

Georgina Jaffee, Department of Sociology, University of the Witwatersrand, Johannesburg, R.S.A.

Terence Moll, School of Economics, University of Cape Town, Cape Town, R.S.A.

Colin Murray, Department of Public Administration, University of Liverpool, Liverpool, U.K.

Vishnu Padayachee, The Institute for Social and Economic Research, University of Durban-Westville, Durban, R.S.A.

Peter Robbins, Third World Information Network, London, U.K.

C.M. Rogerson, Department of Geography, University of the Witwatersrand, Johannesburg, R.S.A.

Colin Stoneman, Centre for Southern African Studies, University of York, York, U.K.

John Suckling, Centre for Southern African Studies, University of York, York, U.K.

Landeg White, Centre for Southern African Studies, University of York, York, U.K.

1. Growth, Crisis and Change in the South African Economy[1]

FUAD CASSIM

INTRODUCTION

This chapter provides an overview of current developments and underlying trends in the South African economy. The role of government policies in the structural failure of the South African growth pattern under apartheid is analysed by examining, at a descriptive level, movements in industrial production, trade and the balance of payments. The chapter ends by looking at the alternatives facing a 'post-apartheid society'.

The assessment is pessimistic. A cumulative deterioration of economic performance has led almost all schools of thought to see the chronic state of the South African economy in terms of 'collapse' or 'catastrophe'. Current difficulties, whether measured in terms of unemployment, inflation, falling output, increasing debt or bankruptcy, warrant the term 'crisis', in that ' ... in order for accumulation to continue, some sort of restructuring of the accumulation process is necessary. ...'[2]

The current crisis may be seen as the outcome of the interaction of four forces: a general recession in the world economy since the 1970s;[3] a specific structural malady of the South African economy characterised by low productivity growth and investment relative to the 1960s; a set of specific government policies which have had the effect of worsening the slump; and an unprecedented political crisis, which has seriously undermined the internal and external legitimacy of the regime.

THE SOUTH AFRICAN ECONOMY: A BRIEF OVERVIEW

The South African economy is classified by the World Bank in the category of developing 'higher middle-income countries' such as South Korea, Brazil, Argentina and Algeria. The single most important sector is manufacturing. The economy has grown rapidly from 1950 onwards through industrialisation, with manufacturing contributing 23% of GDP in 1980, compared with 14% in 1946. In contrast, agriculture's contribution fell from 13% in 1946 to 5% in 1983. As a whole, the share of the primary sector in GDP declined from 31.7% in 1950 to 18.4% in 1984, while the share of the secondary sector rose from 14.1% to 25.5% over the same period (see Table 1.1).

Mining and agricultural exports are the underlying basis of the economy in terms of both aggregate demand and the surplus generated for reinvestment in other sectors. These effects are subsumed in the key role of supplying foreign exchange to what is by any standards an extremely open economy. For example, mining contributed on average only 11% to GDP in 1985, but was responsible for 70% of foreign exchange earnings.

A parallel feature of the output pattern is the pattern of demand. First, international markets for export products are dominated by capital imports from the metropolitan economies, which means that expansion of mining production has always been easier than attempts to export manufactures, particularly if foreign investors are involved. Second, internal consumption demand is highly concentrated in the white sector. The location of manufacturing plant and spatial allocation of the workforce are immediate consequences of the narrow-based demand pattern, with 80% of production taking place in four metropolitan areas. An important effect is to sustain a particular style of consumption which relies for its satisfaction upon foreign technology, 'modern goods' (such as cars and televisions) and imported brand names, thus justifying the presence of multinational corporations in the postwar period.

The changes in the pattern of output reflect a period of unbalanced growth and associated political crises. The rapid expansion in the 1950s was inhibited by the political events of 1960 and 1961, but by 1962, the forces making for expansion were on the move again with the state playing a major role. The annual growth rate in real GDP over the periods 1962-72, 1972-81 and 1982 onwards was 5.5%, 3% and negative respectively. The three points of major economic disequilibrium were also those of political crisis in 1961, 1976 and 1984. Whilst simple causality is not inferred in these events, these crises certainly did influence political events by heightening class and racial conflict.

THE CURRENT RECESSION: THE SHORT TERM

The current economic recession which threatens to be more serious and persistent than any other in South African economic history indicates a decisive break with the relatively stable growth of the Sixties. At the end of 1981 the South African economy entered a major recession. Policy makers claimed that the solution to this decline lay in certain policy changes. However, since then inflation has not abated, output and investment have slumped, and an unprecedented foreign debt crisis has further constrained the balance of payments. The question as to who is responsible is important. It will be argued that as a result of the policies of this government, the malaise of the South African economy is iatrogenic — the disease has been induced in the patient by the physicians. In the final analysis, it is both the policies and the framework which constitute the problem.

Let us examine some indices of the crisis. In the most superficial sense, the contemporary problems of the economy can be characterised in terms of a decrease in annual growth rates of GDP, as the figures below show:

Growth Rates of Real GDP

1980	1981	1982	1983	1984	1985
7.8	5.1	-0.9	-3.3	4.7	-1.1

The decline in the rate of growth of GDP since the end of 1981 has resulted in a slowdown of demand. The negative rate of growth since 1982 means that per capita income must be falling. Unemployment rates have risen dramatically. Simkins's estimates indicate an upward trend in the unemployment rate, reaching 22.5% in 1982 (see Table 1.2).

To understand why demand deaccelerated in the economy, we need to look at the broad objectives of the government's economic policy, the measures used to achieve those objectives, and finally the effects on companies in South Africa. Financial reforms, started in March 1980, included the abolishing of deposit rate controls and ceilings on bank credits. Interest rates were relatively free: whereas real long-term rates were negative for much of the 1960s and 1970s, this position was reversed in the 1980s. The state's economic managers expected that the liberalisation of the domestic financial market, accompanied by the gradual opening of finance to the external sector, would lead to an increase in saving and investment. The result has been markedly different and places financial reform at the heart of the crisis that surfaced subsequently.

During the latter part of the Seventies, the government committed itself to the defeat of inflation as its primary goal, as part of a wider programme for restoring market forces as the basis for achieving growth. The government adopted a two-pronged strategy. On the one hand this aimed at controlling the supply of money to reduce inflation. On the other hand, an attempt was made to control government expenditure, to reduce the deficit before borrowing. So the policy decision was to restrict money supply and cut borrowing. This, it was argued, would inhibit monetary growth and also lower interest rates.

Reducing the growth of the money supply raised the cost of borrowing.[4] Bank rate increased from 9.5% to 17% in the course of 1981, rose immediately to 18% and subsequently rose to 20% through most of 1982, reaching an unprecedented rate of 25% in August 1985.

This policy had a crippling effect on industrial and commercial companies in South Africa. A large number of companies were unable to cope with the impact of interest rate increases on their cost structure. In particular, inventory demand in the company sector fell dramatically. Total investment in inventories fell from R1,562 million in 1981 to -R836 million in 1982, of which industrial and commercial inventories fell from R775 million to -R829 million.

For companies running large overdrafts, the government's monetary policy, and the interest rises which it entailed, was a disaster. At the same time, companies faced increased wage and salary costs. With costs rising fast, something had to give, and it was company profits. The rate of return on U.S. manufacturing investments in South Africa declined from 31.7% in 1980 to a reported loss of $143 million in 1984.[5] Many firms began making losses. In the period 1980-85 bankruptcies increased by 500%.

Firms responded by reducing current output and stocks. This reduction led to massive retrenchments in the workforce. The objective for firms was to lower running costs and to reduce bank debt, but the effect was to create a recession. The government had, in effect, created this response by attacking the financial positions of companies.

So a monetary policy resulting in high interest rates produced an immediate recession. However, the rise in interest rates did not produce a capital inflow since the austerity measures had shaken investor confidence due to the squeeze on company profits and liquidity. The impact on saving and investment was equally severe. From 1981 to 1984 the ratio of real gross domestic fixed investment to GDP declined from 27.2% to 24.6%, and the ratio of gross domestic saving to GDP from 28.6% to 22.8%.

Two trends characterise the response to the crisis: first, the rise in speculative activity and, secondly, the rise of mergers and takeovers that increase the concentration of capital. With total output in the economy falling, the demand for funds in the economy, particularly since 1980, has been for purchase of assets in the property market and stock exchange, resulting in an unprecedented expansion of the financial sector. Activity in the financial sphere is largely reflected in existing assets rather than new assets, or real productive activity, as reflected by the upward climb of indices on the Johannesburg Stock Exchange.

A basic feature of the South African economy is monopoly, which has been enhanced by the recent wave of mergers. Early in 1982, two of South Africa's leading sugar producers, Tongaat and Huletts, merged, giving rise to a R1,000 million company, which brings the sugar industry under the control of Anglo American. Soon thereafter, the formation of Anglo American Life Assurance resulted in the creation of another R1,000 million company. Barlows' C.G. Smith company took control of Tiger Oats, thus strengthening the relationship between the two giants, Anglo and Barlows. By April 1982, 45% of the total market capitalisation of the top one hundred industrial companies was controlled by ten of them.[6] It was estimated in 1983 that seven companies controlled 80% of the value of the R90 billion shares listed on the Johannesburg Stock Exchange.[7]

Alongside this process is an equally large number of divestitures, whereby corporations sell assets of less profitable subsidiaries to streamline their operations, or they divest to raise cash and reduce their commitments to the domestic economy. Since the beginning of 1985, about 46 United States firms with 7,815 local employees have ceased operations in South Africa or sold their equity in South African subsidiaries.[8] Structural change proceeds through a combination of diversifications into more profitable industries and divestiture/disinvestment of assets in unprofitable industries. The 'restructuring' of capital in the South African economy is not simply a uniform process of centralisation and concentration, but is simultaneously accompanied by the divestiture of capital.

The other crucial element in the government's economic strategy has been an attempt to control and reduce government spending. The argument here was that government spending was excessive, both inhibiting the operation of the free-market economy by distorting demand, and raising interest rates and fuelling inflation through government borrowing. The government has not succeeded in its attempt to cut expenditure, but has redistributed it away from such areas as social welfare towards defence. This has altered the pattern of government demand for goods and services.

Economic policy since the inception of the Nationalist government has continued the interventionist trend that characterised economic development since the mid-1920s. The application of market oriented policies was heralded in the Wiehahn Report (1979) and the De Kock Commission on exchange rates. Generally the shift has been from a detailed regulation of certain markets to a general withdrawal and greater reliance on the private sector and spontaneous market forces.

The shift in policy heavily influenced by monetarist ideology has subsequently had an acute destabilising effect on output, employment and income. In particular, the production base has narrowed. The consequence has been to benefit speculative activity to the detriment of production and investment. The presence of destabilising forces in the adjustment processes has exacerbated costs in the social and economic dimension.

THE INDUSTRIAL DECLINE

Manufacturing industry is the sector of most rapid and sustained output growth in the economy and is central to economic development. Manufacturing growth has come from three sources — increasing domestic demand, import substitution and export demand. In South Africa its growth has been characterised by a durable goods sector and it does not yet possess a true 'capital goods' branch.

The most significant structural change in the manufacturing sector took place in the late Sixties as part of the process of import-substituting industrialisation. Much of the growth in the subsequent phase utilised excess capacity. Moreover, the particular manner of industrialisation involved a dominant role for foreign firms and technology, with capital-intensive output geared towards the needs of a narrow market. In consequence, even though manufacturing emerged as the largest single production sector it remained concentrated spatially, providing relatively sophisticated goods for a minority of the population without being integrated into the rest of the economic structure, and heavily reliant on imports for its input requirements. From 1919 to 1976, the growth of industrial output averaged 5.9% per annum in real terms.

The annual growth rate of manufacturing output which, at 8% p.a., reached record levels for the period 1960 to 1968, declined to 6% between 1967 and 1975. Subsequently it declined further. The boom of the Sixties transformed manufacturing into the leading and most important sector, accounting for 24% of GDP in 1970, though the protection it enjoyed through import tariffs also became very expensive as the deteriorating balance of payments showed. As manufacturing growth slowed down, so did the overall rate of growth of output and employment.

Over the decade 1973-83, output increased by only 3.2% p.a., whereas the capital stock expanded at a rate of 5.6% p.a. Over the ten-year period capacity utilisation averaged 86% in manufacturing, explaining in part the decline in productivity growth of capital. Labour productivity, on the other hand, recorded a positive growth over the past decade, although at a low rate of only 0.8% p.a.[9] The prime cause was the shortage of skilled labour in the 1960s and the resulting increase in the capital:labour ratio.

However, when the rate of growth of productivity falls short of the increase in the capital:labour ratio, the capital:output ratio rises, and thus tends to reduce the rate of profit.[10] The initial growth of the capital:labour ratio led to an improvement in labour productivity and, initially, to a decline in the capital: output ratio. But as changes in technology became more costly in terms of capital, the capital:output ratio began to rise, more than offsetting gains in productivity (see Table 1.3).

The fall in real manufacturing investment was most pronounced between the middle of 1980 and late 1984. From 1980 total fixed investment had fallen from R2,346 million to R1,408 million in 1984. The index of the physical volume of manufacturing production decreased from its peak of 135.6 in 1981 to 119.6 in 1985. There was a 50% fall in the output of the motor vehicles and other transport equipment sector and at least a 30% fall in the semi-durable and capital-goods sectors.

This decline in output has been accompanied by falls in employment. Though the manufacturing sector is seen as the key generator of employment, and though manufacturing employment doubled from 644,000 to 1,238,000 from 1960-80, employment growth fell from 5% p.a. between 1958 and 1977 to 3.3% between 1968 and 1977. Between 1981 and 1985, manufacturing actually lost 20,000 jobs. The sectors that showed significant employment growth have been the mining sector, financial services, and the institutions and the state sector.

In the popular conception, 'deindustrialisation' appears to be undercutting the foundation of the industrial structure in South Africa. However, the notion of deindustrialisation for an open economy may be analytically inadequate in that a decline in manufacturing employment, or even output, or a fall in their rate of growth may reflect no more than a normal adjustment of the economy to changes in the domestic and world market conditions. Thus, the question as to whether deindustrialisation in this sense implies any structural maladjustment of the economy can be understood in terms of the interactions of the domestic economy with the rest of the world, i.e. in terms of its overall trading and payments position in the world economy. Singh defines an efficient manufacturing sector as 'one which currently, as well as potentially, not only satisfies the demands of consumers at home, but is able to sell enough of its products abroad to pay for the nation's import requirements'.[11] So the link between the domestic and external sectors must be examined.

THE EXTERNAL SECTOR

In the postwar period, there was a tremendous expansion of manufacturing behind import controls and tariff barriers. From 1946-71, South Africa had almost continuous deficits on the current account of the balance of payments (see Table 1.4). Overall equilibrium was maintained by large capital inflows: during 1946-71 these equalled R3,632 million (despite a net loss of R579 million from 1959-64). The balance of payments had thus become a serious constraint on growth by the late Sixties.

The Reynders Report (1972) attributed this to a basic lack of manufacturing sector competitiveness in export markets. Manufacturing exports were small, about 10% of the gross value of 1970 manufacturing production, and a quarter of total export in 1970. At the same time, manufacturing had become a net user of foreign exchange. The exhaustion of import substitution by the early Seventies led to a reassessment of industrial strategy and an emphasis on the role of exports.

The current account of the balance of payments only improved from a persistent deficit situation when the price of gold rose, providing a temporary balance of payments surplus and masking the crisis facing the economy. The spectacular rise in the gold price from 1978 resulted in huge surpluses in 1979 and 1980, but when the price fell in 1981 a R3 billion deficit resulted, thus indicating the volatility of the balance of payments in reacting to the price of gold (see Table 1.5).

1983 measures towards trade liberalisation and further deregulation of the foreign exchange market did not have the desired impact. The rand shifted from an overvalued to an undervalued position, and the structural problems facing the trade sector were exacerbated. Export volumes declined by 20% between early 1980 and late 1983, and the terms of trade (including gold) worsened by 20% over the same period.

In the 1970s, the world economy entered a period of slow growth and general instability. Growth in the industrialised countries dropped extremely sharply, the volume of world trade contracted, and unemployment rose simultaneously with inflation. The fall in the growth of world trade led to a slowdown in the growth of South African exports, worsening the domestic slump. World trade in manufactures grew by 5.7% in 1979 and by 4.6% in 1980, yet South Africa faced a decline in manufacturing output.

FOREIGN CAPITAL

Foreign investment is crucial to the South African economy, though its pattern has changed over time. In the 1970s the proportion of portfolio and direct investment declined, while that of *loans* increased. The main demand came from public corporations and the government. In 1972 63% of South Africa's foreign liabilities were accounted for by direct investment. By 1977 this had fallen to 41%. Whilst direct investment rose by three-quarters over that period, non-direct investment more than tripled, despite the relative decline of portfolio investment. While the investment-income ratio increased enormously, the domestic savings ratio remained fairly constant. Hence, the demand for investment expenditure could not be met by domestic savings, and public corporations became more reliant on foreign borrowing to finance their investments in the Seventies.

Long-term loans from abroad increased from 20% of foreign liabilities at the end of 1956 to 28% at the end of 1981. Short-term liabilities (to be repaid within 12 months) increased from 16% of foreign liabilities at the end of 1956 to 27% at the end of 1981. Between the end of 1973 and 1981, South Africa's foreign liabilities rose by 212%. As the Nedbank Report shows, 'hard core' foreign liabilities increased by 143% while foreign borrowings more than quadrupled. As Table 1.6 shows, by the end of 1981 total foreign borrowings amounted to R17,972 million.

The government found it increasingly difficult to finance expenditure domestically, which led to greater reliance on foreign sources at the same time as South Africa's standing in world financial markets was seriously affected. Table 1.7 indicates that South Africa's financial crisis is not new: ever since 1974 the increase in foreign issues has been almost entirely an increase in non-marketable stock, i.e. loans rather than bond issues. The net result is that South Africa's foreign debt has been mounting rapidly. The magnitude of borrowing was such that by 1976 the country as a whole was 'overborrowed': its indebtedness to international banks reached the high level of 20% of GDP, a higher ratio than, for example, Chile or Zaire.

To resolve the crisis, the government had to adopt measures to redress the current account imbalance and finance investment from domestic sources. This led to a tightening of credit, an import deposit scheme, cutbacks in government expenditure, and a tightening of exchange control to reduce the capital outflow. Manufacturing output and real wages fell, interest rates and unemployment increased. Imports fell and the balance of payments improved. These deflationary measures drove the economy into deep recession, enabling the government to strengthen its international financial position.

The conclusion that emerges is that this remedy helped to restore the viability of the financial system. The IMF Staff Report (June 1978) on South Africa approved of the policy measures, and suggested that the rand should become a freely floating currency,[12] a suggestion followed up by the De Kock Commission.

In February 1983, South Africa abolished foreign currency control for non-residents, as part of the broader objective contained in the De Kock Commission of emphasising deregulation and, hence, market-related interest and exchange rates. With this, the financial rand disappeared. Non-residents reacted quickly by selling stocks and shares and transferring funds to higher earning assets in America and elsewhere. Demand for US dollars rose and the rand fell against the dollar. Whilst the falling rand helped increase export volumes, the costs of imported raw materials, capital goods and services all increased, as did the rand value of overseas loans, credits and interest payments. The foreign debt burden increased, together with the rate of inflation. From mid-1981 to late 1985, real GDP fell, while foreign debt increased 30% from $18 billion to $23.7 billion. Since 1980 the foreign debt-GDP ratio has more than doubled to about 45%.[13] A high proportion was short-term bank debt, incurred by local companies in the 1980s.

Against this background of deflationary policies, it becomes easier to understand why the Vaal Triangle erupted in September 1984 and unrest spread throughout the country. Political 'ungovernability' was, in fact, preceded by economic mismanagement or rather lack of management and guidance. On 20 July 1985, the government declared a State of Emergency, and as investors began switching funds out of South Africa, imposed a debt freeze and a two-tier exchange rate. At the same time, resistance in the country reached a new stage. Though it has become fashionable to blame political events for the debt crisis, the economic developments outlined must be seen as interacting and intensifying political instability.

The recent pattern of growth of the South African economy has been accompanied by worsening deficits and mounting external indebtedness. The integration of the South African economy into the world economy was based on continued primary export production (in particular, gold) accompanied by import-substitution in which multinational corporations were closely involved. It is clear that this model of accumulation was betraying morbid symptoms by the mid-1970s: the restricted domestic market, the foreign exchange constraint on accumulation, and upward pressure on wages and social expenditure as a result of industrialisation. The slowdown in industrialisation was made worse by the deflationary stabilisation policies and the reduction in the flow of foreign finance.

What does the new model of accumulation look like? The shift from the import substitution or endogenous development of the 1960s to a new development pattern characterised by increased participation of large-scale foreign capital has required access to foreign markets, and increased inputs of foreign capital and technology to achieve higher levels of output. The need for foreign markets arises because of the narrowness of the domestic market resulting from the highly skewed distribution of income. The regulation of the economy through monetary stabilisation, privatisation and deregulated markets aims at a reduction in aggregate demand through a fall in real wages, and at a reduction of both government spending and the budget deficit. This leads to a further concentration of capital caused by bankruptcies of the smaller enterprises whose assets are absorbed by big industrial and financial enterprises. Demand-deflation creates an overstocking crisis which further makes small enterprises more vulnerable. The effect is compounded as trade liberalisation measures remove some of the previous protection enjoyed, rendering firms more uncompetitive. Such a structural change brings about a new form of insertion into the world economy: the export profile of the economy changes from one reliant on primary products to one with a greater share of manufactured goods. However, the structural adjustment is contingent upon an increasing role for foreign capital, because of the economy's modern integration with the international economy.

STRUCTURAL CRISIS — CAPITALISM AND APARTHEID

The nature of the absolute decline that characterises the South African economy can be referred to as a 'structural crisis', meaning that the crisis originates from within the economy. This involves a break in the structurally stable path of accumulation which, in this case, lasted from the end of World War II to the early Seventies.[14]

However, to speak of the structure of the economy is also to refer to its mode of organisation, i.e. the pattern of ownership and wealth, its institutions (financial, business, unions, government agencies, etc.), and its political legal character. Thus, the term 'structural crisis' could embrace a wide variety of features. In this chapter, the term 'crisis' means that South Africa is no longer capable of sustaining the structure of production, employment and trade. It follows that South Africa will not be able to sustain present levels of income and consumption.

Having discussed the process of growth (capital accumulation) at an economic level thus far imposes a limitation on our analysis. Capital accumulation means not only the quantitative growth of the stock of physical capital (i.e. productive capacity) but also, more importantly, the concrete social relations leading to, and resulting from, the economic growth. Instead of restricting the discussion of accumulation to abstract macro-variables such as aggregate investment, production, savings and so on, we need to look at broader social conflicts and the way in which they are generated and/or affected by capital accumulation.

The concept of capital accumulation includes a fundamental element of social and political relations, and therefore does not refer to an economic process only. The process of capital accumulation must be seen as the structural framework within which options for action and policies are opened to social actors. Within the South African context, a unique, specific and persistent feature of the structural framework is the interaction between race (apartheid) and capitalism.

The relationship between apartheid and capitalism has been the subject of intense debate between liberal and marxist schools of thought. The former assert that there exists an incompatibility between apartheid and capitalism, whereas the latter have seen apartheid as an essential factor in the development of capitalism. However, the aim of this chapter is not to review this debate, but rather to suggest that the structural changes which are occurring in South Africa's political economy are generating certain contradictions within the established economic, political and ideological order, and imposing limits and constraints on the role of the state.

Contradictions set in motion forces to modify the system. But modifications through reformist trends have not necessarily or spontaneously stemmed from an advanced stage of growth *per se*: if this were so, they should have appeared ten years ago, in the booming Sixties, though this is not to deny that the continued 'development' of the forces of production has in some ways contributed to such trends. What these trends seem primarily to stem from are historical changes during the 1970s in the overall international, regional and national balance of class power, and in the balance of costs and benefits of contemporary apartheid for capitalism.[15]

Major changes have taken place in the South African political economy. The traditional structure of the economy was based on gold mining and migrant labour, which had the effect of restricting the growth of the domestic market and therefore constituted an impediment to the development of industrial and agricultural capital. At the same time, the largely unskilled migrant labour force could not fill the industrial sector's need for stable, trained and skilled labour. An important contradiction generated here was the fact that migrant labour extracted from the rural areas had the effect of eroding the productive base in the reserves which formed the backdrop of the system. The impact of the system was also to reduce urbanisation costs in housing, education, etc., increase policing costs, and produce a highly unstable workforce.

As the manufacturing sector became more dominant in terms of contribution to GDP and employment, the nature of labour demand changed. Manufacture became interested in a more educated, trained and stable labour force. Significant technological changes have also taken place in agriculture, mining and the financial sectors of the economy. In short, this transformation of the economy has generated economic and political contradictions which call into question the relationship between capitalism and apartheid and the reproduction of apartheid itself.

Pressures which emanate from the economy as a result of structural change have simultaneously led to tensions in the political arena. In more recent times, the restructuring of the division of labour and its partial deracialisation have modified the traditional caricature of apartheid. Political changes entail the recognition of black trade unions, urban black councils, and the tricameral parliament.

The dominance of the Nationalist government has been expressed through its control over the disposition of the country's economic surplus, which has implied the subordination of the mass of the black majority. This required a state that could guarantee stability to business. Once this was achieved and rooted in a whole range of institutional and ideological forms, the special economic surplus extraction features of racial controls in the reserves come to be of secondary importance. Yet the overall system of racial subordination remained intact. This process occurred with the combination of a growing demand for black labour as part of the industrial proletariat.

From the point of view of maintaining national control, the disturbances in the existing order, more so than any other factor, have threatened the dominance and social hegemony of the Nationalist government, not only over the black majority but also over their fellow whites. The threat of disruption in the given pattern of racial accommodation has serious implications because the uncertainty it generates reduces the predictability that is necessary for the long-term operations of business corporations.

Under these conditions the state is unable to maintain an equilibrium. The reformist philosophy of government and business has been one of seeking a dynamic or smoothly shifting racial equilibrium, i.e. a system that attempts to reduce the shocks to a manageable frequency and to incorporate them into the existing order in a non-disruptive manner. Such a strategy can best be pursued by fostering a series of small incremental changes that are mediated by a market mechanism or in non-market spheres.

In general, it can plausibly be suggested that the costs of maintaining the racial order have come home to roost. The crises of contemporary political economy are cumulative and emerge at different political and ideological levels. To counter this, interventions have been made to maintain equilibrium, so preventing economic and political collapse. Herein lies a central contradiction that plagues the basis of South Africa's political economy.

The contradiction that characterises the dynamic nature of the economy is that the economic and political shifts have transformed benefits into costs, and thus produced the dysfunctionality of the South African growth model. To put it differently, industrialisation in South Africa (which has incorporated the majority of the working population into the wage economy) is still characterised by a system of racial regulation and control, thus constraining its growth capacity. As Greenberg has suggested:

> the insufficiency of state capacity and the rising costs of control have produced recurrent and growing political turmoil within the state. The elaboration of the state in this contradictory context has produced not unity but doubts and, increasingly, a struggle over the best means for preserving privilege and maintaining order. Some actors have responded to the insufficiency of repressive and racist methods with demands for more. Others, against the dominant presumptions favouring increased control, have given tentative voice to new policy directions: less evidently coercive ways for allocating labour, new mechanisms to reduce the costs of state regulation, and new approaches to inducing compliance and building broader support for the social order. These struggles have proved endemic since the late 1930s and now have become so intense and indeterminate that they threaten the coherence of the state response.[16]

Any economic structure or system which is successful and well adapted to its task at a certain stage of historical development may not be so at another stage. It may become inflexible and incapable of change, so that when material conditions alter it is slow or unable to adapt. South Africa, in particular, is vulnerable to this failing because of its reliance on the market mechanism, which acts imperfectly to induce adaptation to major changes in the economic and political environment, and incurs major social and economic costs in the form of stagnant production, bankruptcies and unemployment. To move to a new path, so as to bring about a regeneration of development, such a system would require a severe shock in the form of war, a slump or determined state intervention — or a combination of all the above. In the absence of such a disturbance, a capitalist economy in this predicament may stagnate indefinitely along its original path.

In the contemporary context, the South African economy provides an apt example of such a situation. The determined state intervention in the postwar period, when the apartheid policy was intensified against the background of a growing international economy and the availability of foreign funds, led to growth. However, the internal crisis of the 1970s and deflationary policies in the latter part of that decade began to result in low investment, falling productivity and a declining industrial structure. Any domestic growth was immediately followed by a deterioration in the balance of payments, much reduced economic growth and increased unemployment. Under these conditions, balance of payments equilibrium can only be achieved at the cost of domestic unemployment and stagnation. This has reduced the incentive to invest and thus productivity has lagged and industry has become less competitive. More fundamentally, the state has been increasingly constrained to meet the growing costs of implementing apartheid policy measures and attendant consequences. The growth pattern of apartheid and capitalism is thus called into question.

The nature of the South African state since 1948 has certainly not remained static but it is still organised on the basis of racial exclusivity. State intervention altered the logic of accumulation through its control over the disposition of the country's economic surplus. It is the exercise of this form of control that has made the political and economic spheres indistinguishable. The question now facing the state is how to uncouple racism and capitalism. How does it win support for a simultaneous programme of partial deracialisation and economic downturn? This is where academic doctrines like monetarism have a role to play. They provide the intellectual and political justification for altering the role of the government, to extricate it from a 'Catch 22' situation.[17]

Within the last few years, the state has attempted to lessen its active role as an organiser of racism. It even engages in partial deracialisation in the economic sphere, such as the lifting of job reservation, the promotion of small black business, and the opening up of the central business districts. Nevertheless, the essential framework of apartheid remains intact in other spheres such as housing, education, transport, health, sport and recreational facilities. However, the economic sphere of activity cannot be separated from the socio-political arena, where racism still exists. Certain sectors of the black middle class have emerged on the basis of racial motivations, and this is functional for a society which has structured white over black relationships.

The real aim of the government is not to harness popular dissatisfaction, nor to reduce the power of the state, but rather to attempt a coherent and radical approach to resolve economic and political difficulties on its own terms. It seeks to cope with the major problems generated by the end of the boom years — increased popular resistance, rising expectations — by shifting the parameters that previously maintained some degree of stability. To recreate conditions for growth and profitability the state is attempting to recast the relations between itself and the rest of society by creating a new balance of forces. In a divisive counter to inter-class solidarity, it has used reformist and repressive methods concurrently.

This is nothing less than an attempt to change decisively the character and nature of class relations. A key tactic is the inculcation of an individualist ethic to undermine the inter-class solidarity of the black people, in particular the cohesion between working class and middle class sectors. The construction of new black middle strata is intended to produce a new hegemony over the working class and a stable source of support for the freedom of the market. Liberal economic policies and a free-enterprise ideology are part of a political strategy whereby the coercive power of the state is strengthened and the state itself withdraws from the pressure emanating from below and immunizes itself from popular demands.

D. Yudelman suggests that the shift in economic policy can be attributed to a more fundamental reason, that is, 'the crisis of legitimation'. It is argued that the ideology of apartheid has had limited success, and thus the turn to free-market policies. 'Apartheid is no ideology for a state that wishes to be a part of the emerging world industrial economy and urgently needs an exponential growth in quantity and quality of skilled labour. This is not to argue that apartheid *policies* are dead: the core policies will be around for a considerable time to come, though the periphery ("petty apartheid") will increasingly be discarded.'[18]

In view of this legitimacy crisis, the state has been forced to seek methods of depoliticisation. And an obvious way to do this is to withdraw and cut back its role in the economy. The consequence would be that the poor and recipients of welfare would be depicted as scroungers, in an overt attempt to blame the victim and assert the discipline of the market. 'These are less explosive scapegoats than the colour of one's skin, or the state's policy of political and economic discrimination. The state hopes that if its roles as accumulator and distributor are reduced, its vulnerability as a legitimator will be reduced.'[19]

PROSPECTS FOR THE FUTURE

Having exhausted the internal conditions that facilitated the earlier cycle of growth, the apartheid model of growth and exploitation is no longer reproducible and can only be held in place at an ever rising cost. The future of the Nationalist government has never been so precarious. Apart from a military solution (or authoritarian repression), a number of other forces make transition inevitable — industrial unrest, political mobilisation, the role of the churches, all severely undermine the legitimacy of the regime. Externally, the isolation and pressures building up impinge upon the perception of costs and the practicality of continuing the *status quo*.

The economy is increasingly affected by uncertainty as to the nature of transition. Except for some ongoing operations, major new medium- or long-term investments are not being undertaken. The uncertainty will not diminish until a transition is determined or is in formation. There may be many strategies posed, but ultimately any alternative will depend on the form that transition takes. But it is also clear that any process of change will not be developed without facing obstacles, contradictions, conflicts and tensions.

South Africa today faces special problems: it knows neither political nor economic democracy. The intensity of the pressure for transition will have to take into account a high corporate surplus share in the GDP, massive racial inequalities and the dependence of capital and technology on external sources. Efforts to avert, limit or manage these factors will have to deal with structural impediments that seem difficult at best.

Given this understanding of the problem one finds that the great task of social and economic development in South Africa does not simply lie in a 'technocratic' manipulation of macro-variables to attain growth, but involves a qualitative change in socio-economic relations both internally and externally. Thus, any alternative has to be about challenging the social relations that have been structured by apartheid and capitalism. Within the limits of existing *laissez-faire* economics, it is impossible for these structural reforms to take place. Such reforms would affect the position of privilege and domination of the ruling oligarchy as well as the interests of apartheid's domestic and foreign beneficiaries.

The question that emerges is how can the impasse be broken? What are the likely directions of movement of the South African economy and society? These are immensely difficult questions to answer, especially as the answers have to make assumptions about a reality which is constantly changing. Any attempt at a detailed policy agenda for a future society would be rash. Though the goals of the broad democratic movement are on record, at this stage (understandably) they have not been worked out in any detail. Instead of speculating on possible scenarios attention will be focussed on the forces operating, since it is these that will determine the particular form of a 'post-apartheid' society.

One can identify two groups whose real and potential power is likely to be decisive. They are the alliance led by the National Party on the one hand and the broad democratic front on the other. From the perspective of the former, the contradictions could be resolved by 'reformist' policies. Of course, reformist policies will have a differential impact and cooption will continue. However, the subordinate classes are even more important as agents of social change. In particular, it is difficult to predict working class strategies because these will be dependent on changing conditions. In turn these conditions will determine the relative position of the contending forces.

At the same time as the legitimacy of the ruling class and the social order increasingly come under question, the government's inability to cope with the problem of consent has served only to infuse greater confidence in the subordinate masses as evidenced by their increasing assertiveness. To what extent this situation will gain momentum and whether it will yield to a fundamental transformation of social relations remains an open question. In this context, the transition from an apartheid to a 'post-apartheid' society is extraordinarily complex. Not enough attention has been paid to objective forces. Research in this area is extremely limited.

It is clear enough, though, that internal domination and exploitation in its present form cannot persist within the existing structural features of capitalism and apartheid and its dependence on international capital. Having said that, we must avoid seeing any 'post-apartheid' framework as the panacea to South Africa's problems of developing the productive system and its ensuing relations. In this context pressures from the international system will be immense.

Any new government will not be at liberty to fabricate an economy. It will, in fact, inherit an economy which imposes a certain logic and rigidity on the course of future development. The rigidity of the international division of labour will act as a constraint, for reasons which include access to technology, the comparative advantages of industrialised nations in manufacturing and the narrow domestic market. The question then is not one of how to insulate or even isolate the domestic economy from the international economy, but rather how to reorganise a society towards a more equitable and just order, so as to challenge the relations which historically structure the South African economy and society.

CONCLUSION

This chapter has attempted to provide an analysis of the nature of the economic and political crisis that plagues South African society. The conclusion that emerges is that the current malaise is not simply an outcome of political unrest and thus a problem of 'law and order' that can be resolved by the growth of authoritarianism and repression. In essence, politics and economics integrally constitute the basis of the deepening and unfolding disintegration of South African society. As has been shown, the economic decline started well before the increased political resistance which therefore exacerbated an already declining political economy. Thus, in current economic conditions the key question is not one of whether economic growth would undermine apartheid but rather the extent to which the South African economy can sustain any real growth at all.

A variety of factors militate against the government's policies to sustain growth. Given the economic constraints and obstacles, coupled with the state's objective of maintaining political domination, the current recession may well engender the collapse of the South African economic order — without international support for economic revitalisation and debt relief. The acute inequalities of South Africa make it impossible to depoliticise economic issues and exclude structural reforms from the political agenda. Thus unrest threatens. However, when this happens the authorities spring to action to put out the fire and in the process spread more inflammable material around, ready for the next flare-up to emerge. Hence, we have another state of emergency; long-suppressed demands will undoubtedly be expressed and lead to further popular political mobilisation and renewed instability.

Finally, the question of a 'post-apartheid' society is on the agenda. As suggested, its particular outcome and form will depend on the balance of forces. There is no recipe for a strategy of transition and it is clear that conflicts and contradictions will appear in the future. Though no concrete blueprint can be prepared, it is nevertheless a priority that research in this area begins to unfold. That task, however, cannot be separated from the people, for it is in their strength and potential that the future lies.

NOTES

1. I would like to express my gratitude to all those who advised and commented on this chapter. Errors remain my own responsibility.
2. E.O. Wright, *Class, Crisis and the State* (Verso, 1978).
3. Ironically, the results of international monetary turbulence during the 1970s had a positive effect on both the balance of payments and growth, particularly because of the gold price.
4. Money supply figures have shown a highly erratic growth, contrary to stated objectives: thus one has to distinguish rhetoric from practice.
5. Bureau of Economic Analysis, U.S. Department of Commerce.
6. D. Innes, 'Monopoly capitalism in South Africa' in *South African Review 1* (Ravan Press, 1983).
7. Mercabank, *Focus on Key Economic Issues*, No. 34.
8. Report by S. Barber in *Business Day*, 1 May 1986.
9. J. Natrass, *The South African Economy — Its Growth and Change* (Oxford University Press, 1981).
10. The notion of a capital-output ratio is none the less fraught with ambiguities, raised by problems of definition and measurement of the capital stock.
11. A. Singh, 'U.K. industry and the world economy: a case of deindustrialisation', *Cambridge Journal of Economics*, June 1977.
12. IMF Staff Report on South Africa, June 1978.
13. Mercabank, *Focus on Key Economic Issues*, No. 39, Nov. 1986.
14. Formulated by J. Saul and S. Gelb as an 'organic crisis', in *The Crisis in South Africa* (Monthly Review Press, 1981) which also offers a more detailed account of social forces.
15. F. Johnstone, 'Most painful to our hearts: South Africa through the eyes of the new school', *Canadian Journal of African Studies*, Vol. 16, No. 1, 1982.
16. S. Greenberg, 'The state and the market', paper presented at the Institute of Commonwealth Studies, London, 1984.
17. F. Cassim, 'The unequal burden in the creation and distribution of wealth', University of the Witwatersrand, Senate Special Lectures, 1984.
18. D. Yudelman, *The Emergence of Modern South Africa: State, Capital and Organised Labour on S.A. Goldfields, 1902-1939* (Greenwood Press, 1983).
19. *Ibid.*.

Table 1.1: Composition and Growth of GDP in South Africa

	1950-54	1960-64	1970-74	1980-84
Agriculture, Forestry and Fishing	14.1	11.3	8.7	7.4
Mining and Quarrying	17.6	21.3	15.7	11.0
Manufacturing	14.7	17.0	22.1	25.3

Table 1.2: Unemployment Rates in South Africa, 1960-82

1960	16.7	1972	18.9
1961	17.4	1973	17.0
1962	17.9	1974	16.2
1963	17.8	1975	16.2
1964	17.0	1976	16.9
1965	17.5	1977	18.4
1966	16.2	1978	20.4
1967	15.9	1979	21.1
1968	18.5	1980	20.8
1969	17.3	1981	21.1
1970	17.5	1982	22.5
1971	17.7		

Source: C. Simkins, 'Structural unemployment revisited', research paper, South African Labour and Development Research Unit, 1982.

Table 1.3: Average Capital:Labour and Capital:Output Ratios for the Economy as a Whole and for Manufacturing Industry (Constant 1970 Prices)

Year	CLR		COR	
	Economy	Manufacturing	Economy	Manufacturing
1970	3,341	2,752	2.35	1.05
1971	3,485	2,867	2.41	1.11
1972	3,616	3,039	2.51	1.18
1973	3,746	3,181	2.57	1.20
1974	3,886	3,274	2.53	1.24
1975	4,064	3,404	2.65	1.30
1976	4,416	3,426	2.77	1.37
1977	4,882	3,647	2.90	1.52
1978	4,940	3,831	2.95	1.53
1979	5,065	3,970	2.95	1.52
1980	5,152	4,389	2.92	1.34

Source of basic data: S.A. Reserve Bank and Central Statistical Services.

Table 1.4: Balance of Payments — Current Account Summary

	1950-59	1960-69	1970-74	1975-79	1981
Merchandise exports	693	1,145	2,180	6,219	9,328
Gold output	367	710	1,451	3,510	8,338
Merchandise imports	-924	-1,546	-3,533	-7,765	-18,171
Visible trade balance	136	309	98	1,964	-505
Service receipts	171	334	819	1,755	3,117
Service payments	-396	-679	-1,578	-3,580	-6,929
Net transfer payments	17	25	47	107	370
Invisible balance	-208	-320	-712	-1,718	-3,442
Balance on current account	-72	-11	-614	246	-3,947

Source: South African Reserve Bank Bulletin

Table 1.5: Terms of Trade (1975 = 100)

Year	Index, Including Gold	% Change	Index, Excluding Gold	% Change
1970	78.5	-4.7	115.8	-1.4
1971	80.1	2.0	109.9	-5.1
1972	85.4	6.6	103.4	-5.9
1973	102.8	20.4	112.4	8.7
1974	111.7	8.7	109.0	-3.0
1975	100.0	-10.5	100.0	-8.3
1976	89.5	-10.5	96.8	-3.2
1977	92.1	2.9	96.8	0.0
1978	94.2	2.3	94.0	-2.9
1979	97.8	3.8	87.2	-7.2
1980	109.0	11.5	80.6	-7.6
1981	94.9	-12.9	78.9	-2.1
1982	84.6	-10.8	74.6	-5.5
1983	90.6	7.1	74.8	
1984	90.8	0.2	76.1	

Source: South African Reserve Bank Bulletin

Table 1.6: South Africa's Foreign Liabilities at the end of 1981

Gross foreign liabilities		
Private sector direct long-term investment of an equity of shareholders' loan nature		10,940
Private sector non-direct long-term investment of an equity nature		3,135
Direct long-term investment in the banking sector		443
Total 'hard-core' foreign liabilities	14,518	
By subsidiaries from their parents		773
By central government and banking sector		1,960
By 'other' public sector borrowers (chiefly public corporations)		6,399
Long-term elements of borrowing	9,092	
By foreign controlled banks from parents		333
By foreign controlled companies from parents		2,456
By 'other' private sector generally		3,044
By central government and banking sector		3,047
Short-term elements of borrowing	8,880	
Total foreign 'borrowings'	17,972	
Gross foreign liabilities	32,490	

Source: Nedbank, South Africa: An Appraisal (1983) p.152.

Table 1.7: Government Foreign Issues and Foreign Holdings of
Domestic Non-Marketable Stock (R million)

	FOREIGN ISSUES		
	Marketable	Non-Marketable	Total
1970	92	136	229
1971	170	246	416
1972	237	265	502
1973	222	138	361
1974	242	267	509
1975	273	613	886
1976	295	1,030	1,325
1977	297	1,059	1,356
1978	297	888	1,185
1979	261	673	934
1980	216	387	603
1981	198	697	995
1982	240	1,215	1,655

Source: South African Reserve Bank Bulletin

2. 'The Limits of the Possible': Macro-economic Policy and Income Redistribution in Latin America and South Africa

TERENCE MOLL

INTRODUCTION

It is widely accepted that South Africa is in the throes of a crisis which can only be resolved through major economic and political transformation. At an economic level, everybody from the ANC to the Urban Foundation agrees that 'structural change' and a redistribution of income and wealth are urgently required.

One of the most important statements on this issue appears in the Freedom Charter.[1] Its central economic demands include nationalisation and extension of public ownership; land reform; increased government social services expenditure; and jobs, education, housing and medical care for all. This chapter will discuss the feasibility of such a programme of economic reform and income redistribution, focussing particularly on macro-economic policies and structures of control and ownership as they establish the fundamental mechanisms by which income is distributed in an economy.

Two questions will be posed regarding South Africa. What are likely to be the quickest and most effective means of redistributing wealth and income in a period of political change? How and where are these means compatible with macro-economic objectives (growth, balance of payments soundness, low inflation)? These questions will be discussed with reference to the experience of Latin American countries which have implemented programmes of 'structural' economic change and income redistribution similar to that advocated in the Freedom Charter.[2] The cases referred to include the military populist Peronist era in Argentina 1944-1955, with attempts to shift wealth from rich farmers to urban industry and workers; Chile 1944-1970 (the Frei period of class reformism) and 1970-1973 (socialist reformism under Allende), with various forms of income redistribution, land reform, higher wages, etc.; and radical military populism in Peru 1948-1975, which aimed at overcoming economic 'dualism' via industrial development with worker participation.

This chapter is based in part on research carried out while the author was a junior research fellow in the Department of Economics at the University of Cape Town, working on a project examining macro-economic policy and poverty in South Africa, funded by the Friedrich Ebert Stiftung. Thanks to Iraj Abedian, Sean Archer, Peter Moll, Nicoli Nattrass, Jenny Robinson, Wolfgang Thomas and John Wells for comments on various versions.

ARGENTINA, CHILE, PERU AND SOUTH AFRICA

These countries are all classified as middle-income economies by the World Bank (1986), with estimated mid-1984 populations ranging from 11.8 million (Chile) and 18.2 million (Peru) to 30.1 million (Argentina) and 31.6 million (South Africa). They have a similar history of incorporation into the world capitalist economy, mainly via trade as exporters of food (Argentina) and minerals (Chile, Peru and South Africa). All attempted import-substitution industrialisation in the 1914-45 period as a matter of necessity, and it became a policy tool after the Second World War with local manufacturing industry growing at around six per cent per annum behind tariff walls during the 1950s and 1960s, often with strong penetration by multinational corporations.

Growth at four to five per cent per annum was steady until the 1970s, during which Peru and South Africa faltered somewhat (under three per cent per annum) and average growth rates in Argentina and Chile fell to between one and two per cent per annum with considerable variation from year to year. A signficant characteristic of the Latin American countries is a history of high and erratic inflation rates, rising to over 100 per cent per annum in Argentina and Chile in the 1970s. All four have had governments playing a strong developmental role via parastatals and a variety of forms of economic intervention, though the Latin American countries have been politically unstable and often experienced significant policy shifts over quite short time periods.

Finally, a notable characteristic of all these countries is a very high concentration of income and wealth with limited 'trickling down' of the material gains from higher output (see Lecaillon et al, 1984, Ch. 2). According to one estimate, the 8.7 per cent income shares of the poorest 40 per cent of the Latin American population in 1960 *fell* to 7.7 per cent in 1975 (Portes, 1985: 25; also Felix, 1983). There appears to have been some reduction in relative income inequality in South Africa over this period, though the poor still have a very low income share (McGrath, 1984). All these countries have a severe poverty problem, with the very poor concentrated in rural or peri-urban areas and usually lacking formal sector employment.

In short, the four countries examined have similar economic structures and processes of income distribution. It thus seems possible that South Africans can learn lessons from Latin American attempts to modify these.

'STRUCTURALISTS' AND INCOME REDISTRIBUTION IN LATIN AMERICA

The emergence of internal and external disequilibria in Latin American economies after the Second World War led to the emergence of two competing sets of analyses and policy recommendations (see Baer and Kerstenetzky, eds., 1964). Monetarists argued that lack of monetary restraint — and in particular, government budget deficits (Harberger, 1964: 322), often financed by foreign loans or printing new money — led directly to inflation and balance of payments (BOP) deficits which served to undermine economic development (Dorrance, 1964: especially 68). Hence strict control over the money supply, domestic credit and government expenditure would best control inflation (Campos, 1961: 69-70), while devaluation, lower real wages and fewer controls would improve the structure of relative prices and the BOP. Inflation should fall rapidly during a strict stabilisation, with fairly low employment and output costs (Campos, 1967: 110-113), and economic recovery and rapid market-oriented growth should begin. In practice, however, adjustment costs of monetarist programs were high in terms of output and employment foregone, and often disequilibria re-emerged once economic growth resumed (Moll, 1986: 62-78).

The basic structuralist argument — which provided the rationale for the redistributionist efforts discussed below — was that economies were far more complex than this. Writers in this vein identified a number of factors in Latin American economies which they felt led to slow growth, inflation and BOP disequilibria via 'structural' channels which freer markets could not remedy. These included food bottlenecks due to rural institutional factors (Grunwald, 1961: 110-111), low and erratic rates of growth of export earnings coupled with rising import demand creating foreign exchange bottlenecks, and a poor government finance and tax position leading to inflationary deficit financing (Kirkpatrick and Nixson, 1978: 132-134). The money supply was seen to respond 'passively' to cost-push inflationary pressures (Canovese, 1982: 523) as an easier alternative than strict monetary policy and open social conflict.

Structuralists argued that attempts to eliminate disequilibria via market processes based on vigorous monetary control would only succeed via brutal quantity-adjustment mechanisms (Prebisch, 1961: 17-20) which would lower aggregate demand and investment, thus *reducing* the economy's long-run growth capacity. Instead, social constraints on development (e.g. inefficient rural oligarchies) should be eliminated and the state should take the lead in helping to develop local manufacturing industry and small-scale agriculture, extend national control over the productive structure to prevent the loss of 'economic surplus', and actively intervene and plan in strategic areas (ECLA, 1961: 4-6; Malan and Wells, 1984).

Income redistribution was seen as a vital part of development. It would lower the unproductive consumption and luxury imports of the rich, it would raise aggregate demand inside the country and stimulate local industry, and by so doing, lower the revenues and repatriated profits of foreign firms. It was thus advocated on economic as well as the usual moral grounds (Balogh, 1961: 52-53).

In practice, structuralists vastly overestimated the efficacy of structural reforms and their work underplayed aggregate demand factors and inflationary expectations. They also underrated the extent to which 'conventional' macro-economic policies — limiting government spending, export incentives, higher internal food prices — could overcome bottlenecks. Instead, their approaches in Latin America led to strategies of autarchy, excessive monetary growth and inefficient controls to handle macro-economic imbalances, while 'structural' reforms to improve the distribution of income often failed to reach the very poor. The relevance of this record to South Africa is discussed below.

In many cases of attempted 'structural' economic reform and income redistribution in the 1950s and 1960s, events followed a standard pattern (Diaz-Alejandro, 1981: 121-122). Typically, reformist-populist governments came to power on the basis of strong nationalist feeling and lower-class support; first moves included attempts to redistribute income and encourage growth via land reforms, introduction of more progressive taxes, attempts to increase the national ownership of the productive structure, higher real wages and social security provisions, and increased government spending and economic planning. Initially, given spare industrial capacity,[3] and populist mobilisation, the raising of aggregate demand and income redistribution stimulated the economy and GDP and industrial output grew steadily for a year or two, while the rate of inflation often stabilised or even fell initially. The share of wages and salaries in national income and government welfare and social service expenditure increased, and various structural reforms were begun. The most ominous sign was a decline in investment due to rising costs and political and economic uncertainty within the capitalist class.

In due course, balance of payments deficits and inflationary pressures emerged and were 'controlled' by supporting the exchange rate and drawing down reserves, administrative import-repressing mechanisms and price controls. Over time GDP growth slowed due to sluggish investment and inefficiencies, inflation accelerated, controls proliferated and there was talk of restrictive fiscal and monetary measures. At this stage reformist politicians changed direction, introducing anti-labour legislation, lower real wages and the IMF, thus cancelling much of the redistributive emphasis of the early days of reformist governments. In practice such policies were rarely politically acceptable, the left being antagonised and the right remaining unconciliated, still calling for conservative or military rule (Ascher, 1984: 213).

In some cases — e.g. Chile 1970-1973 or Bolivia 1952-1956 — the radical reformists retained power and precipitated the economy into the stage of structuralist disaster. Inflation escalated as the money supply zoomed out of control, exports fell, imports necessary to domestic industry were cut off, urban services faltered and the urban food supply was sometimes halted. Some from the populist coalition argued for centrally planned socialism (further discouraging investment and inducing capital flight) while defections to the right accelerated. In a situation of general disequilibrium, inflation and erratic relative prices, real wages fell, mass disaffection grew and the right moved in for the kill, leading to a military coup, monetarist stabilisation, and the reversal of the wealth and income redistribution originally achieved.

MACRO-ECONOMIC LIMITATIONS ON 'STRUCTURAL' REFORMS

To structuralists, reforms in productive activity and the redistribution of wealth and income were the best way to ensure long-run development and growth, raising aggregate demand and market size and solving 'structural' bottlenecks constraining the economy (see Lustig, 1980). Such a process, however, is subject to severe limitations.

Firstly, radicals often plan to revitalise the economy by raising aggregate demand to utilise excess capacity. In practice, as applied in Chile 1970-1973, the first — or output-rising — stage seems rather brief, firstly for 'structural' reasons: bottlenecks in and interrelationships among particular industries lead to early price rather than output effects, even with spare capacity in many areas; secondly, the structuralist model assumes industrial monopoly with prices as a constant mark-up over unit costs, but given excess aggregate demand, such mark-ups become flexible upwards; thirdly, the model assumes a fairly well-behaved investment function, but where investor confidence is lacking short-run output may rise but investment decline, undermining the long-run prospects of the model (see Griffith-Jones, 1981: 130-133). Instead, capacity utilisation levels can perhaps best be raised via selective incentives to industrial exports, a more open current account of the balance of payments, and the removal of explicit or implicit subsidies on capital-use (Schydlowsky, 1979: 348-351; 1981). General economic expansion is too blunt a tool to yield the desired results.

Secondly, structural reforms affecting the productive structure and the distribution of income tend to undermine short-run output and efficiency in the economy,[4] and disrupt the price system as means of resource allocation (Griffith-Jones, 1981: 7). This implies a politically unpopular need for revolutionary governments to maintain strict fiscal and monetary control (Seers, 1983: 118, also Ellman, 1983: 108-109), as only within a very stable macro-economic framework can long-run changes be smoothly instituted and redistributive gains preserved.

Thirdly, the hope is often expressed that output and investment will rise following nationalisation and expropriation of the 'surplus' lost to foreigners. While this is conceivable in the very long run, the short-run costs are often high (disruption of production processes and markets, sabotage by previous managers), there are knotty questions concerning compensation or otherwise, and the new state managers may often be incompetent or lose the 'surplus' to worker wage demands (see Horvat, 1981: 957). In both Chile and Peru in the 1970s, nationalised firms were inefficient and unprofitable, consuming resources rather than providing a surplus for investment (De Vylder, 1976: 154; Fitzgerald, 1979: 194-195).

In *macro-economic* terms, it seems many objectives that underlie nationalisation can be more efficiently achieved in other ways, e.g. shrewd use of taxation (Nattrass, 1985: 28-31) or joint ventures with multinational corporations (Faber, Green and Harvey, 1983: 8-9), without necessarily undermining the socialist ideals of the state. It is clear, however, that a socialist case can be made for a considerable degree of state *supervision* over finance and banking and perhaps large-scale mining.

Fourthly, at or approaching supply capacity there is a short-run trade-off between growth and wages. Real wages might need to be constrained to allow a surplus for investment and to ensure investment in the non-socialised sectors of the economy. Wage restraint is critically important in the public sector where the trade-off between government investment (e.g. infrastructure, public works) and social services (which can have desirable output and employment effects, e.g. health and housing expenditure on the poor), and high wages for organised public sector workers is particularly vivid (Ascher, 1984: 238). This, of course, presented a difficult political problem for regimes which came to power precisely on the basis of lower class — especially organised urban worker — support, as with Peron in Argentina (1946-55) and Allende in Chile (1970—73).

Fifthly, structural programmes vastly underestimated the importance of the external sector and the balance of payments, the argument usually being that trade immiserised and undermined the local economy, and that self-reliance was preferable. Autarchic development strategies often led to inefficient and excessive industrialisation efforts, prevented the growth of manufacturing exports, forcibly curbed import levels via balance of payments crises (jeopardising essential capital and intermediate inputs), and permitted excessive increases in government expenditure, thus encouraging rapid growth in internal demand and inflation.

Sixthly, income redistribution changes the structures of demand, raising particularly the demand for basic manufactures and food[5] (Griffin and James,

1981, 15-17). Where these are in inelastic supply, prices may soar, leading to popular resentment; if they are held down, excessive imports may result. This occurred in Chile, where food imports came to 19.6% of export earnings 1965-70 and 56% in 1972 (De Vylder, 1976: 202). This constraint could only be solved by a concerted combination of rationing, producer subsidies, marketing and development assistance, and efforts to raise savings.

Finally, the costs of right-wing and business opposition to redistributive policies were high. Disinvestment and capital flight was the common economic response to reform: for example, private investment fell from 43% of total investment in Chile in 1970 to around 15% (of a falling total) in 1972. This was in reaction both to lower expected returns in activities adversely affected by government policy, and to perceived threats to the return or ownership of investments hitherto untouched. The former is to an extent unavoidable but the latter can be lessened by cunning and subtlety, e.g. Peron's division of capitalist opposition and only partial destruction thereof (Ascher, 1984: 113-114). In some cases state sanctions against firms which exported capital or refused to invest may have been possible, but were rarely attempted.

Within these constraints, however, the structuralist record also seems to imply there is definite scope for redistribution in peripheral economies, without growth and investment suffering greatly. Once certain economic fundamentals are ignored, however, structural reforms and income redistribution grind to an abrupt halt.

ASSET REDISTRIBUTION, MARKETS AND GROWTH

Asset redistribution may be a prerequisite to rapid egalitarian growth in the four economies under discussion. For example, it seems the impressive growth-with-equity record of East Asia relates to a significant extent to a position of initial economic and social equality resulting from post-war US intervention (cf. Morawetz, 1980: 353); where this is absent an export-oriented growth path may be exceedingly inegalitarian, as in the case of post-1968 Brazil (Knight, 1981: 1067-68; Taylor *et al*, 1980, Ch. 10).

The costs of such redistributive efforts, however, can be high. Two major positions on their *timing* can be distinguished. Some argue that 'if a major redistribution of assets and income is to be successful it will almost certainly have to be done rapidly . . . creeping reformism is almost certainly doomed to failure' (Griffin and James, 1981: 1) under pressure from asset 'mining' and organised capitalist resistance (Elliott, 1984: 3). On the other hand, an abrupt approach could destabilise the economy over a lengthy period where new managers of productive assets lack the necessary skills and experience, previous users sabotage sectors of the economy, production processes are complex and delicate, and links to the world economy are close. The actual path chosen would have to depend crucially on local economic and political conditions.

Some 'rules' regarding redistribution processes can, however, be posited. The first is that redistribution should not be permitted needlessly to damage private sector investor confidence: where possible its final limits should be very clearly defined when it begins. Failure to define the extent of nationalisation and reform in Peru and Chile led to massive disinvestment and destabilising uncertainty (see Morawetz, 1980: 354). A clearer policy appears to have been followed in post-1979 Nicaragua (Irvin, 1983: 127-129).   •

The second rule is that there are good economic reasons why land should be eminently redistributable — there is evidence that land reforms in fact tend to raise agricultural output in the medium-term (e.g. Dorner, 1972: 110ff.; Nguyen and Salvidar, 1979). Such reforms can lead to considerable labour absorption, especially of the rural poor, land is less easily 'mined' than industrial assets or minerals, and frantic attempts to sell simply lower land prices and make land reform easier.

Third, the role of market relations in the redistribution process is a problem. Griffin and James argue that radical redistribution leads to major economic disequilibria and breakdown of market processes which can only be effectively overcome by resorting to controls and direct allocation of resources (1981, Ch. 4), e.g. price controls and rationing. While this can be an important *transitional* strategy, particularly in the form of limited price-controlled rationing for the very poor, it is far from obvious that it is viable in non-agricultural countries; it had a far better chance of working in the case they stress, post-war China (*ibid.*: 93-97).

Finally, there is ample evidence that land reform and nationalisations are effective in raising production and permitting its socialisation only when there is substantial involvement, organisation and initiative 'from below', e.g. tenant, farm labourer and sharecropper organisations and peasant land invasions (Dorner, 1971: 29-31), trade unions and active worker participation in decision-making (Espinosa and Zimbalist, 1978: 158-161), self-management in rural development schemes (Griffin and James, 1981: 60-66), and so on. Where this crucial *political* element is weak or missing, redistributive efforts are likely to be greatly hampered by conservative opposition and do little for productivity — this is clearly seen in the experience of Chile and especially Peru (Fitzgerald, 1979: 123-128).

THE IMPACT OF REDISTRIBUTIVE INSTRUMENTS

In practice, redistributive efforts in Latin America often had a highly selective impact on poor groups in society. This section discusses why and posits some criteria for evaluating redistributive measures.

Redistributive programmes attempted to shift income from capitalists and foreign-owned firms to the working classes and the poor. Reforms to this end were often short-lived, not lasting much beyond the lifespan of the governments introducing them. Apart from political opposition by the rich, one of the reasons for this was that a main form of redistribution was simple increases in nominal wages or social service spending funded partly by private firms and partly by the fiscal budget. Such redistributive efforts *directly* boosted total nominal expenditure,[6] leading to inflation and balance of payments crises. Where these took place gradually, workers were sometimes able to achieve and preserve real income gains without reducing growth rates much (e.g. Chile under Frei). Where they happened rapidly, however, they were neutralised by rising prices, since firms can better defend themselves against inflation than workers.[7] Peron's Argentina (1946-48) is among the few cases where redistribution actually took real income from the rich and transferred it to the poor, in part because his efforts to raise wages took the form of gradual selective state intervention in wage negotiations rather than blanket decrees applying without considering profits earned and productivity (Ascher, 1984: 57-58).

Redistributive efforts in Latin America faced a fundamental difficulty: the nature and dispersion of poverty. Poor people tended to be those excluded from the relatively prosperous high-wage 'modern' sectors of the economy — the unemployed, informal sector operators, rural workers and peasants. These groups are notoriously difficult to reach in any social reform programme.

For example, large real wage rises in Chile in 1964-72 were of benefit mainly to (better-off) sectors of the population working in large urban firms; such transfers within the modern sector failed to reach the urban poor working in the informal sector, slum dwellers and the unemployed, and hardly applied to rural workers (Ffrench-Davis, 1976: 111). These families lacked access to market-oriented income channels, and within households the allocation of income was determined in part by patriarchal power relations such that women and children often failed to benefit. Better poverty-oriented policies might have attempted to transfer income directly to women in poor households, e.g. via rural employment creation. Likewise, high minimum wages (or high wage levels in the state sector) may have had an adverse effect on the supply of low-paid jobs, but evidence on this point in less-developed countries is ambiguous and depends on the suddenness, levels and methods of application of minimum wages regulations (Lecaillon *et al*, 1984: 187-191).

Asset redistribution had similar results. Policies of nationalising large and capital-intensive industries in Allende's Chile had the effect of privileging around 20% of the industrial labour force — improved working conditions, fringe benefits, child care, medical services, etc. — while leaving the majority of workers untouched (De Vylder, 1976: 154-155) and in fact harming them via draining the state budget and inducing inflationary deficit financing. Land reform in Chile (on the basis of 'land to those who work it') succeeded in redistributing parts of huge, poorly utilised estates to existing cultivators (tenants, sharecroppers, etc.) but often left out others with weaker links to the land (e.g. day-labourers) and tiny smallholders; further, most Latin American land reforms directly benefitted only men in households (Deere, 1985). De Vylder estimates that around 8% of Chilean workers would have been affected by nationalisation and land reform programmes between 1970-73 if they had been carried through as envisaged (1976: 212-213).

Another common Latin American pattern concerns the sectoral benefits of redistribution. The many laws on land reform and income redistribution in Peru after 1968 amounted to a redistribution of income *within* each sector or enterprise, but given widely differing labour productivities and earnings between sectors (to the detriment especially of agriculture), the impact on the poor was severely limited (Webb, 1975: 121-123). Summarising the Velasco reforms in Peru of 1968-75, Figueroa observes:

All together they apply to 45% of national income and transfer between 3% and 4% of it to approximately 18% of the country's labour force. This transfer takes place almost entirely within the wealthiest income quartile (1976: 171).

In short, wage- or asset-based redistributive efforts in Chile and Peru succeeded in raising worker incomes at the expense of capitalist and foreign interests, with significant direct and indirect effects on the poor (e.g. via stimulating the urban informal sector). As a poverty-alleviation strategy, however, they were inherently constrained by the fact that in developing countries, many or most poor people do not earn stable wage incomes.

Government expenditure was a far more effective means of alleviating absolute poverty. Higher government social spending — especially on housing, education, health, pensions — can significantly assist the poor, as is shown by studies of Chile 1965-70 (Foxley et al, 1979, Ch. 6) and Peru 1963-73 (Webb, 1975: 108-120). Even small changes in government expenditure can have significant welfare effects: Selowsky, for example, argues that in 'semi-industrialised Latin American countries', an additional 5% of GDP devoted to education, health, nutrition and housing could cater for the basic needs of the poor without radical social transformation and at an estimated cost of 0.5% lower GNP growth (1981: 84-90).

In Latin America, however, such expenditures tend to have a strongly urban bias and there is always a danger that they may be appropriated by politically organised middle classes (Pinto and Di Filippo, 1976: 103); this was increasingly the case over time in Frei's Chile (Ascher, 1984: 127-128). It may also be cancelled with later stabilisation or where government revenues do not rise correspondingly. In general, of course, high progressive taxes were vital if possible inflationary effects of higher government social expenditure were to be countered (cf. Lecaillon et al, 1984: 176-181), but taxes were rarely seriously used as an instrument of redistribution — political commitment to this end was usually lacking (Cline, 1975: 395) and structuralist regimes found it exceedingly difficult to introduce and administer tax increases.

A variety of large-scale redistributive instruments can be implemented to reduce poverty in semi-industrialised countries. Apart from the usual efficiency criterion, two considerations come to mind in evaluating them: *specificity* (to what extent can they be aimed at particular groups of poor people?) and *substantiality* (can they be maintained over time?).

Large nominal wage rises fail both these criteria: they benefit wage-earners rather than the very poor, and can only be maintained at the cost of lower investment and inflation — which may erode real wages below their original levels. Employment creation via public works or selective stimulation of labour-intensive sectors (e.g. construction) tends to be (self-) selective but its sustainability depends in part on bureaucratic efficiency and the extent to which it boosts the local economy and encourages capital formation. By contrast, for example, successful measures to raise peasant productivity are fairly specific and — almost by definition — sustainable; likewise efforts aimed at bringing about health, educational and food consumption equality among children (Ffrench-Davis, 1976: 131-132).

In general, demand-oriented instruments do poorly in terms of these criteria, supply-oriented ones do far better but are far more difficult to implement, while extra-market distribution channels are an intermediate case. Clearly, the use of a variety of reasonably specific redistributional measures is likely to have the maximal impact on poverty, while if these are chosen to reinforce each other (e.g. land reform, agricultural extension work and rural food rationing) and have a high *investment* component (e.g. rural public works, 'human capital' improvements), their long-run viability is increased (see Griffin and James, 1981, Ch. 3).

REDISTRIBUTION AND POLITICS

The long-run record of structuralist economic management and redistribution of income is rather disappointing. The most effective case discussed above was that of Peron, operating in uniquely favourable economic circumstances, though Frei also had some successes. Redistributionist regimes tended not to survive, however, and were often replaced by right-wing governments implementing inegalitarian poverty-*creating* programmes (Moll, 1986: 66-74).

There are several reasons for this. Firstly, redistributionists often lacked real mass support; all too often they had the executive and administrative power to introduce anti-poverty programmes, but lacked the power to raise taxes to fund them. Likewise, conflicts within ruling coalitions led to excessive expenditure on sectional support groups, as in the case of Allende's Chile. These had harmful macro-economic consequences and encouraged right-wing political mobilisation. Secondly, rightist forces were able to gain international aid and the CIA's help in their struggles. Thirdly, redistribution attempts were administered by inefficient and corrupt bureaucracies which consumed resources and often prevented the masses from benefiting. Finally, severe policy errors were made in some cases — with high economic and political costs.

In conclusion, then, income redistribution is possible but requires large-scale political mobilisation, especially if radical changes are made. Where possible, sectors of the well-to-do (e.g. the petty-bourgeoisie) should be incorporated into such programmes, or at worst neutralised. Redistributional strategies with a high degree of popular control and input, which limit revenue passing through bureacratic channels, or which have a 'once and for all' state involvement (e.g. land reform) may be optimal, reducing corruption and maintaining political support for the regime. Finally, where political support is lacking, well-publicised gradualist redistributional policies may help build up political legitimacy and provide for a better future than rash radicalism followed by economic collapse and/or right-wing backlash.

LESSONS FOR SOUTH AFRICA

Reformers and radicals in South Africa have much to learn from the Latin American redistributionist record. Firstly, in economies with excess capacity, expansion and redistribution via higher total nominal expenditure may initially have positive effects via raising output, wages and social services. However, if this is not carefully done through developing exports, limiting real wage rises[8] and maintaining investment, the full-capacity stage of inflation and falling real wages is likely to appear quite soon and will undermine the economic and political support of the ruling regime.

Secondly, radical governments attempting to equalise income distribution significantly in a highly unequal economy might find it necessary to redistribute *before* growth (at the time of significant political change) as it is difficult to modify the structure of the economy later. The method of redistribution is important (for example, it is generally preferable to redistribute productive assets rather than subsidise private consumption) and it has the maximum effect on poverty if particular initiatives are aimed at specific groups.

Such redistribution can follow two paths. On the one hand, governments might attempt a radical redistribution of wealth and income while preserving the overall allocative role of the market; in such cases they should maintain medium-term fiscal and monetary balance while watching out for the three evils of disinvestment, inflation and balance-of-payments crises. The alternative is a move towards controls and direct (state-directed) allocation of resources. In fairly advanced trade-dependent, market-sensitive economies this would be likely to entail very high — and perhaps permanent — transitional costs.

Thirdly, the structure of ownership, production and distribution in the economy will determine which group will benefit from or be harmed by particular macro-economic or redistributive policies. For example, nationalisation will not reach the unemployed and rural poor; higher wages may not help the families and children of migrant labourers; a changed exchange rate may redistribute income from and to particular groups or government (Johnson and Salop, 1980). Macro-economic policy formulation is not a neutral process and a variety of distributional and welfare trade-offs exist which should be taken into account by politicians.

Finally, economic growth is vitally important for less-developed countries, as only in this way can the potential be created for satisfying the material needs of the majority of the population in the long run. There seems, however, to be some 'looseness' or latitude in any economy such that a considerable degree of redistribution is possible with largely neutral effects on growth and investment:

> The orthodox fear of a decline in the savings rate with equalisation is found empirically doubtful. The unorthodox 'structuralist' hope that redistribution will stimulate growth is also found dubious (Cline, 1975: 395).

Economic reformers should also be willing to learn from the major *mistakes* of Latin American structuralist economic programmes. One of the most important of these was export pessimism. Latin American countries often had scope to raise their exports considerably in the medium term; this would have made it easier to fund capital and intermediate goods imports necessary for economic development, as import-substituting industrialisation could provide only a part of these. Some monetarist regimes succeeded in vastly improving the trade balance via devaluation, a higher ratio of traded/non-traded goods prices and export incentives (Cline and Weintraub, 1981: 12; Bird, 1984: 103-106); structuralist regimes could perhaps have done the same at lower social cost.

Secondly, structuralist regimes tended to rely too much on an active developmental role for the state. State involvement in production often undermined efficiency and vastly increased government spending, with limited economic benefits. While there is an overwhelming case for some state economic regulation and anti-poverty efforts, it seems its productive activities should be limited; alternatively, forms of administering state sector firms other than centralised state control should be considered.

Finally, structuralist regimes often attempted to do too much too soon and were unable to deal with the consequences. Poor or excessively abrupt expansionary policies (and supply-side shocks) tended to lead to rapid inflation, large government deficits and BOP deficits. In such cases some form of stabilisation was required, reducing the real incomes of various sectors of the population. Structuralist regimes usually lacked the economic discipline and political support to carry this out, resulting often in right-wing resurgence and monetarist stabilisation, with harmful effects on output, growth and the distribution of income. Instead, there was a strong case for using several demand- and supply-side tools in circumstances of disequilibria, with gradualism particularly important when imposing fiscal and monetary discipline. Various means — e.g. careful use of government investment, taxation and social welfare — could have been used to ameliorate short-term adverse social effects (Cline and Weintraub, 1981: 13).

THE FREEDOM CHARTER

Returning to the questions posed in the Introduction, two categories of economic policies can be evaluated. The first can be termed 'the gentle option' and includes a variety of efforts to redistribute some income and ameliorate absolute poverty without significantly changing property relations in society — e.g. selective taxation, food aid, public works, better social security and even higher wages in some circumstances. These would be unlikely to materially affect growth rates, investment levels and macro-economic balance, and their costs and benefits are fairly easily estimated. Their effect on poverty could be considerable if the measures were carried out by an efficient and committed state apparatus, but they would have little impact on inequality and the structure of power relations in society. Finally, of course, they would totally fail to satisfy the demands of the oppressed black majority for a just and democratic society in South Africa.

'The radical alternative' is of a very different nature. It entails major structural transformation and wealth redistribution from rich to poor — land reforms, various forms of nationalisation of mines and industry, massive increases in government expenditure on education, housing and job-creation, generalised wage increases throughout the economy, and so on. It is difficult to evaluate their effects, and the dangers associated with the indiscriminate usage of these tools have been stressed above. The central point is that the medium-term necessity for reasonable macro-economic balance imposes major limitations on them. Moving rapidly towards direct allocation of resources by the state offers little hope for an economy as complex and sensitive as that of South Africa.

How does the Freedom Charter fit in with this discussion? Two positions regarding it can be discerned. The first views it as a short-run policy programme along the lines of 'the radical alternative' — with immediate and significant economic implications. These include domestic reflation via higher government spending, controls over trade, capital movements and prices, greater public ownership of industry and decentralised worker control where possible, higher government investment and large-scale land reform (cf. Gelb and Innes, 1985: 15ff.) The similarities to Popular Unity's approach in Chile 1970-73 are disconcerting; the likely outcome would be inflation (open or repressed), extension of government and bureaucratic power, an investment slump, BOP crises and slow economic growth, with little benefit to the poor. Such an approach might well lead *away* from democratic socialism.

It seems preferable to view the Freedom Charter as a statement of long-run policy goals while recognising that trade-offs and compromises are inevitable in the short run. The best approach for a strongly redistributionist regime after liberation might then be to utilise 'the gentle option' to the full to alleviate absolute poverty, and use elements of 'the radical alternative' to begin restructuring society in a more democratic direction. In the short-term this might involve bringing strategic areas of the economy under state influence (though perhaps not ownership), improving *priority* areas in education, housing, health and social security, selective land reforms and efforts at improved worker representation in firms. Explicitly socialist ideals of democratic workplace participation, socialisation of industry and economic equality would be seen as long-term goals to be worked towards.

There is clearly much scope for debate on these issues. The single most important element needed is the realisation that bringing about significant economic change is a slow, difficult process. In this respect, five areas of particular importance to South African socialists can be identified.

1. The transition period

The real incomes of the majority of the population are likely to *fall* in the transitional period to a new non-apartheid economic order in South Africa due to political and military conflict, the emergence of large economic disequilibria (e.g. in the export sector) and general economic disruption. Where combined with wealth redistribution, such a period may last some years. (It may, of course, be shortened via aid and assistance from a welcoming outside world.) Disseminating an awareness of all this within the liberation movement is a crucial political task of radical politicians, one which was disastrously handled by Popular Unity in Chile (Pedraza-Bailey, 1982: 47).

2. Monopoly capital

It is often argued that the real enemy of the South African people is monopoly and international capital:

> All classes, the working class, in particular, the small peasant, the small business people, even the small manufacturer, are caught in the vice grip of the massive monopolies . . . . (Billy Nair, quoted in Suttner and Cronin, 1986: 180; also Freedom Charter, paragraph 3.2).

In many circles a conception appears to prevail that aggregate demand and real wages can be considerably raised if external links are weakened or severed and the monopoly 'surplus' is appropriated locally rather than lost or wasted. Instead it seems such 'surplus' is quite small and claiming it could weaken essential trade links, undermine investment and lead to protecting the industrial sector inefficiently in a more closed economy.

It is also clear that monopoly firms can be confronted in various ways. Blunt nationalisation largely on principled grounds may be expensive and inefficient, especially where factories are large and production processes complex. South African socialists often fail to evaluate this problem fully.[9] Instead, there is scope for bargaining with multinationals (cf. Schatz, 1982; Green, 1978), and controlling them via taxation and joint ventures, a tactic attempted in Rumania, China and other socialist countries (Spigler, 1973: 60; Yahuda, 1982: 38-39).

3. Aggregate demand

Reasonably open political systems face conflicting pressures for higher wages, high government expenditure and easy credit, and can only survive in the long run if such demand-side claims are reconciled with the supply capacity of the economy. As Sheahan remarks,

> Some sense of a maximum feasible rate of growth of final demand, and of real wages, must be established in quantitative terms and accepted by the majority if . . . an open system is to remain viable (1982: 27).

What should be avoided, above all, is the tendency for distributional conflicts to be 'resolved' simply by raising the nominal incomes of all politically powerful groups; this is highly inequitable and ultimately economically destructive.

4. International economic relations

External links dominate the South African economy and will both help to provide the basis of development here for many years to come and constrain internal economic transformation. It is essential that these financial and trade links be well managed to provide the most favourable context possible for reform and redistribution.

5. The poverty problem

Absolute poverty in South Africa is widespread, and those most affected are people outside the formal labour market — farm labourers, women and children in rural areas, the unemployed, much of the 'informal sector'. These groups also lack political influence. Special efforts — e.g. land reform complemented by rural credit and infrastructural investment for small farms, rural job-creation, food aid — will have to be made to reach them, otherwise it is all too likely that redistribution will occur entirely within the upper ranges of the income distribution, to already better-off urban workers.

Clearly, however, a variety of interests conflict in these debates. Bureaucracies might hope to extend their powers via nationalisation, organised urban workers might push for higher minimum wages, the rural poor might propose extensive and rapid land reform, while the middle classes might favour higher government housing and education expenditure. Some political compromise would need to be reached between them, since these demands are not all compatible with each other — especially in the short run. It is to be hoped that the kind of economic limitations on structural change and income redistribution discussed above will delimit the parameters of debate on these issues.

NOTES

1. The Freedom Charter was drawn up by the Congress of the People in Kliptown, outside Johannesburg, on 25-26 June 1955. It summarised the political and economic prerequisites for a free South Africa put forward by hundreds of organisations and meetings all over South Africa (Suttner and Cronin, 1986), and has been adopted by many organisations, including the ANC.
2. This chapter is a shortened version of Moll (1986), which discusses the Latin American debates at greater length.
3. This has been common in Latin America. Schydlowsky has suggested a variety of causes including limited economies of scale, capital-cheapening tax and credit systems, excessively high wages, monopolies, use of advanced technologies and large plant-sizes, and rent-seeking (1979). Many of these are linked to import-substitution industrialisation programmes over many years (see Little, Scitovksy and Scott, 1970: 93-99).
4. Even in the obvious case of land reform, output may only significantly rise after some years and may need to be encouraged via training, credit, markets, etc. (Dorner, 1972: 19).
5. 'Structuralists' argued that since this would raise the weight of basic goods and lower that of luxury goods in total demand, economic growth would be encouraged due to basic goods having lower import propensities, being labour-intensive and more subject to economies of scale (Cline, 1975: 375). The evidence on this point is far from decisive (Morawetz, 1977: 127-130).
6. Efforts to raise savings could play a useful role here (as in China in the 1950s), soaking up inflationary pressures, providing resources for investment and easing BOP pressures (Griffin and James, 1981: 46).

7. In some such cases, as in Allende's Chile, real wages ended up well below their original levels (Pedraza-Bailey, 1982: 42).

8. A useful principle is that 'to the maximum possible extent earnings should be related to production, even in the difficult early days of asset transfer' (Elliott, 1984: 3).

9. For example, the ANC has been quoted as advocating 'an anti-monopoly democracy in which monopoly business is nationalised without disruption of the economy' (NUSAS, 1986: 25), while it has also been claimed that socialism is 'inconceivable' without the nationalisation of banks and large industry (McLean, 1986: 12).

REFERENCES

ASCHER, William, 1984. *Scheming for the Poor. The Politics of Redistribution in Latin America.* Cambridge, Mass. and London, Harvard University Press.

BAER, Werner and Isaac KERSTENETZKY (eds.), 1964. *Inflation and Growth in Latin America.* Homewood, Illinois, Richard D. Irwin.

BALOGH, Thomas, 1961. 'Economic policy and the price system', in *Economic Bulletin for Latin America*, Vol. 1, pp.41-53, March.

BIRD, Graham, 1984. 'Balance of payments policy', in Killick, Tony (ed.), pp.86-127.

CAMPOS, Roberto de Oliveira, 1961. 'Two views on inflation in Latin America', in Hirschman, Albert O. (ed.), pp.69-73.

CAMPOS, Roberto de Oliveira, 1967. *Reflections on Latin American Development.* Austin, University of Texas Press.

CANOVESE, Alfredo, J., 1982. 'The structuralist explanation in the theory of inflation', in *World Development*, Vol. 10, No. 7, pp.523-529, July.

CLINE, William R., 1975. 'Distribution and development. A survey of literature', in *Journal of Development Economics*, No. 1, pp.359-400.

CLINE, William R. and Sidney WEINTRAUB, 1981. 'Introduction and overview' in Cline and Weintraub (eds.), pp.1-42.

CLINE, William R. and Sidney WEINTRAUB (eds.), 1981. *Economic Stabilisation in Developing Countries.* Washington, Brookings Institute.

DEERE, Carmen Diana, 1985. 'Rural women and state policy: the Latin American agrarian reform experience', in *World Development*, Vol. 13, No. 9, pp.1037-1053, September.

DE VYLDER, Stefan, 1976. *Allende's Chile.* Cambridge, Cambridge University Press.

DIAZ-ALEJANDRO, Carlos, F., 1981. 'Southern cone stabilisation plans', in Cline, William R. and Sidney Weintraub (eds.), pp.119-141.

DORNER, Peter, 1972. *Land Reform and Economic Development.* Harmondsworth, Middlesex, Penguin.

DORRANCE, Graeme S., 1964. 'The effects of inflation on economic development' in Baer, Werner and Isaac Kerstenetzky (eds.), pp.37-88.

ECLA (United Nations Economic Commission for Latin America), 1961. 'An agricultural policy to expedite the economic development of Latin America', in *Economic Bulletin for Latin America*, Vol. 6, No. 2, pp.1-11.

ELLIOTT, Charles, 1984. 'The economics of transition: some notes on the supply side', Carnegie Conference Paper 137, University of Cape Town, April.

ELLMAN, Michael, 1983. 'Monetarism and the state socialist world', in Jansen, Karel (ed.), pp.96-109.

ESPINOSA, Juan G. and Andrew S. ZIMBALIST, 1978. *Economic Democracy.* New York, Academic Press.

FABER, M., R.H. GREEN and C. HARVEY, 1983. 'TNC — state relations and negotiations: fiscal and financial issues', in *Namibia High Level Workshop on Transnational Corporations*, Brazzaville.

FELIX, David, 1983. 'Income distribution and the quality of life in Latin America: patterns, trends and policy implications', in *Latin American Research Review*, Vol. 13, No. 2, pp.3-33.

FIGUEROA, Adolfo, 1976. 'The impact of current reforms on income distribution in Peru', in Foxley, Alejandro (ed.), pp.163-178.

FITZGERALD, E.V.K., 1979. *The Political Economy of Peru 1956-78*. Cambridge, Cambridge University Press.

FFRENCH-DAVID, Ricardo, 1976. 'Policy tools and objectives of redistribution', in Foxley, Alejandro (ed.), pp.107-134.

FOXLEY, Alejandro (ed.), 1976. *Income Distribution in Latin America*. Cambridge, Cambridge University Press.

FOXLEY, Alejandro, Eduardo ANINAT and Jose P. ARELLANO, 1979. *Redistributive Effects of Government Programmes. The Chilean Case*. Oxford, Pergamon.

GELB, Stephen and Duncan INNES, 1985. 'Towards a democratic economy in South Africa', Association for Sociology in Southern Africa Conference, draft paper, July.

GREEN, R. H., 1978. 'A guide to acquisition and initial operation: reflections from Tanzanian experience 1967-74', in Faundez, Julio and Sol Picciotto (eds.), *The Nationalisation of Multinationals in Peripheral Economies*. London, Macmillan.

GRIFFIN, Keith and Jeffrey JAMES, 1981. *The Transition to Egalitarian Development*. London and Basingstoke, Macmillan.

GRIFFITH-JONES, Stephany, 1981. *The Role of Finance in the Transition to Socialism*. Totowa, NJ, Allanheld, Osmun.

GRUNWALD, Joseph, 1961. 'The "structuralist" school on price stability and development: the Chilean case', in Hirschman, Albert O. (ed.).

HARBERGER, Arnold, 1964. 'Some notes on inflation', in Baer, Werner and Isaac Kerstenetzky (eds.), pp.319-351.

HIRSCHMAN, Albert O. (ed.), 1961. *Latin American Issues*. New York, Twentieth Century Fund.

HORVAT, Branko, 1981. 'Establishing self-governing socialism in a less developed country', in *World Development*, Vol. 9, Nos. 9/10, pp.951-964.

IRVIN, George, 1983. 'Nicaragua: establishing the state as the centre of accumulation', in *Cambridge Journal of Economics*, Vol. 7, No. 2, pp.125-139, June.

JANSEN, Karel (ed.), 1983. *Monetarism, Economic Crisis and the Third World*. London, Frank Cass.

JOHNSON, Omotunde and Joanne SALOP, 1980. 'Distributional aspects of stabilisation programs in developing countries', in *IMF Staff Papers*, Vol. 27, No. 1, pp.1-23, March.

KILLICK, Tony (ed.), 1984. *The Quest for Economic Stabilisation: The IMF and the Third World*, London, Heinemann.

KIRKPATRICK, C. H. and F. I. NIXSON, 1978. 'The origins of inflation in less developed countries: a selective review', in Parkin, Michael and George Zis (eds.), *Inflation in Open Economies*, Manchester, Manchester University Press.

KNIGHT, Peter, T., 1981. 'Brazilian socio-economic development: issues for the eighties', in *World Development*, Vol. 9, Nos. 11/12, pp.1063-1082, November-December.

LECAILLON, Jacques, Felix PAUKERT, Christian MORRISSON and Dimitri GERMIDIS, 1984. *Income Distribution and Economic Development*. Geneva, ILO.

LITTLE, I.M.D., T. SCITOVSKY and M. SCOTT, 1970. *Industry and Trade in Some Developing Countries*. London, Oxford University Press.

LOWENTHAL, Abraham F. (ed.), 1975. *The Peruvian Experiment. Continuity and Change Under Military Rule*. Princeton, New Jersey, Princeton University Press.

LUSTIG, Nora, 1980. 'Underconsumption in Latin American economic thought: some considerations', in *Review of Radical Political Economics*, Vol. 12, No. 1, pp.35-43, Spring.

MALAN, Pedro and John R. WELLS, 1984. ' "Structural" models of inflation and balance of payments disequilibria in semi-industrialised economies — some implications for stabilisation and growth policies', in Csikos-Nagy, Bela, Douglas Hague and Graham Hall (eds.), *The Economics of Relative Prices*, pp.391-414. London and Basingstoke, Macmillan.

McGRATH, Mike, 1984. 'Global poverty in the South African economy', in *Social Dynamics*, Vol. 10, No. 2, pp.38-48, December.

McLEAN, Hugh, 1986. 'Socialism and the Freedom Charter', in *South African Labour Bulletin*, Vol. 11, No. 6, pp.8-20, June-July.

MOLL, T.C., 1986. 'Macroeconomic policy, income redistribution and welfare in Latin America'. Unpublished manuscript, Department of Economics, University of Cape Town.

MORAWETZ, David, 1977. 'Employment implications of industrialisation in developing countries: a survey', in Royal Economic Society and Social Science Research Council, *Surveys of Applied Economics*, Vol. 2, London and Basingstoke, Macmillan, pp.115-168.

MORAWETZ, David, 1980. 'Economic lessons from some small socialist developing countries', in *World Development*, Vol. 8, No. 5/6, pp.337-369.

NATTRASS, Nicoli Jean, 1985. 'Bargaining with mineral multinationals: the case of an independent socialist Namibia'. Unpublished, Magdalen College, Oxford, May.

NGUYEN, D. T. and M. L. MARTINEZ SALVIDOR, 1979. 'The effects of land reform on agricultural production, employment and income distribution: a statistical study of Mexican states, 1959-69', in *Economic Journal*, Vol. 89, No. 3, pp.624-635, September.

NUSAS (National Union of South African Students), 1986. *NUSAS talks to the ANC*, Cape Town.

PEDRAZA-BAILEY, Silvia, 1982. 'Allende's Chile: political economy and political socialisation', in *Studies in Comparative International Development*, Vol. 17, No. 2, pp.36-59, Summer.

PINTO, Anibal and Armando DI FILIPPO, 1976. 'Notes on income distribution and redistribution strategy in Latin America', in Foxley, Alejandro (ed.), pp.91-106.

PORTES, Alejandro, 1985. 'Latin American class structures: their composition and change during the last decades', in *Latin American Research Review*, Vol. 20, No. 3, pp.7-39.

PREBISCH, Raul, 1961. 'Economic development or monetary stability: the false dilemma', in *Economic Bulletin for Latin America*, Vol. 6, No. 1, pp.1-25, March.

SCHATZ, Sayre, P., 1981. 'Assertive pragmatism and the multinational enterprise', in *World Development*, Vol. 9, No. 1, pp.93-105, January.

SCHYDLOWSKY, Daniel, M., 1979. 'Capital utilisation, growth, employment, balance of payments, and price stabilisation', in Behrman, Jere and James A. Hanson (eds.), *Short-term Macroeconomic Policy in Latin America*. Cambridge, Mass., Ballinger, pp.311-355.

SCHYDLOWSKY, Daniel M., 1981. 'Comments by Daniel M. Schydlowsky', in Cline, William R. and Sidney Weintraub (eds.), pp.326-332.

SEERS, Dudley, 1983. 'Structuralism versus monetarism in Latin America: a reappraisal of a great debate, with lessons for Europe in the 1980s', in Jansen, Karel (ed.), pp.110-126.

SELOWSKY, Marcelo, 1981. 'Income distribution, basic needs and trade-offs with growth: the case of semi-industrialised Latin American countries', in *World Development*, Vol. 9, No. 1, pp.73-92, January.

SHEAHAN, John, 1982. 'Early industrialisation and violent reaction: Argentina and Brazil', IDS Discussion Paper, Sussex, August.

SPIGLER, Iancu, 1973. *Economic Reform in Rumanian Industry*, London, OUP.

SUTTNER, Raymond and Jeremy CRONIN (eds.), 1986. *30 Years of the Freedom Charter*. Johannesburg, Ravan.

TAYLOR, Lance, Edmar L. BACHA, Eliana A. CORDOSO and Frank LYSY, 1980. *Models of Growth and Distribution for Brazil*. Oxford, Oxford University Press.

WEBB, Richard, 1975. 'Government policy and the distribution of income in Peru, 1963-1973', in Lowenthal, Abraham F. (ed.), pp.79-127.

WORLD BANK, 1986. *World Development Report 1984*. Oxford, Oxford University Press.

YAHUDA, Michael, 1982. 'China's foreign relations and the modernisation programme', in Gray, Jack and Gordon White (eds.), *China's New Development Strategy*. London et al, Academic Press, pp.37-54.

3. The Political Economy of Forced Relocation: A Study of Two Households Through Time

COLIN MURRAY

INTRODUCTION

The Surplus People Project published, in 1983, a five-volume report which represents the most comprehensive, detailed and damning indictment of forced relocation and of the human misery which it creates. In June 1985 the findings of the main report were presented in a more selective and accessible manner in *The Surplus People*.[1] While neither could be a definitive account of forced relocation, since the process continues, the strength of both the main report of 1983 and the later book of 1985 lay in the explicit and systematic attempt to relate the evidence of the experience of individual households and communities to a macro-analysis of the political economy of apartheid. It is clear that, as Cosmas Desmond put it in his foreword to *The Surplus People*, 'the resettlement policy is the cornerstone of the whole edifice of apartheid'. It is also clear that no single explanation on its own — whether it is the dumping of the structurally unemployed, the relocation of labour, or the political elimination of black South Africans — adequately embraces the astonishing variety and complexity of the phenomena collectively understood as forced relocation. Many 'types' of relocation have been analysed, ranging from farm evictions to the elimination of 'black spots', to influx control, to strategic and infrastructural relocation.[2] Case studies demonstrate that appropriate analytical frameworks must embrace not only macro political economy — in the form of the history of industrialisation, the Land Acts and 'native policy' under successive governments — but also particular regional histories — of ethnic conflict, of the experience of political resistance, of repressive Bantustan administrations, etc.

The argument in this chapter is a simple one. An understanding of forced relocation is profoundly important for the construction of a different society in South Africa in two senses. The first sense is an immediate political one. So many people have been directly and indirectly affected over the last two or three decades. The SPP estimated in 1983 that three and a half million people were relocated, in one way or another, between 1960 and 1982, and that nearly two million were threatened with removal in the future.[3] These people are scattered in remote and isolated dumping grounds all over the country, but they are also concentrated in huge rural slums (KwaNdebele, QwaQwa, Moretele-Odi, Onverwacht/Botshabelo, etc.), and their desperate struggle for jobs and housing will be the most pressing political and economic challenge facing a new government in South Africa. The second sense relates to longer-term strategic planning. The physical distribution of members of households based in the rural slums demonstrates (1) the fundamental inter-connectedness of all sectors of the economy — 'white' farming, mining and manufacturing industry, domestic and other services, and poverty in the Bantustans; but also (2) the significant patterns of differentiation within the labour force as a whole — between 'insiders' and 'outsiders', between men and women, between migrants, commuters and the unemployed. There are of course well-established conventional methods for studying both the sectoral inter-connectedness and the structural differentiation of the labour force — those of macro-economics, statistical demography or political economy. This paper suggests that detailed household studies are an alternative method of mapping structural tendencies over time that should be integrally developed within a framework of political economy. Two case studies are presented from the largest relocation slum in South Africa — Onverwacht/Botshabelo outside the Thaba 'Nchu district of Bophuthatswana in the eastern Orange Free State.[4] The justification of this approach is simply that such households represent, in aggregate, an accumulation of past history and a distribution of present experience that are vital for planning the future.

HOUSEHOLD MM: NARRATIVE

MM is the dominant figure in a household of refugees from Kromdraai (in Thaba'Nchu) who live in the A section of Onverwacht. She was born in 1927 on a farm in the Zastron district, but the family moved repeatedly and she married her husband, born in 1922, at Dewetsdorp. She bore fourteen children, of whom seven died very young and seven survive: three boys and four girls. She is severely affected by high blood pressure. In a varied working life her husband has moved from farm work to mine work — three shaft-sinking contracts at Virginia, presumably at the time the OFS gold mines were being opened up after World War II — and back to farm work. Their last place was on a farm in the Wesselsbron district. The family spent about five years at Kromdraai but the move was a protracted one, with MM herself travelling frequently between Wesselsbron and Thaba 'Nchu. Initially her eldest daughter B3 (see Figure 3.1 for numbered letter references) was living at Kromdraai on her own, while MM's husband A1 was still working on the Wesselsbron farm. He finally left the farm in 1977 when a new owner expelled many of the old workers and their families. MM and her husband were arrested at Kromdraai during one of the raids by Bophuthatswana police in 1978, but were released after persuading the authorities that they did not intend to stay. Her husband found a cooking job later in 1978 but it did not suit him and he got another job at Welkom in February 1979, with a firm involved in dam construction. The family moved from Kromdraai to Onverwacht late in 1979.

In mid-1980 the eldest son B1, born in 1950 in the district of Virginia, was a driver at Crown Mines, Johannesburg. He had been married but his Xhosa wife deserted him and took their two young children to the Transkei. MM's next son B2 worked at Western Holding gold mine as a surface worker in the reduction plant, earning R194 per month. He had not joined on contract but directly, he said, from the farm in Wesselsbron district. He would prefer to stay at home and 'make a business', if he got the chance. The eldest daughter B3 was a Moposetola — an adherent of an Independent (Zionist) Church — in Pretoria. The next daughters

B4 and B5 were both at school at Virginia, staying with their father's sister in the township. Their younger brother B6 was at school in Onverwacht, as was the youngest child B7.

MM's younger brother, A3, born in 1942, began his working life as a farm labourer, moving with his family from the Dewetsdorp district to farms in the Brandfort and Wesselsbron districts. At the beginning of 1974 he took a mine contract at Welkom, paying R14 a month to rent a place for his family to stay on a white-owned farm outside the town. In addition, his wife A4 had to work for the farmer without payment in the weeding and reaping seasons. At the end of 1975, through knowing some of the workers there, he was able to get a job with Boart Drilling for R120 a month, compared with his earnings at the mine of R70 a month at that time; and he was able to fix his pass accordingly. His family remained on the farm, his children unable to go to school, until December 1979, when they were evicted by a new owner who did not want to farm his land as a labour reserve. His wife and children were arrested and fined R90. He was eventually able to arrange for them to go and stay in Onverwacht where his brother-in-law was already established with his family. Their stand was intolerably crowded as a result, and A3 was anxious to register at Onverwacht so that he could be allocated a stand of their own. His wife could not do this in his absence because the office would insist on seeing her husband's reference book, and he could not risk remaining in his job at Welkom without this. So in February 1980 he gave up his job and came 'home' where he was only able to find occasional piece work. They registered for a stand in June 1980 but were told, along with everyone else resident at Onverwacht already, that they were unlikely to be given a stand until August 1981, since the priority was to remove people from oppression by the Barolong in Bophuthatswana. It was then extremely difficult for A3 to find another job.

By August 1981, B1 had recovered one of his sons from his wife's family in the Transkei, and this boy C1 was now living in the household. B2 had got married, while on leave, to a girl B11 from the D section of Onverwacht who had just moved in with the family. B4 and B5 had both returned from Virginia to Onverwacht where, within several weeks of one another in June 1981, they both gave birth to baby daughters by men who were working respectively at Virginia and Welkom and whose prospects were relatively good, although it was unclear at the time whether marriages would take place. A3 was away on a one-year contract on one of the new gold mines in the OFS. His wife's sister A5 had been staying in the household for eight months. Thus there were fourteen *de facto* residents by August 1981, by contrast with eight in June 1980.

In early September 1983 MM's husband A1 was on weekend leave from his job at Welkom. B1's son C1 was in the Pokolo sanatorium at Thaba 'Nchu for long-term disabilities arising out of a bad fall as a baby. B2's wife had had a baby C4 in September 1981. B4 was living at Virginia at her husband's place with her child C2. B5 was still resident in the household while the family of her child's father were near neighbours in the A section. A3 was still working at the new mine near Theunissen, and his family still had no stand of their own. The walls of a cement-block house were half-finished.

By July 1986 the household had significantly contracted in numbers. A3's family and two of MM's children, B2 and B5, were now established in their own stands in other sections of Onverwacht, reflecting an extended sprawl north-westwards and south-westwards that had taken place in the previous three years.

B2's wife B11 lived on her own in the J section, in the absence of her husband at work in Welkom, while her child C4 spent most of his time at his grandmother's. B5's husband was similarly absent at Welkom, and both B4 and B5 had had another child. B6 had completed his Matric and was anxious to find some way of further pursuing his studies. B7 had a child in 1985 and also spent two months in hospital as a result of severe burns from a flaring primus stove. It is now possible for individuals to buy stands at Onverwacht. Significantly, B5 distinguished between those who have bought stands — a once-only payment of between R60 and R80 depending on size and situation; they then build for themselves as they can afford to — and those like herself who have bought four-roomed houses as well and are locked into a heavy long-term financial commitment: R52 per month in 1984, R58 in 1985 and R75 in 1986. The former, she reflected, was the sensible thing to have done, given pervasive insecurity of employment.

HOUSEHOLD MM: COMMENTARY

Kromdraai was a concentrated informal settlement of 'illegal squatters' on part of the original Thaba 'Nchu reserve. By the late 1970s it contained nearly 40,000 people, predominantly Basotho immigrants who had come from white farms all over the OFS and some small town locations. Throughout 1978, after 'independence', they were repeatedly harassed by the Bophuthatswana police, and their predicament as a numerical majority but a political 'minority' within the 'land of the Barolong' was the immediate reason for the establishment of Onverwacht, through tripartite negotiations between the central government and the authorities of Bophuthatswana and QwaQwa. The inhabitants of Kromdraai were all removed to Onverwacht in the second half of 1979 and by December of that year Kromdraai was razed to the ground. The experience of these refugees is a classic example of the vicious absurdities of 'separate development'. They brought with them to Onverwacht a virulent terror of 'MaYB', the Bophuthatswana police, a bitter resentment of Barolong exploitation of their insecurity in Thaba 'Nchu, and a pathetically disproportionate sense of gratitude to their 'saviour', Chief Minister Mopeli of QwaQwa, the South Sotho Bantustan. Mopeli's political credit rapidly evaporated, however, as it became clear in the following years that he could not provide jobs, services or proper housing. It was announced on 9 July 1986 that Onverwacht would indeed become another part of QwaQwa. Mopeli does not dare to show his face there today.

The working lives of MM's husband A1 and brother A3 suggest a degree of mobility between farms, and between farms and industrial employment, that is not altogether consistent with the assumption that farm workers, being formally precluded from access to the urban areas, are tied either to particular farms or to farm work in general. Such mobility reflects the well developed intelligence networks by which farm workers and their families know very well which farmers treat their employees well and which badly, and it explains the otherwise paradoxical but common observation through the decades that labour shortages have coexisted with labour abundances. But the constraints are severe nevertheless. People brought up on farms experience the enduring structural disadvantage in the labour market of very little education, relative illiteracy and the non-transferability of limited skills. And when they do attempt to establish a foothold in urban employment, as A3's case demonstrates, they and their families

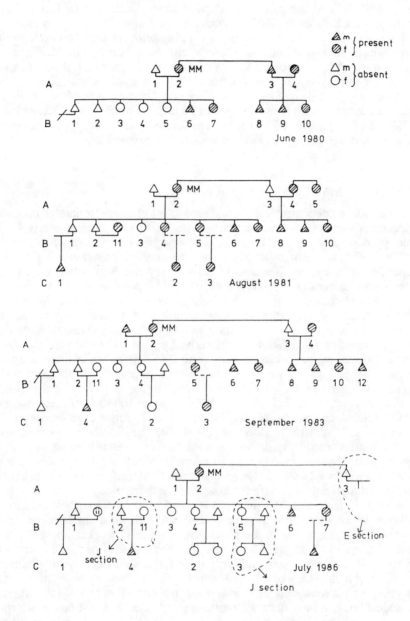

Figure 3.1 *Household MM, Onverwacht*

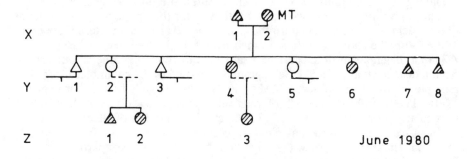

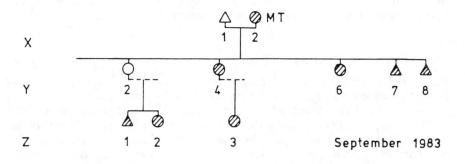

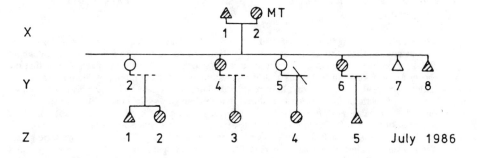

Figure 3.2 *Household MT, Onverwacht*

are exposed either to official harassment or to the arbitrary whims of landowners with a monopoly of state power on their side. It should be remembered that evictions under the pass laws do not simply move people from 'white' towns to Bantustans, they destroy years of patient accumulation of family livelihoods.

Having seen his family expelled from a rented site on a white farm, A3 was forced to give up his job as well in order to wait for the opportunity to register at Onverwacht, by which procedure the family *might*, at some indeterminate point in the future, be allocated a stand of their own. It took three years to achieve that. A3 could begin again from scratch, meanwhile, to compete in the labour market from a distance that enforced the migrant as opposed to the commuter mode. It is possible, however, to observe MM's family rebuilding their lives through the 1980s. The household was well off, relatively, having at least three male members in regular paid employment in 1983. The crucial condition of such rebuilding is having a secure place to stay, albeit at the cost of physical distance from centres of industrial employment that will be rightly intolerable in a post-apartheid society. In view of the enormous cost of state provision of housing, and in view of the comparative evidence on the impressive capacity for self-improvement amongst slum and shanty town dwellers who have security of tenure,[5] the first and fundamental necessity in this area of strategic planning is surely to legalise informal settlements wherever they are established in South Africa.

HOUSEHOLD MT: NARRATIVE

In October 1979 MT and her family were evicted at 24 hours' notice from the farm Ngoanyana south of Tweespruit, close to the eastern boundary of the modern Thaba 'Nchu district of Bophuthatswana. They had no food at the time, and no money. The owner had gone bankrupt at the beginning of 1979, and the farm workers had not been paid for eight months. During the winter, pending negotiations for a bond, the man who was trying to buy the farm, who had himself been expropriated by the South African government in the area which became Onverwacht, several times invoked the Tweespruit police against 'squatters' on Ngoanyana, and finally expelled eighteen families. Nine months later, settled in a rough corrugated sheeting shack in the D section of Onverwacht, MT described the experience:

> When we were staying there we suffered a long time! We had no food, we were scratching around for ourselves in such distress. It was appalling, staying there. Then we saw the lorries come, about to take us away — we were thrown off the farm. We sorted out our stuff in pain, we saw that the lorries would take us and dump us in difficulty and hunger, without money, without anything. We hadn't been paid there, we hadn't been paid on the farm, we were living in acute distress. When we arrived here without food, but with children dying of hunger, we lived on water, we spent three days without maize meal. It was terrible. Our baggage was taken in great haste, we spent a whole night packing our stuff. Our kids had nothing to eat, they didn't understand what was going on. We climbed on, our skirts half off, not knowing where we were being taken or where we were going. We arrived here, lost, in despair. When we came, what a struggle it was! We left there — it was a shame! — our Baas didn't tell us at all that we had to go away, he just left us as if he'd thrown us away. We suffered then in a way we didn't know.

A visit to Ngoanyana in July 1980 revealed that the majority of the huts were rubble. The resident black community then consisted of remnants of the 'old' families and the families of farm labourers recently moved in by the new owner. They all felt acutely insecure: someone remarked bitterly, 'We live by the gaol.'

There had been another raid by the Tweespruit police in February 1980; and people were in constant fear of being hauled off to gaol, or fined from R30 to R50, for being illegally resident on the farm. It was of course impossible to find that sort of money. On the morning of 9 July 1980 the new owner had delivered an ultimatum to three unemployed youths, that they must be off the farm by nightfall. Where were they to go to? Their parents lived and worked in a 'white' area, and the boys could not go and reside with them. So they stayed on the farm with their grandmother, who had been born there, had grown up there, married there, lived there all her life. She asked rhetorically, with simple dignity, why should she move? She and her grandsons had nowhere else to go. On the same day, a vehicle from Onverwacht had also been at the farm, to register those who wished to go there. Opinion was divided: some wished to go, on account of the continuing insecurity at the farm; others wished to stay.

MT has eight surviving children. In June 1980 two older sons Y1 and Y3 (see Figure 3.2) were living with their families elsewhere in the OFS, with jobs at Virginia and Welkom. Her husband X1, who had been a tractor-driver on the farm, had been unable to find any employment. MT's eldest daughter Y2 was a domestic servant in Johannesburg, able to visit home only once a year, and her two children Z1 and Z2 were resident in MT's household at Onverwacht. Another daughter Y4 had been made pregnant at Ngoanyana by a youth who then deserted her, and her child Z3 was born in May 1978. In June and July 1980 this child had a severe chest infection. MT's youngest daughter, Y6, aged 17, and two youngest sons Y7 and Y8, aged 14 and 12, were also living in the household. Another daughter Y5 was married on a farm near Ngoanyana. Thus MT, with her husband, was immediately responsible for four of her own children and three of her grandchildren. Remittances of about R10 per month from the eldest daughter Y2 in Johannesburg were the household's only regular source of cash income at the time. MT was desperate, and explained why. As she talked about their circumstances, she was cleaning sheep's intestines:

> I'm running about even at night. I lie awake the whole night worrying about how we can survive, what I can do, what I can sell in order to look after these mites deserted by their menfolk. They depend on me, if I don't get up even at night, they don't eat, they just stay as they are. So I get up and go to the white man and beg him, 'Hao! Baas, if you would only give me meat on credit, I'll pay you when I've finished selling it.' Well, he hands it over, so that I can sell it and pay him off, and struggle to find maize meal for my children. He writes me down in his book, that I'll pay him another time when I've sold the meat, and with what's left over I buy maize meal. That's the truth, there's no-one who can say I'm lying. ...

In September 1983 MT was still hawking meat, the shack had been extended to three sections in an L-shape, and foundations had been dug for a proper house, but the family could not afford to build. MT's husband X1, extraordinarily at his age, managed to find a job at the Saaiplaas gold mine in April 1983. By July 1986 he was permanently at home, physically infirm with arthritis; MT's second daughter Y4 was employed at the Onverwacht chicken farm at a wage of R40 a fortnight; her younger sister Y5 had returned to her parent's household with her child Z4 following desertion by her husband, and was working as a domestic servant in Bloemfontein; and the youngest daughter Y6 had borne a child in March 1984; Y7 had taken up his first mine contract at Virginia (with his eldest brother probably exerting some influence on his behalf); and the youngest son Y8 was still at school — although continuing administrative chaos and the takeover of schools by the police and army in July 1986 brought this status into question. The household had built and furnished a four-roomed cement-block house in the front of their stand. The corrugated sheeting shack was a storeroom and shebeen, with a high turnover in both bottled beer and Sesotho beer. This is the most lucrative activity in the informal sector. It is also illegal, and MT had been harassed from time to time. After years of struggle to establish a precarious livelihood, however, things were looking up.

HOUSEHOLD MT: COMMENTARY

The first point raised here is that farm removals are the single largest category of forced relocation, yet arguably they are the least clearly understood. SPP estimated that 1.13 million people were moved off white farms between 1960 and 1983.[6] They went to the Bantustans. Although no direct comparison can be made, this figure is at least consistent with the findings of Charles Simkins's demographic study of the distribution of the domestic black population at different points in time, and with Mike de Klerk's study of the mechanisation of maize farms in the western Transvaal. Simkins estimated that the *proportion* of the black population resident in rural ('white' farming) areas outside the Bantustans declined dramatically from 31.3% in 1960 to 20.6% in 1980, while the proportion in the Bantustans increased from 39.1% in 1960 to 52.7% in 1980. The most important implication of De Klerk's study is that black unemployment in 'white' agriculture is manifest in the rural slums in the Bantustans and not on white farms, since residence on farms is generally tied to employment there.[7] A place such as Onverwacht, therefore, is a vast repository of oral history. It is indeed difficult for historians to interview current farm workers about their wages and conditions and experience of change over the years. But it would be a fascinating challenge to reconstruct significant 'moments' of transformation in the relations of production in 'white' agriculture in different districts by interviewing some of the hundreds of thousands of redundant farm workers and their families who are now concentrated in rural slums around the country.

Many of these people were not 'forced' to move in the narrow sense of being directly evicted by the landowner or of being transported and dumped by GG lorries. They invoke a wide variety of particular circumstances to explain their decision to leave. But the implied distinction between 'forced' and 'voluntary' removal is misleading, here as elsewhere. For individual decisions to leave are commonly taken under acute structural pressure. For example, farmers seldom tolerate the presence on the land of adult men who are not employed on the farm. Typically, then, an elderly farm worker with adult sons still resident on the farm but employed as migrants elsewhere will be under strong structural pressure to leave, although the actual decision may be triggered by any one of a number of particular incidents or by a combination of circumstances that is perceived as unique. The point is that the particular circumstances differ widely but they work themselves out within a framework of law enforcement which allows, indeed encourages farmers to evict on the slightest whim. Farm workers may decide they will no longer put up with arbitrary impositions by the farmer, even though the only defence they have is the ultimate one of rendering themselves homeless and jobless.

The second point that must be drawn out of this case study relates to the position of women. MT's family exhibits striking evidence of the differentiation of the labour force by gender and of the extent to which 'family life' is articulated by women. The five grandchildren resident with MT in July 1986 were all daughters' children, while her two married sons had established families elsewhere. The eldest daughter Y2, who had never been formally married, was a domestic servant in various suburbs of Johannesburg throughout the period 1980 to 1986. Her youngest sister Y5 became a domestic servant in Bloemfontein on the failure of her marriage, and both rely on their mother MT to look after their children in a distant rural slum. Y4 was also deserted by the father of her child, but she remained at home where the only possibility of employment was on the local chicken farm where wages were appallingly low — as is typical of 'border' industries established with generous tax or wage incentives for employers from central government. MT herself, on whose broad shoulders rested the immediate responsibility for feeding and clothing this large household, entered the informal sector with vigour and desperation but initially with very low returns from long hours invested. She graduated, in due course, to the most lucrative part of that sector: the concentrated weekend booze. But it is a risky business, and often violent and sordid as well.

This household encapsulates, then, the structural disadvantages in the labour market experienced by women. They have three options only: domestic service under conditions of extreme exploitation by white employers beyond the reach of daily commuting; residual employment at very low wages in a Bantustan or 'border' industry established to take advantage of an unlimited local supply of cheap labour; or an informal sector at home subject to strong competition and official harassment.

CONCLUSIONS

What then, may be learned from case studies such as these two? What is implied, in practice, in the phrase 'dismantling forced removals'? There may be half a million people living in Onverwacht/Botshabelo today. Their stories are extremely diverse, and there is of course no suggestion that households MM and MT are representative in any sense. But typical themes emerge: the pervasive bureaucratic obstruction of everyday life; the marginalisation of women in the labour market, and their centralisation in household survival; the grotesquely disproportionate necessity for farm labourers (and indeed other workers) to render themselves homeless and jobless in order to resist the arbitrary impositions of employers; the unremitting and exhausting struggle to connect more closely a place to work and a place to live. The experience that is *common* to everyone in the rural slums is the experience of insecurity. Above all, they want security: firstly, of a place to stay; secondly, of a mode of livelihood.

Nevertheless, insecurity takes many different forms; it is more or less acute, more or less pervasive. It is therefore vital to understand particular hierarchies of insecurity within the context of detailed regional studies. The history of Onverwacht/Botshabelo is instructive in this respect. It began in 1979 as a 'place of refuge' (*botshabelo*) for non-Tswana immigrants into Thaba 'Nchu who were not welcome in Bophuthatswana. But it was rapidly appropriated by the several tentacles of the state's planning bureaucracy. Housing in Mangaung (Bloemfontein's black township) was already frozen by 1980, long before the strategy of 'orderly urbanisation' emerged in September 1985 as a substitute for the pass laws.

Onverwacht/Botshabelo became the site of concentration of all black 'urban' expansion in the OFS. The economic region which embraces Bloemfontein, Onverwacht/Botshabelo and Thaba 'Nchu has been analysed recently by William Cobbett as a test case for 'orderly urbanisation', and he argues convincingly that Onverwacht/Botshabelo shows 'how far labour provision has moved from the simple traditional division between urban workers and long-distance migrants. Peripheral labour pools form part of extended labour markets, by complementing controlled residential exclusion with labour market inclusion'.[8] Thaba'Nchu is part of Bophuthatswana, and people who live there remain 'foreign' with respect to their access to the labour market in 'white' South Africa. Onverwacht/ Botshabelo has grown up, so to speak, on Trust land but in December 1987 became part of QwaQwa, a 'non-independent' Bantustan. How 'foreign' will its inhabitants be in future, in respect of their access to the labour market?

Whatever the immediate outcomes of state reformism, state repression and popular resistance, the question remains for the longer term. For poverty, inequality and unemployment will not, of course, disappear in South Africa with the collapse of the institutions of apartheid. Places like Onverwacht/Botshabelo — objectively appalling as they are — will not simply fade away in response to the overwhelming pressure of 'disorderly urbanisation', not least because people have already invested very substantially in making their homes there. No presumption is made here to lay down guidelines for a coherent strategy for the future development of South Africa. The case studies do, however, demonstrate that 'dismantling forced removals' is *not* a matter of upgrading or improving the odd rural slum. It *is* a matter of restructuring agriculture and industry and the relationship between them; of undermining race and gender inequalities; of developing a strategy of urbanisation in response to genuine political participation.

NOTES

1. *Forced Removals in South Africa*, The SPP Reports, 5 volumes (Cape Town, 1983); L. Platzky and C. Walker for the Surplus People Project, *The Surplus People* (Ravan Press, Johannesburg, 1985).
2. G. Maré, *African Population Relocation in South Africa* (South African Institute of Race Relations, Johannesburg, 1980); *Forced Removals in South Africa*, Vol. 1.
3. *Forced Removals in South Africa*, Vol. 1, pp.6-7.
4. These are drawn from field visits in 1980, 1981, 1983 and 1986. Onverwacht/ Botshabelo is described and analysed in *Forced Removals in South Africa*, Vol. 3.
5. A. Gilbert and J. Gugler, *Cities, Poverty and Development: Urbanization in the Third World* (OUP, Oxford, 1982); P. Lloyd, *Slums of Hope?* (Penguin, Harmondsworth, 1979); P. Harrison, *The Third World Tomorrow* (Penguin, Harmondsworth, 1980).
6. *Forced Removals in South Africa*, Vol. 1, p.6.
7. Figures adapted from C. Simkins, *Four Essays on the Past, Present and Possible Future of the Distribution of the Black Population of South Africa* (Southern African Labour and Development Research Unit, Cape Town, 1983), pp.53-57; M. de Klerk, 'Seasons that will never return: the impact of farm mechanization on employment, incomes and population distribution in the western Transvaal', *Journal of Southern African Studies*, Vol. 11, No. 1, October 1984, pp.84-105.
8. W. Cobbett, 'A test case for "planned urbanisation" ', *Work in Progress*, No. 42 (1986), p.27.

4. Ownership and Control of Agriculture in South Africa

DAVID COOPER

There seems to be an assumption that rapid urbanisation will provide prosperity for a future South Africa. Yet the urban job market is shrinking. If the economy continues to run down, it will be a long time before urban job opportunities can absorb current urban unemployment, let alone those unemployed in the rural areas.

This chapter examines inequalities in land ownership. I have concentrated on the white farms, because they will be the area where most work will be necessary in a restructured economy. The white farms and the Bantustans are part of one system of land use. White farmers have used the Bantustans as a dumping ground for tenants when they have adopted a capitalist system of production. They continue to depend on the Bantustans and neighbouring countries for a supply of ultra-cheap labour for plantation agriculture.[1]

OWNERSHIP AND RACE

Ownership of land is defined by the 1913 Natives Land Act. Along with the Population Registration Act, the Group Areas Act and the Bantu Authorities Act, the Land Act is a pillar of the apartheid system in South Africa. Land ownership is divided on a racial basis.

Table 4.1: Private Ownership of Land in South Africa outside Bantustans, According to Race

	No.	Area (hectares)	Owned	Rented
Whites	65,972	77,000,000	63,000,000	14,000,000
Coloureds and Asians	2,487	515,000	230,000	285,000
Africans		157,000	157,000	

Sources: 1978 Census; Black Development in South Africa (Benbo, 1976).

The laws governing racial ownership of land were introduced soon after the formation of the Union of South Africa in 1910. The Land Act set aside a mere 7% of the land for occupation by 'natives'. Prior to this Act, Africans were able to buy land on a freehold basis in the Transvaal and the Cape, and had done so to a limited extent. In 1936 the Native Land and Trust Act extended the area for African occupation to 13% of the total land in South Africa.

In areas set aside for white occupation — most of the country — a system of freehold tenure ypredominates. A relatively small proportion of land is held by the state as forest reserve, railway reserve or municipal land. Non-state land is under either private or company ownership, most of it being owned by private farmers. Table 4.2 shows the number of farms owned by white farmers, and the area of these farms.

Table 4.2: Number and Area of White Owned Farms, According to Type of Ownership

	Number	%	Area	%	Average
Individuals and partners	68,459	95.6	77,515,000	90.7	11,321
Private companies	2,599	3.8	5,813,000	6.8	2,236
Public companies	150	0.67	388,000	0.45	2,586
Public corporations	3	—	4,952	—	1,650
Cooperatives	27	—	10,766	—	398
Municipalities	46	—	856,458	1	18,618
Govt. enterprise	207	—	680,653	0.8	3,288
Other	130	—	195,239	—	1,501
TOTAL:	71,621		85,447,000		

Source: Census on Agriculture, 1978 and 1980.

Although the number of privately owned farms is surprisingly high — comprising 95% of the total — company owned farms are relatively more productive.

TRENDS IN OWNERSHIP OF LAND

Agriculture in South Africa, as in other industrialising countries, produces a decreasing proportion of GNP, as manufacturing and service industries assume a greater role in the economy. Nonetheless, the rate of growth of agriculture over the last 40 years has been quite consistent.

Table 4.3: Value and Index of Volume Growth of Agriculture by Sector 1950-85

	Rand Value (Total in Millions)	Crops	Horti-culture	Animal	Index Volume Total	Crops	Horti-culture	Animal
1950	618.9	207.9	69.9	341.1	—	—	—	—
1960	855.6	364.8	125.5	365.3	62	56	51	74
1970	1,499.4	700.0	258.7	540.7	88	82	88	95
1980	7,036.4	3,436.7	984.6	2,615.1	117	120	122	112
1984/5	10,602.9	4,529.1	1,678.7	4,395.1	119	93	136	140

Source: 1986 Abstracts on Agriculture   (Note: 1975=100)

The number of farmers in South Africa peaked in the 1950s and thereafter declined steadily until the 1970s and 1980s when the rate of decline increased.

Table 4.4: Number of Farm Units 1950-1985

Year	Number
1950	116,848
1960	105,859
1970	91,000
1980	69,372
1985	59,088

Sources: 1986 Abstracts on Agriculture; Hattingh, Lanvokon 1986 conference paper.

The rate of growth of farm size has been accompanied by an even more rapid concentration of the production arising from farms. The reasons for this concentration, and the process which has brought it about, are very complex. To understand them it is necessary to examine the structures which organise agriculture, and the political forces which govern state intervention in that field.

White farmers are remarkably well represented in the white parliament which governs South Africa.[2] The ruling National Party and the opposition parties have a large number of farmer MPs. Until the 1970s farmers were the most important sector of support for the Nationalists. Through delimitation of constituencies, farmers were significantly over-represented. In recent years some of this bias has been corrected as merchant, mining and industrial capital has become more influential. Hence, farmers have now become a major source of opposition to the state from the right, especially in the less productive farming areas like the Northern Transvaal and the Orange Free State (OFS).

As part of the ruling elite, farmers have demanded a high standard of living in return for their allegiance. The state has only been able to provide this through generous subsidies to agriculture.

Table 4.5: Subsidies to Agriculture (Rand Million)

Year	Total	Grain	Stock Farming
1950	19.4		
1960	30.5		
1970	65.8		
1980	174.6		
1985	500.1	410	90

Source: 1986 Abstracts on Agriculture.

The government's stated policy is to maximise the number of farmers on the land, while conserving water and soil resources. Starting in the 1930s subsidies were designed to help poor farmers survive. Farmers were offered cheap loans to capitalise agriculture, loans or grants to conserve soil and water resources, loans to improve conditions for farm workers, and subsidies to boost production through price support for maize, wheat and dairy products. In 1970, the government appointed a commission of inquiry into agriculture. Called the Marais/Du Plessis Commission after its consecutive chairmen, it noted that the policy of subsidisation had failed. Subsidies provided 20% of average farm income. Rather than helping agriculture as a sector, it had held back the productivity of agriculture by keeping poor, 'unscientific' farmers on the land.[3] It would be better, the commission said, for a small number of more efficient farmers to control agriculture. Not only would agriculture then be more productive, but those farmers would require fewer workers to live on the farms, and a second objective of the government — the displacement of Africans from the white rural areas — would be achieved.[4]

In some instances, the Du Plessis/Marais Commission was rubber-stamping policies already in effect. For example, from the 1960s the government laid down the maximum number of farm workers that could reside on any single white farm. These numbers were generous enough for mechanised production, but were designed to enforce production based on wage labour on all farms and end tenancy agreements and squatting, which still persisted on the less capitalised farms. In other instances, the Du Plessis/Marais recommendations, when given the force of law, effectively subsidised richer farmers through generous tax concessions and freer access to Land Bank loans, which were previously restricted to poorer farmers. As these farmers proceeded with mechanisation they were able to buy up more land and bring it under mechanised production, effectively displacing thousands of workers. Mostly the process seems to have been one of richer farmers buying out their neighbours.

If one examines the structures of white agriculture, it is not surprising that private farmers benefitted most from these changes. Farmers are represented by the South African Agricultural Union (SAAU) which is made up of delegates from the four provincial (and the Namibian) unions on the one hand, and the large cooperatives on the other. Politically, the union is very close to the ruling National Party and in effect represents richer farmers. Although at odds with some government policies, like the use of land for industrial puporses, in general the union is very close to the government, and policies which have favoured the accumulation of wealth in the hands of a smaller number of farmers have been welcomed. It has also worked closely with government on issues opposed by many poorer farmers, like the ending of labour tenancy and the consolidation of the Bantustans.[5]

Most farmers also belong to at least one cooperative, which represents the major source of farmers' economic power. There are 294 farmers' cooperatives, but 18 central marketing and 26 large trading cooperatives, representing 63% of members, are dominant. The cooperatives take up an increasing share of sales to farmers and farmer credit. Between 1970 and 1981, the share of credit given by the cooperatives increased from 8% to 23% of the total. The cooperatives buy and sell all produce, and are the major input suppliers to agriculture. They are funded by the Land Bank. This means they have access to capital at below commercial rates. Until recently, the cooperatives enjoyed special tax concessions which enabled them to consolidate their monopoly position in the agricultural economy.[6]

The third area of interlocking interests is the marketing boards. These are dominated by producers and control the sale of 86% of all produce. There are 26 boards, controlling most produce to some degree. Freer marketing practices have been encouraged in recent years, but the state still subsidises losses and actively controls marketing. Since the cooperatives are the main agents for the marketing boards, the richer farmers who control the boards, the cooperatives and the farmers' unions exercise a very great degree of control over agricultural production, largely to their own benefit.

The concentration of production has been accompanied by increased commercialisation. Farming is now big business, a transformation which began with the involvement of banking in agriculture. In the main commercialisation was accomplished through bank credit from the cooperatives, from the Land Bank and from the commercial banks. From 1970 until the drought years of 1982-85, farmers spent this money on intensifying production, particularly arable production. Expenditure on inputs into agriculture increased dramatically as farmers bought more tractors, equipment, fertiliser, herbicide and seed.

Table 4.6: Expenditure on Short-Term Requisites (Rand Million) 1950-1985

	Total	Packing	Fuel	Fertilisers	Feeds	Dips, Pesticides
1950	69.2	11.0	22.0	16.0	18.0	2.2
1960	159.3	25.4	47.2	34.3	43.7	8.7
1970	285.8	34.3	50.2	83.0	97.8	20.5
1980	1,795.1	94.6	378.5	512.1	544.6	265.3
1985	2,790.7	131.5	625.7	603.0	1,077.7	352.8

Source: 1986 Abstracts on Agriculture.

Capital expenditure on tractors, buildings, cars and irrigation equipment increased even faster.

Table 4.7: Gross Capital Formation — Investment in Fixed Improvements, Tractors and Machinery, and Number of Tractors Imported

	Fixed Improvements (R million)	Tractors (1,000)	No. of Tractors Imported
1950	37.5	35.2	—
1960	44.2	58.6	11,095
1970	77.8	120.9	18,137
1980	298.7	580.9	20,860
1984	330.6	558.0	5,666

Source: 1986 Abstracts on Agriculture.

As agricultural expenditure increased, land values rose. The largest expense that farmers incurred was on repayment of loans for land purchases. Even during the drought years, land values continued to rise ahead of inflation.

Table 4.8: Gross Land Values in South Africa

Year	R million
1950	1,958.7
1960	3,404.8
1970	7,288.3
1980	22,448.0
1984	30,893.4

Table 4.9: Index of Values of Land in Recent Years in Different Sectors,
Compared with Index of Producer Prices

	Land	Maize	Wheat	Land	Grapes	Land	Cattle Grazing	Land	Sheep Grazing
1975	100	100	100	100	100	100	100	100	100
1980	159	185	202	128	135	145	232	219	157
1983	267	294	258	259	175	217	256	252	220
1985	330	343	303	425	217	270	344	425	283

Sources: 1986 Abstracts on Agriculture; Kassier, 'Tendense in Landbou', Lanvokon 1986 conference paper.

In the process of this expansion, farmer debt rose to all-time record levels.

Table 4.10: Agricultural Debt

	Land Bank	Commercial Bank	Co-ops	Agricultural Credit	Private Persons and Other	Total
1970	278.0	281.8	113.4	136.2	574.6	1,384.0
1975	394.7	384.0	197.8	148.2	665.7	1,790.4
1980	675.6	801.5	866.9	180.0	1,314.6	3,838.6
1984	1,923.0	2,968.8	2,233.7	443.3	1,926.5	9,495.3

Source: 1986 Abstracts on Agriculture

Since 1980, farmers have been squeezed by high inflation, in which input prices have been rising faster than producer prices, and by high interest rates. In an attempt to control inflation, the Reserve Bank set high interest rates which contributed greatly to farmers' debt. Since 1984, the collapse of the South African rand against other currencies has resulted in greatly increased import costs for agriculture. Even with this year's fall in fuel prices, inflation caused by expensive imports into agriculture is considerable.

Table 4.11: Value of Imports and Exports into Agriculture (Rand Million)

	Imports	Exports	Processed and Raw
1960	49.5	293.1	168.1
1970	60.5	431.5	229.9
1980	158.4	2,052.5	1,008.9
1984	853.6	1,842.3	788.6

Source: 1986 Abstracts on Agriculture

Over the past five years, production has stagnated, food imports have become necessary and farmer debt has increased geometrically.

LAND OWNERSHIP AND PRODUCTIVITY

South African agriculture can be divided into a productive core sector and a large, unproductive periphery. This periphery exists partly because of ecological considerations: there are large parts of the country in the arid west and north-west where farming is uneconomic except on very large units. These areas are the most ecologically damaged in South Africa. In many areas the ecology is fragile, and extensive overgrazing and the ploughing of grazing land has led to widespread erosion. Conservation authorities have attempted to improve the situation by imposing a ban on new ploughing without permission and stricter control on livestock numbers; any gains have, however, been offset by the severe drought.[7] The problem is a structural one — exclusive white ownership has fostered a system of agriculture unsuitable to the ecology. An open, pastoral system as practised by precolonial farmers was more suitable.

This sector is also unproductive because of the break-up of large farms in the 1960s. In some areas, units are too small for farmers to earn an income equivalent to town incomes. So farmers abandon their farms to look for work in town. In other cases, they attempt to grow crops in areas which are ecologically unsuitable. This leads to soil erosion and makes the land uneconomic for farming.[8]

In some areas regional underdevelopment makes farming unviable. Farms may be too distant from markets, or there may be a lack of infrastructure to provide agriculture with the necessary means of production. These backward regions are widespread — in the northern Cape, the south-eastern and northern Transvaal, northern Natal, the southern OFS and part of the eastern Cape. In these areas, farmers tend to rely on more extensive methods of production — cattle and sheep ranching predominate.

In many of these areas farms are unoccupied by whites. As early as 1960 24% of farms in the OFS were unoccupied; in four northern Natal districts the figure was 42%.[9] On these farms, Africans survive by subsistence farming or as managers for white owners living in towns. In the northern Transvaal there have been reports of people living on some farms without permission of the owner. In the border areas the government perceives absence of occupation as a security threat and offers incentives for white farmers. These are as follows: R500 per month living allowance for resident farmers; 80-100% subsidy for drilling boreholes; 50-70% subsidy for stock feed in drought listed districts; 70% subsidy for rented grazing and transport to such grazing; 80% subsidy for landmine resistant vehicles; 50% subsidy for fortification of farmhouses; and a subsidy of R822,000 paid to the northern Transvaal Cooperative.[10] In 1980 alone, the government gave interest-free loans totalling R20.9 million to 212 farmers and companies starting farms in border areas.[11]

Another unproductive sector is part-time farming. Around most major cities people live on small farms and work in the cities, their urban income subsidising the farm. The state discourages part-time farming, so no financial, advisory or marketing services exist, and the farms produce very little. The farms are occupied by a large number of African tenants, some rent-paying, who migrate to urban employment. Unlike the larger farms, these peri-urban areas have seen an influx of population over the past 20 years.

THE PRODUCTIVE CORE

The overall position of farmers is as follows:

	No. of Units	Capital Value	Debt	Net Value
1976	75,562	250,741	30,407	220,334
1980	69,372	422,516	55,334	367,182
1985	59,088	728,490	184,334	544,156

Source: Hattingh, Lanvokon 1986 conference paper

Net farm income in the same period is as follows:

	Gross Farm Income	Total Costs	Net Income
1976	40,783	24,154	16,629
1980	84,791	49,344	35,447
1985	163,557	129,212	34,345

In addition to this, income from outside farming is estimated as R12,000 per farm unit in 1983.

However, these overall figures do not show the distribution of income within the sector. According to a 1983 study,[12]

- 1% of farmers, or 590 units, contributed 16% of gross farm income, or an average of R2.62mn per unit in 1985;
- 6% of units produced 40% of G.F.I. at an average of R1.09mn per unit; and
- 30% of farmers, or 17,700 units, produced 75% of income or R409,500 per unit.

In 1970, the equivalent figures were 2.2% producing 21%, 9% of farmers 49%, and 40% of farmers 87%.

Hattingh, a government economist, argues that the reason why 18,000 farmers produce 70 per cent of agricultural produce, is that they control 75 per cent of the resources of agriculture in the country. This tendency is on the increase largely because of biases in financial policy, marketing practices and pricing policies. Particularly in years of good harvests, grain farmers can earn very large amounts, and this is translated into large-scale land acquisition. The tendency to large-scale mechanised farming has been accompanied by a move away from diversified agricultural production. Pricing policies, as well as the nature of mechanised production, have seen a growing concentration on maize and wheat production at the expense of other grain production.[13] Production per hectare has not necessarily kept pace with the increased size of farming. Hence it appears that production in the major farming sectors has stayed the same over the last ten years, while the cost of production has risen rapidly.

Within this core sector, large farms are owned by private farmers and monopoly capital companies which have diversified from mining and industry into agriculture. There are a number of large public companies involved in agriculture. These include:

- Anglo American Corporation, which as Soetevelde Farms runs 'mega farms' in the eastern Transvaal, southern Transvaal, northern OFS and northern Natal, and also controls Rhodes Fruit Farms in the western Cape;

- Kanhym Estates, a beef and maize company with farms in the eastern Transvaal, owned in part by Gencor;
- C. G. Smith Foods, a subsidiary of Barlows, owning sugar farms in Natal;
- Tongaat-Hulett, owned by Anglo, with sugar and vegetable farming interests;
- poultry companies like Farmfare and Stein Bros, owned by the food industry companies; and
- SAPPI and Mondi (an AA subsidiary), major planters in the forestry sector.

These companies, along with the input suppliers to agriculture and the food processing conglomerates, are taking control of agriculture in an increasingly integrated way — supply of inputs, production, sale of raw materials, processing and packing, wholesaling and retailing. The five major food companies are C. G. Smith, Premier Foods, Tiger Foods, Federale Foods, and the Cooperatives.[14] The involvement of these conglomerates shows that a part of South African agriculture is highly profitable.

EMPLOYMENT IN AGRICULTURE

In examining employment on South African farms, it is necessary to make two sets of distinctions. The first is the distinction between 'core' farms and those on the periphery. The second is the distinction between different sectors of agriculture. After a brief description of the overall position of farm workers, we will look at employment in different sectors in more detail.[15]

Table 4.12: Rural Population, Level of Employment and Remuneration on White Farms, 1980

	Total	Regular Employees	Casual	Domestic
Number in Employment	1.238mn	669,086	483,679	85,636
Remuneration White		R87mn	—	—
Coloured & Asian		R 84mn	R 22mn	R4mn
African		R251mn	R63mn	R15mn

Sources: 1978 Census on Agriculture; 1986 Abstracts on Agriculture

From the time of the initial commercialisation of agriculture, white farmers have complained about labour shortages. Certainly there have been shortages, especially at the wages which farmers were prepared to offer. The desire for a cheap labour force lies at the root of much of the legislation passed by successive governments. As early as 1890 the Transvaal government drew up a *Plakkers Wet* (Squatters Act) to attempt to force Africans off Crown land, mining land and farms which encouraged rent-paying tenancy. The farmers wanted Africans to live on their farms under labour tenancy agreements. The 1913 and especially the 1936 Land Acts contained similar provisions. Chapter IV of the 1936 Act forbade squatting and only permitted existing squatting agreements to be renewed.

In 1954 an amendment to this Act made tenancy still more difficult, to encourage wage labour. In the 1960s tenancy was outlawed, and only wage labour permitted. Influx control was tightened up, and after 1960 farm workers found it increasingly difficult to leave and seek alternative employment outside agriculture. Farmers with 'labour problems' were also helped by labour bureaux: in 1959, 87,996 workers were 'recruited' to agriculture, and in 1976 the numbers were 45,570 men and 5,502 women. State prisons are also an important source of farm labour. By 1966 farmers had built 23 farm prisons accommodating some 6,000 long-term prisoners. According to one estimate, in 1980 there were 90,000 prisoners working on farms. This included parole prisoners and those hired on a daily basis from regular jails. Farmers can hire labour from the prisons department for 42 cents per prisoner per day.[16] Although this cheap labour policy did not provide farmers with quite the captive labour force they desired, farm wages were significantly lower than those in other low-paid sectors like mining and construction.

In 1980 a government study estimated farm wages as follows:[17]

	Cash	In Kind	Total p.a.
Transvaal and O.F.S.	R 360	501	861
Western Cape	795	861	1,556

On highly mechanised farms — the core group characterised above — wages increased by 250% in real terms beween 1970 and 1981, to R1,737 p.a. As wages increased, a greater proportion was paid in cash. When Soeteveld Farms started in 1973, wages were R480 compared with a regional average of R249.[18] These increased wages were accompanied by a great reduction in permanent employment. On Soeteveld, labour usage fell from 34.1 per 100 hectares to 1.8. In the western Transvaal, increased earnings were accompanied by a halving in the number of jobs.

Outside these 'core' farms, wages and conditions of employment are much worse. Incomes of R200 p.a. (1980) are common. Farmers rely on more repressive labour relations. In a submission to a commission on farm labour, workers in these areas said they initially welcomed the advent of cash wages and an end to tenancy, but that wages had been so low that their situation was worse than before. Before 1960, people living on these farms were protected by tenancy agreements. Since the abolition of tenancy, they are more exposed than ever to the whim of the landlord.[19]

Conditions for farm workers vary greatly. On a minority of farms, workers are well housed. The state provided R15.5mn between 1977 and 1982 for housing, loaned at one percent interest to 1,540 farmers. Since this represents two percent of farmers one can conclude that the majority of farm workers live in houses which do not meet even the standards of township houses.[20] Most farm workers lack amenities. There is no basic health care, no clean water, and very little schooling for their children.[21] The only health care freely available is for birth control. Farmers show great interest in controlling the population on their farms.

Farm workers are tied to the farm through housing. But they have no security of tenure and can be dismissed at the farmers' whim. Most workers enter into verbal agreements with farmers, and in the event of disputes there is no access to arbitration. Farm workers are specifically excluded from the provisions of employment legislation affecting urban workers, and are also excluded from the Unemployment Insurance Act. A 1982 commission of inquiry into the position of farm and domestic workers has still not made its findings public, presumably because it recommends legislation which is anathema to white farmers.[22]

EMPLOYMENT AND TECHNOLOGY

Farm mechanisation has slashed the level of farm employment, especially in certain sectors. The most affected sector has been grain, which constitutes almost a third of all farming. De Klerk, in a study of western Transvaal farms in the period 1968-81, gives five related reasons for this change in technology.[23]

1. The technology for grain harvesting was available from the USA and Europe and by 1969 was economical if the crop was larger than 250 tons, which was true on most farms.

2. There was a shortage of labour. In the face of competition from other sectors, real wages on grain farms in western Transvaal rose by 250%.

3. Farms increased in size by 74%, to 1,115 hectares.

4. The cost of capital fell. High inflation and low interest rates made it cheaper to buy machinery rather than continue with labour-intensive methods.

5. The construction of bulk silos for storing grain made it more economical to deliver grain in bulk.

The consequence of mechanisation was a sharp fall in labour demand. In the whole region, which has a diversified economy, permanent farm employment fell from 30,000 in 1969 to 26,000 in 1978. Seasonal labour fell from 105,000 in 1969 to 45,000 in 1981, while seasonal wages rose by only 20% in real terms.

Employment also fell because more farmers preferred to plant maize or wheat, because of the ease of planting and harvesting, their wide adaptability, and the attractions of a fixed price. Other crops are subject to quota restrictions, or prices are regulated by supply and demand. The price index of groundnuts, a labour-intensive crop, increased from 42 to 210 between 1970 and 1980, but the area planted decreased from 300,000 to 250,000 hectares. In these maize growing areas, more seasonal labour was drawn from the families of permanent workers. The biggest decrease in employment has been in long distance and seasonal migration. The lengths of seasonal work changed from all season to harvesting only.[24]

Cotton, which does not compete with maize but is a labour-intensive crop, was grown on 108,000 hectares in 1980, up from 42,000 in 1965. Similar increases in the planted area occurred in citrus and sub-tropical fruit and in vegetable production on irrigation schemes. Farmers of these labour-intensive crops were able to rely on a seasonal labour force drawn from the Bantustans. The population of the rural Bantustans grew by 66% between 1970 and 1980 as forced relocations of farm workers and tenants, communities evicted from 'black spots', and urban communities took place. Farmers could recruit seasonal labour from these Bantustans and pay very low wages. Women and children desperate for any employment and cut off from urban jobs are willing to accept wages of R1 per day or less to try and feed themselves and their families. They work extremely long hours doing arduous physical work, harvesting cotton or vegetables, planting trees or irrigating and hoeing.

This change in employment — from grain farms to sub-tropical and irrigated farming — probably represents the most significant shift in agriculture in the last

20 years. It has been accompanied by a huge shift in population from the white farms to the Bantustans. White farmers have been able to draw on an ultra cheap labour force to develop new, highly productive farm land. When farmers in these areas have been threatened by labour troubles they have responded by withdrawing from labour-intensive agriculture, not by offering improved employment conditions.[25]

The livestock industry represents a third of all agriculture. It also serves as an important agricultural consumer — 50 per cent of grain is sold to livestock farms. Overall employment in this sector has not changed much in the last 20 years. Large-scale capital intensification has taken place. Some of this has resulted in increased production, which has been accompanied by a growth in employment.

Among the graziers, there has been a steady increase in farm size and use of capital (fencing and watering points) rather than labour. But there has been a marked increase in the feedlot industry as well as in poultry and pig production, all of which are labour-intensive. The poultry industry has come under the control of the food industry conglomerates, and labour practices have to some degree been influenced by urban employment practices as workers have become unionised. However, workers only have limited legal protection. The dairy industry has also become more mechanised.

The beef and mutton industries operate a quota system of slaughtering, which is to the advantage of the larger-scale graziers and the feedlot operators, who control this sector of agriculture. Following the drought, imports of mutton increased from 2,797 tons to 9,688 tons, while imports of beef remained constant at about 50,000 tons. The national sheep herd decreased from 30.67mn to 26.83mn. The national cattle herd decreased from 8.35mn to 7.83mn.

The wool industry remains one of South African agriculture's leading export sectors. The value of wool exports increased from R226mn to R319mn, although production fell by 3% per annum between 1983 and 1985. The main importers — for those interested in boycotts — are Italy 12.7%, U.K. 19.3%, West Germany 20% and France 14%. The much smaller mohair industry is going through a similar boom.

The wool-buying cooperatives have organised most of the shearing, and they have chosen to rely on manual shearing. The organisation of shearing by the cooperatives, and the increasing size of individually owned flocks, has resulted in the loss of many seasonal jobs. But South African farmers have chosen not to adopt the international technology available (used, for example, in Australia). This technology is only efficient if performed by highly skilled operators. The absence of training facilities for African and coloured workers, and the availability of cheap hand shearers, have encouraged South African farmers to retain existing technology.

Wool farmers are probably among the wealthiest farmers in South Africa at present. The high price of wool, and the low level of imported inputs makes this sector of farming very profitable. There have not been any reports of related increases in the wages of sheep-farm employees.

Sugar cane production is concentrated along the Natal coast, with additional cane planted in the Natal midlands and the eastern Transvaal. The technology used in cane production varies from large-scale capital-intensive, through plantation labour-intensive, to peasant-based production.

Less than 5% of cane is harvested by machine: most is cut by migrant workers. Until 1976, with increasing labour costs, machine harvesting was increasing, but since then, a freer supply of cheap labour has meant that most cane is cut by hand. The preharvest processes have been extensively mechanised. Although some hand planting is done, weed control is almost entirely reliant on the use of herbicide, and burning reduces the labour involved in cutting. Bulk loading also reduces labour requirements. Overall, this has meant a considerable reduction in labour usage per hectare planted. Overall area planted has increased from (1978) 342,000 to 409,500 hectares (1986), but production has remained at about 2.1 million tons. Of this, 800,000 tons is exported, and 1.2 million used locally. World sugar prices have been low until late 1985, and the local price of R275 per ton has subsidised exports. With the low value of the South African rand, and improved world sugar prices, this is likely to change in 1986-87.

The sugar industry is one of the best integrated agricultural industries. The SA Sugar Association represents millers and growers. It has its own research and training facilities, sets quotas and prices, and promotes sales and exports. Miller interests dominate, as the millers are also among the largest growers.

The western Cape is the home of the other large export industry — deciduous fruit and wine. This industry has the highest wage structure in agriculture, because all its resident employees are 'coloured' and thus not restrained from seeking alternative employment by influx control legislation. The industry also makes use of long-term labour migrants from the Transkei. They make up 70% of the labour force and do not have residence rights. Many farmers have diversified production because of long-term labour migrancy. Farmers are adopting micro-jet irrigation which is capital-intensive and also efficient. This will mean a far more seasonal demand for labour.[26] Between 1975 and 1985, production of all deciduous fruit increased from 390,700 to 568,700 tons, while prices increased from R169 per ton to R501 per ton. Net farm income per carton dropped during the same period from R1.68 to R1.40, after allowing for inflation. Only exports helped to maintain profitability. Exports increased from 241,000 to 331,000 tons. Payments from exports were R64mn in 1975 and R339mn in 1985/86.

Forestry is a major employer, and an expanding sector of agriculture. Forests occupy 1,100,000 hectares, along the east coast of South Africa. A minimum rainfall of 800mm per annum is a requirement of forestry. In addition, there are 70,000 hectares of forest land in the independent bantustans of Transkei, Ciskei and Venda. Thirty per cent of plantations are state-owned. Although the greater number of the remaining plantations are owned by private individuals, 53% of all plantations are owned by companies. Forestry contributes 5.8% of all agriculture's gross domestic production. Consumption is largely on the internal market, with imports of wood and wood products amounting to R606mn in 1984, offset by exports of R500mn.

UNDERDEVELOPED AREAS

The areas discussed so far display all the attributes of an advanced capitalist economy — increasing wage labour, albeit at a low level, increasing capital investment accompanied by a concentration of ownership.

In contrast, in the under-developed sector, it would appear that agriculture remains rudimentary, characterised by the absence of a wage labour system. Many of these farms are small; there is poor cropping and low-value sheep and cattle-ranching. Owner absenteeism is frequent. The farms are run by African managers, who may get very low wages or no wages at all, nothing more than a place to stay. Conditions of employment are very bad. In addition to physical brutality, people living on these farms starve. They are far from towns and they depend upon the farmer for purchases of basics or for access to medical facilities.

Many people on these farms are classified as illegal squatters. In reality, they are labour tenants or rent-paying squatters. They may hire grazing from the owner for a few head of cattle or sheep, and plough a small piece of land to produce food for the household. As with families in the Bantustans they depend for survival upon remittances of migrant workers who find work in mines or in towns. On these farms, women are forced to do domestic work for the farmer's wife, often without pay. The position of women on all farms is particularly bad: without ultimate employment opportunities, they take the lowest paid work. They are paid less than men for equal work. They have to do household work as well as farm work. If they want to seek work in town, they must have the permission of the farmer.

WORKER ORGANISATION ON THE FARMS

Farm workers do not enjoy even the minimal benefits of industrial legislation. As a result of this, and the repressive way South African farms are run, very few agricultural workers are organised into trade unions. Where organisation has taken place, it has been on farms run as large estates by multinational companies, public corporations or state-owned bodies.

Farm workers have to struggle for many rights on farms — housing, health care, education and working conditions. But they are most vulnerable: if they do organise and protest, they are subject to dismissal, which means the loss of not only a job, but also a place to live and education for their children.

The unions which have organised agricultural workers are the Orange Vaal General Workers Union (on farms owned by Anglo in the Highveld); the National Forestry Workers Union (on the eastern Transvaal plantations); the Eastern Cape Farm Workers Union (on farms and estates in the region); the Food and Allied Workers Union (on estates owned by canning companies and on sugar estates owned by milling companies); and the Food and Beverage Workers Union.

Organising farm workers has been stated as a priority by COSATU. The basic demands of these workers are: unrestricted choice of industrial employment and free mobility; happy and healthy working conditions; inclusion in provision of social security; decent housing; and equal opportunities.

The abolition of influx control may have a considerable impact on farm worker organisation. If farm workers are not tied to the farms by legislation — and farm workers are still suspicious that additional legislation to this effect will be introduced — farmers, at least in the productive case, will be forced to compete with other sectors for workers. Even in a situation of high unemployment, workers with skills, on profitable farms, will be able to demand decent wages and working conditions. This will offer trade unions a much better basis from which to organise on farms.

THE BANTUSTANS

The 1913 and 1936 Land Acts restricted ownership of land to whites only, except for small areas of coloured and Asian occupation and the 13% of South Africa set aside for exclusive African occupation. Before the 1960s some 157,000 hectares of land was in private ownership by African communities. Since then these areas, designated 'black spots', have been systematically expropriated and the people residing there forcibly removed to land adjoining the Bantustans as part of the policy of 'Grand Apartheid'.[27]

Most land in the Bantustans is state-owned. In a few areas, private ownership was encouraged on land released for African occupation in the 1920s. Other land is under the control of church missions. There are two types of state land — tribal land, where the original reserves fall under the control of the Tribal Authority system; and Trust land, which is land bought by the S.A. Trust and subsequently released for African occupation. However, this land falls under the direct control of the magistrate or district commissioner. Until the 1950s the Tribal Authority constituted a system of government whereby the chiefs and headmen represented the interests of, and were responsible to their tribes. Control over land allocation and grazing rights were fundamental to this system.

As early as the 1930s government officials attempted to introduce a different system of land allocation, called 'Betterment'. This was widely resisted by chiefs and commoners because it included control over livestock numbers.[28] In 1952, the Nationalist government introduced the Bantu Authorities Act. Under this Act, Betterment was used to consolidate the power of state-appointed chiefs and break up the pockets of independent peasant production which existed. Although it was widely resisted, Betterment has been introduced in 70% of the Bantustans. Its effect is pervasive. It gives the government, through the chief, the power to allocate land and to restrict numbers of livestock. This has become a means of political control.

Land in the reserves is severely overcrowded, eroded, and underdeveloped. A system of one family, one plot exists. The prime function of the Bantustans is to provide a subsistence base for the migrant labour system. Under the strain of migrancy, population pressure, lack of capital and the corruption of the Tribal Authority, this is impossible. Only 30% of subsistence, even at starvation levels, is provided by the Bantustans.[29]

In the 1950s, the Tomlinson Commission suggested that the Bantustan population be divided between full-time farmers and people living in rural towns. This would have required massive capital investment and massive urbanisation. Neither was acceptable to the government. Without urbanisation, no change in the land tenure system is possible either. Although a system of private tenure has been suggested, it has never been politically viable. The chiefs tend to lose too much if they don't control land allocation, and commoners stand to lose even their meagre rights. Even now, private tenure is proposed in areas of the KwaZulu and KwaNdebele Bantustans.

The chiefs benefit enormously from this power. In a situation of scarcity of resources, the right to own and graze cattle is one of the few sources of wealth. In one Transkei village, 14% of families owned 71% of cattle.[30] In another, in Herschel, the headman owned more cattle than the rest of the villagers together. Although there is such scarcity of land — landlessness of up to 50% in rural areas is reported — there is also widespread underutilisation of land. This occurs because those allocated the land don't always have the means to work it. Often it is old age pensioners who have land, but they may not have labour. Agriculture in the Bantustans depends on outside capital, so it is mostly landholders with an alternative source of income who are able to farm with any success. The other reason why land is so underused is that it is so eroded or infertile that it is simply not worth farming at existing levels of technology.

The Trust areas tend to be less crowded, as access to land is more closely controlled by the state. Much of this land consists of larger-scale landholdings, an attempt to generate the class of full-time farmers envisaged by Tomlinson which has largely failed for lack of infrastructure. Trust land has also been used to resettle removed communities, and then it is often very overcrowded, as only landowners — not tenants or squatters — are entitled to compensatory land.

STATE AND CAPITAL INTERVENTION IN THE BANTUSTANS

In recent years the state has become more concerned with boosting production in the Bantustans, partly as a way of providing a base for their 'independence'. All the Bantustans have agricultural departments, which concentrate on assisting better-off farmers, or on running state plantation schemes on land which should be used for subsistence production. In the 1960s the state started a series of sisal plantations and, more recently, it has concentrated on other forms of plantation agriculture: tea, cotton, citrus. There have also been some attempts to start settled schemes, especially on Trust land. On the whole, the peasant sector in the tribal areas has been left untroubled, except for inappropriate extension advice to use high cost inputs which the landowners can't afford. Some of these schemes have been successful in production terms, especially the Sheila project in Bophuthatswana and one or two small irrigation schemes. The majority have been spectacular failures, even in high potential production areas. It seems that an authoritarian state has been quite unable to find ways of cooperating with subsistence producers.[31] One exception has been in the sugar growing areas of KwaZulu, where a grower scheme launched by SASA has been quite successful, given the limitations of the land base.[32]

Present agricultural production from the Bantustans is estimated at 6% of South Africa's GAP; since the Bantustans have 14% of the arable land and 13% of all land, there would appear to be room for development. According to the Development Bank of South Africa, now the major source of development capital in South Africa, both large-scale corporate models and support for subsistence farmers should be considered.[33] In reality, it seems that to date almost all development aid has gone to corporate farming. Unless the Development Bank or the Bantustan governments come up with very different approaches to development, there would appear to be little chance of the situation improving for subsistence producers in the Bantustans. The major beneficiaries of development efforts would appear to be the multinationals involved in the supply of inputs like seed, fertiliser and tractors, and the chiefs who use the system to benefit personally through their larger landholdings or through bribes extracted in the exercise of their authority.

LOOKING TO THE FUTURE

About 15mn South Africans live in the rural areas — 9.5mn crowded into the Bantustans and the remainder on farms owned by whites. Of course, not all are equally poor, but on the whole they are poorer than their urban counterparts, in terms of earnings and the availability of facilities. Even in the remotest areas, the network of apartheid laws controls their lives completely.

What is the future for people in the rural areas? At the moment, it looks very bleak. The Bantustans are being controlled by increased use of repressive power, while what 'development' aid exists, is concentrated on expropriating land for plantation agriculture, and turning the landholders into low-paid wage labourers.

Farmers in areas near the Bantustans have expressed their concern about the 'trouble' nearby. Electric fences are being erected within South Africa as well as along its borders. Farmers are preparing for a siege. The outcome of this could be to lower the level of white farmer production significantly and to precipitate the abandonment of large areas of less productive farmland.

On the white farms, the core sector workers have managed to maintain their rather low standard of living. However, there is a decreasing level of permanent employment. Already corporate employers like Soetevelde Farms rely on 'casual' employees to defeat their own stated employment standards: while permanent workers get decent wages, casuals are employed at a fraction of that rate and are becoming increasingly impoverished.

A boycott of South African farm produce could create havoc in the entire agricultural economy. It would lower the level of employment in the agricultural sector as well as having a 'knock on' effect in the agricultural supply industries and processing and packaging plants. Of course the effect would not be comparable with a precious metals boycott, but it would hurt an important constituent of the ruling elite.

There are now increasing demands for the abolition of the 1913 Land Act. This would allow free ownership of land. Although it is an important principle to fight for, in itself it would solve nothing, for very few of the impoverished rural people could afford to buy farms. If its consequence were to maintain land prices, it would surely have the effect of enabling more white farmers to withdraw capital from agriculture. Only if the state embarked on large-scale settler schemes could such a prospect be seen as an improvement by rural people. In the immediate future this seems unlikely. It is more likely that more people will occupy nominally white-owned land which has been abandoned, but lacking capital and infrastructure they will only be able to eke out a subsistence income on that land.

A progressive future government would make a real change in land use likely. Such a government would surely have the objectives of social justice and the maintenance of a reliable supply of food. Experience in Mozambique shows that the first without the second is not very liberating.[34] Zimbabwe's experience would encourage a government to rely on its existing producers to carry on producing if its only criterion was to maintain food production.

One common demand for the future is to nationalise the assets of large corporations, within the context of the Freedom Charter's statement that 'the land belongs to those who work on it'. It has been said that private ownership of land will be retained. With agriculture, this would be problematic, as at least 80% of agricultural land in South Africa is privately owned.

Unionised workers on large farms have indeed said that they want state-owned land, handed over to worker control in production cooperatives. On smaller farms workers have said their demand is for a family plot, to be able to feed their families. In the Bantustans the most common demand is just for more land. These may be the demands, but it still remains to be worked out how they are to be achieved. There must be redistribution of production, but on what basis remains to be resolved.

Three areas need to be explored by people seeking a democratic, just future.

1. *Research*. We need to know a lot more about what happens in the rural areas — ownership, labour relations, state intervention — to plan properly for the future. We also need to study the experiences of other countries, to develop ideas about possible ways of going forward from here.

2. *Building experience of different ways of working on a small scale*. There are three sectors in which new work relationships must be developed. Modest initiatives have started but there is still a long way to go.

(a) *In the Bantustans*. The Luncedo Farm Centre project at Herschel is one example. A Farm Centre offers tractor, milling and seed supply services to five organised farmers' groups. The project helps people to organise around their own problems.

(b) *In the 'black spot' areas*. On one 5,077 morgen farm, 400 families manage to subsist as peasant/workers.[35] Each family has its own plot, which provides it with most of its subsistence needs. The land is not eroded or overgrazed; the main shortfall is in a supply of firewood. All the families depend on migrant labour — either in town or on farms. The community, having won security of tenure, is now starting up a cooperative to farm two blocks of land together. Until now, this land has been fallow because they lack the resources to farm it properly.

(c) *Farm workers taking over white farms*. One such farm exists, to my knowledge. The Catholic Church has handed over a farm of 800 hectares to the 50 families who reside there. The workers are trying to farm it as a cooperative and have just finished their first season. The aim is to build up organisation so that the workers can farm adequately. Secondly, they are improving health and educational facilities. Thirdly, they are attempting to maintain production in the maize, wheat, export asparagus and dairy divisions on the farm.

We need many more similar projects to build up a set of possible models. A study in Natal is investigating church-owned farms, and it is likely that some farm projects will be set up out of this study. One workers' cooperative has already established a small irrigation farm on church land.

3. *Union organisation*. The potential exists for farm workers to achieve improvements in their living and employment conditions through union organisation on farms which are highly profitable. One strategy which unions could adopt is to identify all farms owned by large companies with interests in other sectors; to organise the workers on those farms; then to identify the remainder of the 690 farms with an average profit of R2.2 million, and so on.

NOTES

1. Neighbouring countries include Mozambique, Zimbabwe, Lesotho, Botswana and Swaziland. The Nkomati Accord made it easier for farmers to register migrant workers from Mozambique as workers. There are reports of farmers paying local chiefs in Gazankulu R10 for a family of Mozambican refugees, whom they offer a place to stay and food.
2. S. Greenberg, *Race and State in Capitalist Development* (Yale University Press, New Haven, 1980).
3. Second Report of the Commission of Inquiry into Agriculture, RP 84 of 1970.
4. Not all farmers shared the government's concern over African tenants. The evidence about occupancy is from the Commission of Inquiry into the European Occupancy of Rural Areas, 1960.
5. South African Agricultural Union, Annual Reports.

6. *Financial Mail*, 'Review of agriculture', 1982.

7. Ross, the author of *Soil Conservation in South Africa* and a director of soil conservation in the 1960s, paints a gloomy picture of the government's attempts to improve matters by erecting conservation works instead of improving farming methods.

8. The state introduced new soil conservation legislation in 1982, to try and restrict the worst farming malpractices. Previously, it had introduced legislation restricting the subdivision of agricultural land.

9. S. Greenberg, *Race and State*.

10. *The Star*, 16 June 1986.

11. Department of Agriculture, Annual Report, 1982.

12. SAAU survey of farmers, 1983, quoted by Hattingh in a paper to Lanvokon 1986, Conference of the Society of Agricultural Economists, Pretoria.

13. *Financial Mail*, 'Review of agriculture'.

14. The information on corporate farming is very sketchy. It is an important area of research.

15. Statistics on agriculture are bad, but on agricultural employment they are terrible.

16. F. Wilson, in *The Oxford History of South Africa* (OUP, Oxford, 1971), Vol. 2; Institute of Race Relations, *Annual Survey 1982*; Defence and Aid, *Akin to Slavery*.

17. Submission to commission of inquiry into farm labour, mimeo, 1982.

18. M. de Klerk, 'Maize farming in the Western Transvaal', in *SA Review 2* (Ravan Press, Johannesburg, 1984); G. Young, 'Labour in Transvaal agribusiness', in SALDRU, *Farm Labour in SA* (David Philip, 1976).

19. Submission to commission, 1982.

20. Department of Agriculture, Annual Report, 1982.

21. Submission to commission; farm workers' seminar, mimeo, July 1986.

22. The commission has apparently tabled its report, but it has yet to be debated in parliament.

23. De Klerk, 'Maize farming'.

24. Most of the quantitative data is from papers presented to Lanvokon 1986.

25. *The Star*, 27 May 1986.

26. D. Budlender, 'Agriculture and technology: 4 case studies', Carnegie Conference Paper 23 (SALDRU, 1984); A. Levy, in SALDRU, *Farm Labour in South Africa*.

27. L. Platzky and C. Walker, *The Surplus People. Forced Removals in South Africa* (Ravan Press, Johannesburg, 1985).

28. J. Yawitch, *Betterment. The Myth of Homeland Development* (Institute of Race Relations, 1983).

29. C. Simkins, 'What has been happening to income distribution and poverty in the Homelands?', Carnegie Conference Paper 7; G. Lenta, 'An area study of KwaZulu', mimeo, University of Natal.

30. J. Segar, 'Social inequality in a Transkei "betterment" village', Carnegie Conference Paper 49.

31. M. Roodt, 'Capitalist agriculture and Bantustan employment patterns', in *SA Review 2* (Ravan Press, Johannesburg, 1984).

32. D. Cooper, 'Looking at development projects', *Work in Progress*, No. 26, 1983.

33. Development Bank of SA, Annual Report, 1985.

34. J. Saul (ed.), *A Difficult Road* (Monthly Review Press, 1985).

35. Transvaal Rural Action Committee, KwaNgema, newsletter, 1984.

5. Land Use and the Community: A Case Study

A RURAL COMMUNITY WORKER

THE HISTORY OF LAND SETTLEMENT IN THE VILLAGE

A is a village in a district of the Transkei. The village lies in a valley in the foothills of the Drakensberg mountains. The village is in the sub-ward of J. There are four villages in the sub-ward, and they all fall under one headman.

The area is semi-mountainous, opening into large valleys. The soil is very variable, being fertile along the rivers and streams, but highly erodable on the slopes. The natural vegetation is scrubland and forest, but constant grazing and burning have restricted the present vegetation to open grassland, with very little bush remaining even in the mountains. Rainfall is barely adequate for arable farming. Like most villages in the district, A is heavily populated. There are about 600 families, of whom fewer than 200 own any livestock, and about 400 have fields.

There is a daily bus service to the nearest town, which is the magisterial seat of the district, the main trading centre, and the place from where migrant workers are recruited.

People in the village say they are Hlubis. The Hlubis lived in Natal and fled from Matiwane's Ngwane in 1819. They settled first in the Orange Free State. Then, as a result of continued strife with Ngwane and Tlokwa people, some Hlubi people moved after 1825. People settled in scattered homesteads in the mountains. Pastoral farming was more important, and only the fertile fields along the river were ploughed.

By the late nineteenth century, the district was an area of thriving peasant production. Farmers sent their produce as far away as Kimberley. Today, it is difficult to believe that this ever happened. There is hardly a family that produces enough to eat, let alone sell. Most people get very little from the land. There are no jobs locally, except a few in shops or in the government service. There is no industry. People depend on migrant labour to survive and because of very low wages and unemployment many families find survival very hard.

Before the 1950s, land was controlled by headmen. The government said that chiefdomship was an hereditary, honorary position. In reality, the chief played an important part in local administration, through settling disputes. In order to reduce the power of the chiefs, the government appointed headmen to administer the affairs of the community. They reported directly to the government district commissioner. In the 1950s, the headman of A was S.M. He had the power to give people a place to make a home and a field for ploughing. He also heard complaints from the people and settled disputes. Every year, boys and girls reaching adulthood would go through initiation school. It was the headman's job to organise these schools. He was seen as a respected member of the community and his opinion was sought on many matters. For instance, he discussed and advised about *lobola* (bridewealth payments). Chiefs, however, retained both prestige and practical authority among the Hlubis.

In 1952 the government in Pretoria decided to change the way the district was run. They created 'Tribal Authorities', reinstating the chiefs as heads of local government. The government built Tribal Authority offices and the chiefs became salaried employees. Their aim was to break the chiefs' role as representatives of the people, and ensure that they became agents of government policy. Before 1952, there had been only one chief in the whole district. In that year Z.Z. put himself forward to become the chief, like his father before him. The matter was discussed at a meeting of the Hlubis. The commissioner passed the proposal on to Pretoria. Pretoria replied that there should be six chiefs, because they said the district had six 'tribes'. So each 'tribe' was invited to choose a chief by Pretoria. The government made these 'chiefs' more powerful than the headmen.

The chiefs and headmen have used their power to become wealthy. Although the government sets out the payments that should be made when people apply for a homestead site, these are seldom followed. The chiefs and headmen demand payments and bribes before they will allocate a site. They are able to use this money to buy livestock, and so consolidate their wealth.

When, in 1960, the government tried to impose 'Betterment planning', there was a big conflict among the people at A. 'Betterment planning' meant that people had to move into a closer settlement near the river. Many believed Chief Z was a sell-out because he agreed, along with other headmen and chiefs, to cooperate with the government over 'Betterment'. However, the village headman, M, boycotted the meetings, as he was instructed to do by the community. The chief reported this resistance to the commissioner, and complained that M's absence meant that people were not informed about the government's plans. So the chief proposed to nominate a new headman, until the 'Betterment' reorganisation was complete. They chose V. N. Some people were prepared to follow him while others still supported the headman they had elected.

By 1963, all the villages in the district except A had been planned. The government wanted A to accept 'Betterment' as well. Instead, A's people cut the newly erected fence separating them from the neighbouring ward and drove their cattle into the mountains. The government sent the police into A. The police and army fetched the cattle from the mountains and took them to the new headman's house. When people tried to take their cattle back, police opened fire, killing one person. They jailed 37 people for six months for resisting Betterment. From then on, the government stopped listening to anything from the people.

Under the 'Betterment plan', the people who followed the new headman were given bigger, fertile pieces of land. Those who stayed loyal to the old headman were badly affected. One of the leaders of the resistance, for example, was told to build his house on a site right on the edge of a *donga* (erosion channel).

Today, the headman of A is a man called C.C. He does not live in A but controls what happens there through a sub-headman. In 1985, C was due for re-election. The people of A agreed, with people from neighbouring villages, to nominate a candidate opposed to C. They won the election, but the results had to be ratified by the Transkei government. Although C lost the election, he was again appointed headman by Matanzima, the Transkei 'prime minister'. People in A have tried to fight against this by hiring lawyers to take the matter to the Transkei supreme court, but the matter has still not been resolved.

Betterment resistance has cost people in A a great deal. Not only is land in A unequally divided, but A has also had land taken away from it and given to other villages in boundary disputes. In 1979 another village, B, was moved when a dam was being built. The people of B were given a piece of land belonging to A, without the people of A first being consulted. When the people of A went to the magistrate with their query, he said that the people of A were well known for opposing the government's plans, so he wasn't willing to listen to them.

The whole village is now above the arable lands. The ground is bare because the area is so densely settled. When the rains come, the water rushes through the village, eroding the lands below. Although the fields are laid out along the contour, proper contour banks and drainage channels were never constructed, so erosion is much worse than before Betterment. Yet the government says that one of the aims of Betterment is to improve farming and reduce soil erosion.

However, people in A have also gained from the experience of fighting Betterment. As well as building up a strong community organisation, they have learnt the need for self-reliance. They know they can't depend on the government to help them, so they try to help themselves.

COMMUNITY ORGANISATION IN A

Men in A have always held meetings to discuss the affairs of the village. Night meetings which provide a forum for small groups of people to discuss issues became popular when Betterment was being resisted. Community organisation in A is based on these meetings. In 1962, for instance, the (now defunct) Labour Party advised people in A to ask the government to build a clinic, provide borehole water and build a school before Betterment could take place. The government refused. From that time, people depended upon the meetings to discuss things like boundaries which were being drawn up as part of Betterment.

Most of the men in A are migrant workers. Ninety-five per cent of families depend upon work in factories or on mines and farms for survival. They have insufficient land for subsistence, and there are no jobs available locally. At the age of 16, children sign a contract from the labour recruiting agencies. Many children go to work in Cape Town, or around Johannesburg, or on the mines or farms. At 18 or 20, boys go to initiation school and then get married. At marriage, boys do not have enough money to feed their families, or to pay *lobola*, so they depend on their families for support. They take a job to contribute to the family income. Those who do not take a job are considered lazy. Only pensioners and small children, the disabled and women stay behind in the village. They depend on migrants for money. Migrants are important people in the community. They are active in community affairs, even if they are only home for a short period each year.

Ibuthwana is an association of migrant workers. They applied to plough together and rear milk cows on 50 hectares of land. Before Betterment, this had been a field for all the people. In the Betterment scheme it was planned as a wood lot but was never planted. The Ibuthwana applied to use this land to grow food. Each member was to pay R500 for ploughing and to buy cows. People in Sunduza agreed that they could use the land. So did the headman and the Tribal Authority meeting in September 1979. They said Ibuthwana had good ideas about working cooperatively.

In 1981, Ibuthwana ploughed about 11 hectares of land and planted it. The Tribal Authority said they didn't have proper permission, and charged them with using the land illegally. So the Ibuthwana had to use the money to hire lawyers to fight the case. The fight between people and the government started again. The members of Ibuthwana went to discuss the matter with the magistrate and showed him the papers from the Tribal Authority. The magistrate agreed with Ibuthwana's cooperative use of the land. The magistrate called the agricultural officer, who also agreed. But the headman insisted that the land was for a wood lot. The agricultural officer had no power to decide on land use without the agreement of the headman. So the whole project has come to a standstill. The Ibuthwana cannot buy more cattle because they have no land.

The headman, C, is still fighting the Ibuthwana because he says they do not support him, and the Ibuthwana is fighting C because they want the land to farm cooperatively.

OUTSIDE SUPPORT FOR THE COMMUNITY

In 1977 the people of A saw SAVS, a student organisation from Cape Town, building a community production centre in the local town. They asked SAVS to come to visit them. At the meeting they discussed the problems that people in A were facing. They agreed to build a clinic together because health care facilities in the area were very limited. The nearest health service was the hospital in town, 20 kilometres away along a bad road. The clinic was built during 1977.

In 1978 one of the students, Peter, came to live in A to work as a community organiser. He was funded by a small rural development organisation, RDO.

Initially, SAVS had been invited to the district by Zenzele, a women's organisation active in most of Transkei. So it was logical for the new community worker to work with Zenzele women in A. Together, they applied to the headman for a communal garden, and began work. But a dispute soon arose because Zenzele wanted the garden for its members alone, whereas Peter wanted the garden to be open to everyone. So Zenzele asked Peter to leave the garden, which he did. Peter began to look for other people to work with. People in A told Peter about problems to do with the land, like not having enough cattle to plough. Some women spoke about wanting to rear chickens and grow vegetables.

Through initiating these small projects, community organisation of land use started. People wanted tractors to plough the land. There was a lot of discussion about why using draft oxen was not possible. One of the reasons was because only a few people owned oxen. Another was that in this district, it is necessary to plant very soon after the spring rains as the summer is quite short. At that time the cattle are very weak because of the poor winter grazing. Some people who had oxen, or could borrow oxen, had no equipment to use for ox-ploughing.

After a lot of discussion, people agreed to buy some ox-cultivation equipment for hire, and two Tinkabi tractors to start a ploughing scheme. The project raised funds for this purpose. According to the sellers, the Tinkabis could manage to plough 50 hectares in a season. So a farmer's association with 50 members was formed and began to organise for ploughing. The association members agreed to a ploughing schedule, set the charges for ploughing and undertook to collect the money. People also agreed to use the tractor to set up a milling service. Many of the people said that they didn't have the cash to pay for the ploughing. They asked whether it was not possible to plough on credit and pay later. This was agreed.

After the first year, it was apparent that the Tinkabis could not cope with ploughing 50 hectares of land. They were not suitable for a ploughing scheme because they were designed for use by smallholders. At the same time, many more people said they wanted to use the tractors. People came from other villages to ask about ploughing, and to use the milling service. Some of these villages were up to 30 kilometres away. Associations were formed in four other villages where people wanted to share ideas of working together on the land. The five associations formed the Farm Centre. A second community worker, from A, was employed. More money was raised and two conventional tractors were bought. The members worked out the policy for the Centre defining terms such as equal sharing among members and between villages, free membership so that everyone could join, and payment for services according to their use.

The Farm Centre committee organised the work of the project. If people wanted seeds, the committee would call a meeting to discuss the amount and type of seeds people wanted. Those on the committees learnt new skills: issuing invoices, making receipts, organising ploughing schedules. But at first, people did not have the confidence to control the project themselves. They came to Peter and asked for lands to be ploughed, instead of going directly to the committee.

The migrant workers were very suspicious about the new project. On visits to A they saw the project and discussed its aims. They said that in the past white people had come to steal their land and that Peter, this new white person, would end up stealing their land. Also, people were used to being employees in projects which benefit whites. It was the first time people had seen an organisation which worked for the benefit of people. This alone made people suspicious. The Farm Centre committee was elected from five farmers' associations, by voting at a general meeting of all the associations. According to the constitution, committee members were elected for two years. The farmers' associations also elected committees to represent their members. There had been a long history of disagreement between people who believed in more progressive ways of working together. The community workers and some community members were able to persuade the associations to elect some members who would represent their interests. But the members were still inclined to vote for people because they were powerful in the community. Thus, some Tribal Authority members were elected onto the committees of the associations and the Farm Centre. This led to a lot of fighting on the committees, which still continues. Although the constitution stressed that all people were equal, those who were more powerful in the committee tried to use the Farm Centre for their own benefit. For example, the rule that the tractors could only plough one hectare of land per member was changed so that those with bigger fields could make more use of the Farm Centre equipment.

Men and women were equal according to the constitution. However, it is still difficult for women to express their opinions openly and even more difficult to get all the men on the committees to listen to their opinions. It is a real achievement that many of the committee members are women and that women have been elected as chairpersons of some of the associations.

The aim of having the project came from the people in A. They would elect committees to run the project. RDO planned for the project to be established over five years. Although people discussed the idea of running the project themselves, initially they did not really believe that the project was theirs. How could someone bring all the equipment and tractors to A and then just leave them there afterwards? This attitude began to change as people became more involved.

Although the policy of using the tractors to plough on an equal basis for everyone has changed, the principle that everyone has to pay for the use of the equipment remains in force. This is different from the system that the headmen and chiefs are used to. The headmen expected the tractors to work their fields free of charge. They also expected not to pay for milling, as other people had to. But they were not given free use of the services because the project was trying to equalise people. This created hostility, and the headman at A started to fight the project, saying it was for the political opponents of the government. He got the security police to visit the project; the police asked people about the way they were working. The security police said the project was practising communism because the project was without a leader. They threatened to ban RDO from the Transkei. But they found it difficult to do anything because they did not have any real evidence.

The project operates with serious constraints. Its aim is to help everyone, and especially poorer people. But the very poorest people do not own any land. Many of those who do have land cannot afford to hire the tractors, especially now that costs have risen. After the first few years credit had to be restricted because people could not afford to pay back their loans. As a result, the Farm Centre tractors ploughed for fewer, richer people. The drought in the last few years has also made it impossible for poorer people to plough their fields. This has meant that the richer people had more say in the project, and wanted it to serve their needs.

The project helped the landowners to plough their fields and transport crops from the fields. It helped people to mill their crops and to order good seed, chickens and varieties of fruit trees. As a result of the project, people have gained new ideas about farming. For example, people used to think that early peaches were for the white farmers only. The project also showed people that planting is better than scattering seed, as used to be the practice.

In the first years of the project, the tractors ploughed the fields of about 300 families in A, and about 200 fields elsewhere. People were able to plant maize, sorghum, beans and wheat according to the season and their personal preference. It used to be the practice that after June the fields were opened for communal cattle grazing. Consequently, no one was able to plant winter crops. But once the tractors came, many people wanted to plant wheat. The associations went to the headmen and demanded that this practice be stopped, so that the fields could be planted in winter.

The project has helped families to get more food from their fields. The tractors plough deeper and better than ox ploughs. The tractors also allow more families to plough their fields. However, because the fields are small, all the food produced is eaten and there is nothing left over for sale. The project has not changed the basic subsistence nature of production in the village. People still need a source of income from outside in order to plant their fields.

Slowly, people have become less suspicious about the project. More people from RDO have come to visit the area, and discussed the aims of the project and different ways of working together. People see that working together gives them confidence, and that they can trust these outsiders. They are pleased to be able to use their fields properly.

The project gives people renewed confidence to confront the Tribal Authority about issues like land control, because people once more see the land as a resource they can use.

It was always the aim for the project to be run by the villagers. In 1981, Peter announced that he was leaving at the end of that year and that the committee must prepare to take over the project. People in the committee recognised that to be able to run a project they needed training in bookkeeping, administration, and tractor maintenance. They also wanted to learn more about the general problems facing agriculture in their area. With the fieldworkers, a training programme was drawn up. This involved the whole association, not only the committees, so there would be a depth of experience about how the Farm Centre was run. The training programme helped people to have the confidence to manage the project themselves. During the training period it became clear to everyone that the project could not be run by a voluntary committee only, as originally envisaged. Two active members of the community from A, who have the confidence of local people, work as RDO fieldworkers. They are busy training three elected villagers to take over the coordination of the Farm Centre.

The project has had many problems. The main problems of the Farm Centre are caused by the conditions which exist in the district. Historically, the role of the district as a labour reserve for the South African economy has made agriculture in the area uneconomic. The land tenure system is based on 'one family, one plot'. This, combined with the limited area of land open to Africans, means that each family has too little land to farm properly. Under the existing power structure, it is impossible to reform the way land is allocated because this allocation is the basis of the power of the chiefs and headmen. The severe overcrowding in the district has led to soil degradation and erosion, worsening the already vulnerable position of agriculture. One should not minimise the effect of drought in such a situation. Drought is an important factor in all southern African agriculture. When combined with poverty, it makes a bad situation desperate.

Any family in the Bantustans which is serious about farming finds itself without the resources needed to farm. There is no credit available, no ready supply of inputs like seed and fertiliser, and the markets for selling any produce are severely restricted by the absence of marketing structures.

The Farm Centre project tries to deal with these problems in a way which helps as many families as possible. It started by offering credit to enable all people to participate. This was done in the hope that people would produce enough to sell their surplus and pay back their loans. However, the committee did not stop giving credit to individuals with poor fields. Some people ploughed their fields on credit, but did not harvest much. Even families with good fields consumed all they produced and there was no surplus for paying back debts. The Farm Centre was soon faced with outstanding debts which threatened the financial viability of the project. The committee followed a policy of refusing further credit until old debts were paid off. After the drought of 1982-84, and the rise in the cost of tractor work, this resulted in a drop in membership of the Farm Centre. People did not leave the Farm Centre but they could not afford to make use of the tractor services. This made people reluctant to participate in the day to day running of the centre. Meetings which used to be well attended, were only attended by a few people, and the tractors worked for fewer people.

The Farm Centre has not been able to reach its aim of economic viability. It is very difficult for a tractor service to work without subsidy.

The Farm Centre is subsidised by the purchase of equipment and the payment of salaries and running costs for the Farm Centre vehicle. The charges for the tractors are meant to recover costs and pay for replacement costs for the project. After five years, even with this subsidy, the centre has about R20,000 in its savings account. A new tractor today costs R40,000 and the centre is due to replace a tractor in two years time. So it is nowhere near reaching self-sufficiency. This is in part due to the rapidly rising costs of mechanisation. It is also due to the nature of agriculture in the district — the fields are small and eroded, so mechanised ploughing is expensive while the returns are low. The Farm Centre is economic in the broader sense. Through its activities, people are able to produce more in food value than could be bought from the outside at the same cost. It is only because of the large number of people and the small size of their fields that a cash return to the Farm Centre is possible.

Many people did not participate in the Farm Centre work because they had no fields. These people felt they wanted to work together and share problems. They approached RDO to help them form groups. There are now eight groups, mostly composed of women, doing homestead gardening. This is all quite new; there are many problems of organisation to be sorted out. The groups collect money to buy seed and then plant a communal seedbed. They work together doing transplanting in home groups. Although the gardens are at the homesteads of each member, a lot of the work is done communally. In one village people have applied for communal land for gardening.

The aim of this work is both to encourage people to grow their own food and, more importantly, to change the way that people see their problems and the way they can be solved. Through working together, people practise a better way of interacting, one which can be built into a more progressive form of organisation. There have also been other benefits. Groups may start with gardening work but it soon becomes clear that there is a close relationship between food and health. Groups have started to discuss ways of improving sanitation and water supply.

COMMUNITY ORGANISATION AND SELF-RELIANCE

There have been many changes in the district since the project was set up. We have explained that the chief and headmen do not like the project. They perceive it, correctly, as a source of opposition. This is because the project organises people in a cooperative democratic way, while the chiefs and headmen use autocratic methods to control people.

When the project started, its tractors were virtually the only ones in the villages where they worked. In 1982, the government introduced a tractor service in many Transkei districts. They sent their tractors to work in the same villages where the Farm Centre tractors were working. In Y village, the chairman of the Tribal Authority was also chairman of the farmers' association. He persuaded the members to use the government tractors. The tractors ploughed and the landholders were told to wait for them to come back and plant. They waited in vain. The agricultural officers told the landholders the tractors had not come because the seed that the government had ordered did not arrive. The landholders still had to pay for the ploughing, even though nothing grew that year. They were told that if they did not, their fields would be confiscated. In the same year, the government introduced a 'tractor tax'. Every taxpayer had to pay R20 per year for three years to pay for the purchase of the government tractors. The people of A wrote to the magistrate applying for exemption as they already had tractors, but they were told that if they did not pay, they would be arrested.

Another tractor ploughing project was introduced by Tracor, a government sponsored organisation, in P village. People were told by the chief that their fields would be ploughed on a share-crop basis. The landholders got very little back from their fields, mainly because the Tracor managers disregarded the advice of the P farmers and insisted on planting maize in all the fields, although sorghum in the summer and wheat in winter are considered better crops for the area. The resultant crop failures have left many landholders facing huge debts. They are expected to pay for the high-cost mechanised production package despite the lack of yield. In P and X villages, the Farm Centre associations have been divided as the government has forced people to use a particular service, whether they want to use it or not.

All land issues in districts of the Bantustans are controlled by the government. The main achievement of the project has been to give people the strength to work together, to share their problems and to work out solutions. The project has consistently tried to increase the self-reliance and self-confidence of people through building community organisation. This has resulted in increasing repression on the part of the government. With the recent 'state of emergency' in South Africa, it has become more difficult to organise openly even around basic issues like production from the land. All meetings are banned in A at the moment, as the headman and the security police try to disrupt the work of the Farm Centre as much as possible. Despite these intrusions, the members of the associations have continued to meet and to organise, having gained confidence in their ability to resolve their problems through working together.

In material terms, the project is helping people meet their daily needs. Milling helps many people in the villages. So does using the tractors for transporting crops from the field and building materials from local suppliers. The biggest change between now and in the past is that people are able to work cooperatively on the land. Whereas in the past, everyone had to care for his or her own field, now people are able to organise together to get fields planted. If it were not for the interference of the government, people would be able to improve the way land is used. They would decide on the best way to share the land which they have. They would plough the best land, and use the lands which are not so good for planting pastures or trees.

People see the way that the project works — by involving members as equals, sharing ideas and decisions. They contrast with this the way the government works — telling them what to do and collecting taxes for which they see no benefit. People prefer the way the Farm Centre makes decisions about land issues.

Projects like the Farm Centre will always be important because people need to share their limited resources to farm the land. Under the present system, it provides people with a means of helping themselves which they really need.

In a future South Africa, we are talking about people having equal rights. We would get rid of the 'Homeland' system because the chiefs and headmen who run the system stop people from organising in the way they want to. A more democratic system would give everyone the right to do things for themselves in South Africa. If we got rid of the repression, we would be able to work much more openly to explain to people what they could do for themselves through various projects.

In the future, such projects would be even more important to people, giving them the opportunity to put into practice the kind of freedom for which we all hope, the life we dream about.

6. Regional Development in South Africa: Towards an Alternative?[1]

DARYL GLASER

INTRODUCTION

Regional development policy in South Africa has come under intense criticism from numerous quarters ever since its inception. Much of the criticism has come from a (broadly) 'free market' direction; by which I mean it comes from people who reject any significant state role in the private economy and believe that 'market forces' should be allowed greater sway in determining where capital locates. This chapter suggests that such a position is wrong in its premises and unhelpful as a starting point for devising alternative policies aimed at uplifting the 'immobile poor' in a country scarred by extremely uneven geographic development. It looks at the alternative of technocratic reforms and at the case for a democratic socialist approach to regional planning. Touching briefly on most of these themes, the chapter is intended to delineate points for discussion rather than to offer definitive conclusions.

REGIONAL DEVELOPMENT AND INFLUX CONTROLS

It is not difficult to find grounds for criticising existing regional planning measures in South Africa. They have, from the outset, been bound up with the political goals of the segregationist, apartheid and neo-apartheid regimes that have successively governed South Africa.

In the 1930s and 1940s proposals for developing the reserves flowed from a concern to regulate, though not necessarily to reverse, African influx into 'white' areas. In the 1950s industrial decentralisation was hitched to the National Party's more elaborate programme of ethnic segregation and blocking further African urban influx. When, from 1960, a fully-fledged industrial decentralisation policy was set in motion, it was closely linked to the apartheid regime's goal of 're-migrantising' the existing urban African population through forced resettlement. In the 1970s industrial decentralisation became a means of extending economic viability and legitimacy to the Bantustans, to which Pretoria began granting 'independence' during that decade. In the 1980s decentralisation is at the heart of the central government's 'orderly urbanisation' and its constitutional 'reform' moves towards some kind of hybrid confederal-federal dispensation.

In each of these periods decentralisation has had an 'influx control' function, designed to prevent Africans from congregating in 'white' urban heartlands.

Even in the 1980s, with the formal abolition of much pre-existing influx control legislation, industrial decentralisation is designed to encourage newly urbanised Africans to settle as far as possible in 'deconcentration points' and 'satellite cities' located in a radius of 30-50 kilometres from 'white' metropolitan cores — as often as possible behind Bantustan boundaries. In all of these periods decentralisation has also been concerned to reinforce macro-territorial racial and ethnic segregation and, as a corollary, to prop up existing, or to create new, African elites in the reserves/Bantustans. Even in the 1980s, with the creation of 'regional' planning units that cut across Bantustan/'white' South African boundaries, the ruling groups remain committed to preserving the Bantustans as distinctive political entities.

Clearly, both the influx control and segregation functions flow from a cardinal and consistent imperative: the desire — until recently the more or less unanimous desire — of South Africa's governing groups to safeguard white minority control of the central state and to relegate Africans to subordinate roles in the state system.

Economic liberals correctly stress this relationship between racial domination and the state's attempts to reorganise the country's economic geography. More questionable is their claim that these policies are incompatible and at odds with the logic of capitalist development. Since this is the premise of their prescribed alternative — less state intervention, more competitive market determination of location — it may be useful to say something more about the relationship between present decentralisation policies and capitalism.

DECENTRALISATION AND CAPITALISM

It is clear, from the available historical evidence, that the South African state formulated its successive regional development policy measures largely independently of organised capital, and that these policies have not sprung into being in order to serve capital's 'objective' interests.[1] Yet, to conclude from this that South Africa's regional development policies are *anti-capitalist* is to seriously misread the complex dynamics underlying them and to confuse any attempt to formulate alternatives.

Regional policy makers in South Africa have, in the first place, always accepted that the state is in a relationship of externality vis-à-vis the capitalist economy, that it cannot directly plan and control the geographical movement of capital. As much as anything else, the size of the financial incentives offered to capitalists to decentralise is a reflection of the lengths to which the state must go to influence private investment decisions which are beyond its direct control: planners are forced to engage in continuous institutionalised bribery, and even then they have no guarantee that capitalists will respond favourably to their lures. The unpredictability is not peculiar to the 'irrational' apartheid state: it is, as Offe and others have noted, endemic to state planning in capitalist societies. Capital's spurning of state incentives in particular growth points thus cannot be taken as 'proof' of the anti-capitalist character of South Africa's regional development programme.

The ambiguity of the relationship between capital and regional policy in South Africa can be illustrated in a number of ways. Firstly, capitalist opposition to the industrial decentralisation programme has never been unanimous. There are segments of organised industry — principally those singled out as beneficiaries of the policy — who have prevented united capitalist opposition to state measures and allowed the state to play capitalists off against each other. A number of regional chambers of industry — those in the northern Transvaal, Pietermaritzburg and Border areas — have strongly favoured the programme, generating major tensions in the Federated Chamber of Industries, while the Afrikaanse Handelsinstituut has given its support to decentralisation policy, albeit less enthusiastically now than in the past.

Secondly, organised industry's influence has helped to shape and change regional development policy. Repeated increases in state-provided incentives are themselves a response, in part, to capitalist requests — even while eliciting fresh rounds of complaints from industry about the decentralisation programme's costs. The Verwoerd government's refusal to allow 'white' capital into the Bantustans under the post-1960 border industry policy was also a response, in part, to capitalist pressure, in this case organised industry's fear of being undercut by mini-Hong Kongs on the South African periphery. One consistent capitalist call has been for fewer, better placed growth points — a preference to which the state has, in its practice if not in its rhetoric, acceded; thus the border industry policy's attention to developing industrial suburbs like Rosslyn and Hammarsdale and substantial towns like Pietermaritzburg in the 1960s; and thus the present stress on developing 'deconcentration points' in the proximity of major urban centres.

Where the state has proceeded with decentralisation measures perceived as particularly anti-business — like the 1967 Physical Planning Act — it has often been forced by capitalist pressure, investment strikes and evasions to rework, reduce enforcement levels of, or abandon altogether its course. And in another instance — that of the Good Hope plan — policies have been explicitly shaped to secure the political and economic cooperation of organised industry, which, in part, it obtained, as witness direct capitalist participation in organs like the Regional Development Advisory Committee. Two writers hostile to state plans, and who in another context have argued that they run counter to capitalist interests, have admitted that business 'is immersed' in the Good Hope effort.[2]

Finally, capitalist investors have never been quite as unresponsive to decentralisation measures as they are purported to have been. In the 1960s the state subsidised (and channelled) what were in effect spontaneous drives towards industrial suburbanisation. The 1970s saw the state assist a steady, and at least partly spontaneous, stream of labour-intensive capitalist investment to well placed border and Bantustan growth points, and the fastest relative increase in manufacturing employment occurred in these areas. And the Good Hope plan has, since 1982, massively boosted the rate of private capitalist investment in outlying areas (though this may now be running out of steam).

Quite clearly, then, the liberal assumption that capital has played no part in the formulation and implementation of South Africa's regional policy measures, or that it has been totally unresponsive and universally hostile to them, is wide of the mark. These are not 'anti-capitalist' measures, and any critique of them, or presentation of alternatives, must begin with a recognition of this premise.

It remains true, however, that South Africa's regional policies are premised on state interventionism, as they are in other capitalist societies. They have indeed imposed costs on, and elicited quite longstanding suspicion from the bulk of organised industry; and they do modify, regulate, even constrain the 'free' operation of the market. This has been sufficient to earn them the intense disfavour of free marketeers. But how credible is the 'free market' alternative to the state's regional policies?

DECENTRALISATION'S 'FREE MARKET' CRITICS

Plausible or not, it is articulated frequently. What I call the 'free market' approach is not one of blanket opposition either to industrial decentralisation or to state intervention *per se*. With regard to the former, a distinction is made between 'organic' and artificial decentralisation. Left alone, the argument goes, the market will initially generate industrial concentrations based on 'economies of agglomeration'. Once the optimal city size has been passed, 'dis-economies' will become evident and industry will begin to disperse outwards. 'The major attraction of the metropolitan industrial zones', writes *Financial Mail*, 'is their highly developed social and physical infrastructure, their established markets and trained labour pool'. These attractions are still very much at work in South Africa. However, when 'the cost of congestion becomes unacceptably high', industries will relocate and capital will be invested elsewhere, initially in 'zones contiguous to metropolitan areas.'[3] Likewise, Van der Horst has argued that

> In the natural course of the growth of an industrial area, a measure of decentralisation both of industries and of housing usually does take place. Thus as the land in the centre rises in value and rents and taxes increase and costs of transport rise because of congestion, factories move out. ... This movement, however, which is genuine decentralisation brought about by economic factors . . . is not, I take it, what is meant by the decentralisation of industry [in South Africa].[4]

What these writers criticise is not state involvement in fostering decentralisation but what they consider to be the government's artificial, politically-motivated, hastening of the dispersal process. Businessmen are, they argue, induced to locate in economic backwaters with few, if any, locational attractions. In the end, 'society' pays a high price: the state is stretched to its fiscal limits by subsidisation of wasteful incentive schemes, the burden of which is borne by taxpayers; at the same time jobs that could have been cheaply generated in the metropolitan centres are destroyed by the government's restrictions on the employment of African labour in 'white' urban areas. Assessing the government's latest regional development policy revisions, the *Financial Mail* writes:

> Its prospects for success depend on the extent to which government will interfere in what should be an organic economic process. ... If the proposals are designed to help the organic process along, the private sector will support the plan.[5]

The *Sunday Times* quotes Harry Oppenheimer as saying that 'decentralisation has merit when it is based upon sound economic principles. If not, it will fail.'[6] In other words: decentralisation policies are acceptable as long as they harmonise with market signals and help capitalists make profits.

There has indeed been an 'organic' dispersal of industry to 'zones contiguous with metropolitan areas' — and the state has in fact intervened to assist and accelerate this spontaneous 'suburbanisation' of industry. We have been shown that, contrary to the underlying assumption of economic-liberal arguments, South Africa's spatial policies have never departed from the basic premises of planning under capitalism, and have often, in fact, buttressed patterns of spatial reorganisation arising more-or-less endogenously from the capitalist accumulation process itself. In spite of this urban-rural inequalities have been exacerbated, 80% of Bantustan residents still live in poverty, and more of them than ever are confronted by absolute destitution. Some Bantustans (like Transkei, Venda, Kangwane or QwaQwa) are beyond the commuting range of major 'white' industrial centres while others, notably Ciskei, are located in economically depressed and declining parts of the country. Bantustans as a whole still (and despite some quantitative improvement in their share) produce no more than about 3% of the country's gross geographic product, despite rapid growth from a low base during the 1970s and 1980s.[7] The South African economy as a whole is mired in a long period of stagnation. Under these conditions it becomes possible to question seriously whether 'organic' decentralisation, helped along by the state, can on its own address the needs of the 'immobile poor' trapped in deeply underdeveloped regions of the country. This question becomes all the more germane if we accept the recent thesis of Bell that spontaneous tendencies towards industrial decentralisation in South Africa are on the wane with the gradual exhaustion of the potential for decentralisation via labour-intensive sectors.[8]

'Free market' approaches to regional development have been discredited by their association with theories of spatial equilibrium. Positing an economic model in which there exists complete freedom of movement of 'factors of production', especially labour power and capital, the equilibrium theorists argue that an equalisation of growth rates and incomes between regions would eventuate in market societies. This conception fell prey to criticisms from within a modernisation paradigm long before dependency theory became vogue. Friedmann, who translated Rostow's 'stages-of-growth' model into a theory of spatial evolution, stated bluntly that '[t]he indisputable fact is that regional convergence will not automatically occur in the course of a nation's development history'[9] while most other non-radical development models — for example Myrdal's 'cumulative causation' — accept that industrialisation in poorer countries is complicated by a tendency towards spatial polarisation. The theory of spatial equilibrium, most of these 'reformist' writers implicitly or explicitly argue, does not recognise the extent to which the diffusion of information is uneven and imperfect; the extent to which investors and migrants alike can be misinformed; or the extent to which spatial distance itself implies a degree of market 'malfunction'. To this the reformist positions counterpose calls for substantial state intervention to arrest market malfunctions and promote regional equality, and many advanced capitalist countries, notably France, Italy and the United Kingdom have indeed initiated regional development programmes aimed at uplifting poorer regions by attracting capital there. A number of writers broadly on the left of the political spectrum — like Stuart Holland — have themselves argued the need for a heavy dose of state capitalism to counteract capitalism's intrinsic tendency towards regional inequality.

Of course radical dependency theorists argued that even state intervention would not be sufficient to ensure the economic development of 'satellite' countries locked into a world capitalist system dominated by a small number of 'metropolitan' centres, and the same obstacles would confront 'satellite' regions vis-à-vis their own metropolitan cores. Others of more orthodox Marxist persuasion hold that imperialism could, in fact, serve as a 'pioneer' of capitalist development, spreading it to backward countries and regions.

During the post-war period, certain capitalist countries — the 'newly industrialised countries' (NICs) — have indeed achieved remarkable success in breaking out of the 'dependency' straightjacket. But many of these 'miracles' — notably South Korea, Singapore, and Taiwan — achieved their gains on the basis of economies that are in certain respects highly regulated by the state.[10] Some post-war mixed and market economies have also achieved a certain limited effectiveness, at least by quantitative criteria, in stabilising or reducing spatial disparities between internal regions. This has been in large measure due to autonomous, market-directed 'spillover' effects, boosted by state intervention.

However, if as Stöhr and Tödtling conclude in a 1977 survey, 'traditional regional policy instruments' in capitalist countries have failed to attack the 'basic parameters underlying spatial inequalities in living levels', it is not *because* of state intervention.[11] It appears, rather, to be the other way round: that state measures have failed because of tendencies in the process of capital accumulation which generate a permanent instability of spatial relations and reinforce (in changing forms) the basic features of 'uneven development'. A number of writers on the Left — Damette, Lapple and Hoogstraten, and others — have attempted to explain this phenomenon theoretically, referring variously to the effects of world competition, the hyper-mobility of capital, the particular way in which modes of production articulate, and other factors. This paper does not propose to survey or assess these explanations. But the empirical evidence of a regional crisis in capitalist countries, in some cases after decades of state intervention, provides ground for pessimism about the capacity of the market alone, or even with state intervention, to arrest spatial disparities.

DECENTRALISATION'S TECHNOCRATIC CRITICS

There is, nonetheless, a reformist tradition distinct from the economic liberal one, which presents the regional problem as essentially a technical one unrelated to the specificities of capitalist accumulation. This technocratic ideology has its adherents in South Africa today.

For these reformers, and in contrast to the free marketeers, the curse is not state interventionism *per se* — not even where state intervention is extensive — but the 'political' or 'ideological' character of present decentralisation policies. What is needed, they argue, is a decentralisation programme which frees state planning from some of the more rigid fetters of apartheid and 'separate development', allowing it to be pursued along lines that are more technically rational and racially neutral. This is the argument favoured by technocrats in the state, as well as by many private planners. It has also achieved some resonance amongst businessmen, who have generally welcomed the technicist bent of the Good Hope plan.

There have always been technocrats aplenty in the state's planning branches, notably in the Social and Economic Planning Council of the later 1940s, the Natural Resources Development Council in the 1950s and early 1960s, and in the Department of Planning from 1964 through to the late 1970s. For much of that time the technocrats deferred to the 'ideological' social engineers in the Department of Native Affairs and its successors. Today the technocrats, concentrated in the powerful Department of Constitutional Development and Planning, are ascendant, shifting the emphasis to more technocratic approaches to, and public presentations of, regional planning. Thus the Good Hope plan, drawing on an idea that has been lying relatively dormant in planning circles for some time, divides South Africa's land surface into eight 'functional' regions organised around development axes that cut across the 'soft' borders of the Bantustans. New emphasis has also been placed on 'cross-border' development organs and projects, and on 'multi-lateral' financing and planning.

How adequate is the technocratic approach as a starting point for thinking about regional planning alternatives? A critique must begin, I think, by stating the obvious: that for all its 'technocratic' pretensions, the Good Hope plan is being pursued alongside a continued central government commitment to maintaining the 'self-governing' Bantustans (indeed extending their autonomy), preserving the 'national states' of Transkei, Bophuthatswana, Venda and Ciskei (TBVC), and possibly even creating black 'city states' in a further extension of racial and ethnic balkanisation. The Good Hope plan was, indeed, closely associated from the outset with schemes for constellations and ethnic confederations in southern Africa, and is also — as I have mentioned — integral to 'orderly urbanisation'.

The technocrats in the planning apparatus either themselves endorse this neo-apartheid framework or, shying away from 'politics', pragmatically take it as a given. The technocrats are thus not innocent of direct collaboration with racial domination.

Nonetheless, currently influential technocrats should not be seen simply as providing a new and more effective mask for an unchanging reality of racial domination. Technocracy is an ideological discourse with a powerful independent logic, sustained by specialised technical strata with genuinely 'scientific' pretensions. Technocrats often come into conflict with key tenets of apartheid, and many, convinced of the essentially neutral and benevolent purpose of their work, align themselves to a pragmatically reformist political position. A critique of the Botha regime's technocratic corps — and of reformist planners and specialists outside the state — must therefore go beyond simply demonstrating their complicity with 'modernised' racial domination. After all, planning specialists and other technocrats will be around long after apartheid really is buried: and so, therefore, will the positivist, apolitical ideological baggage they carry around with them. It is the ideological baggage itself which needs to be unpacked.

As is often noted, technocratic ideology, offered unchecked sway, gives way all too easily to the 'rule of experts'. This is not meant to imply literally that scientific and technical strata become a ruling class; their apparent 'rule' almost always conceals the dominance of other social strata whom they serve. Nonetheless rule by experts does entail a preponderant role in the planning process for experts, economic managers and organised interest groups; as a corollary, it entails the insulation of the planning process from public political scrutiny and popular participation. This 'depoliticisation' seems to be the central intention behind the new administrative and planning organs hatched by the Botha regime, for example the Regional Services Councils and Regional Development Advisory Committees. This has been recognised as a problem even by some of the more advanced members of the reformist camp in South Africa. Reflecting on this technocratic reform approach, the Buthelezi Commission worried that multi-racial planning through development councils and development banks would be dominated by 'economists, accountants and planners', putting 'grass-roots representatives of Black South African communities at a disadvantage' and ensuring that 'economic and technical considerations' swamp 'expressions of the political opinion of rank-and-file Black South Africans'.[12] It hardly need be said that not only now, but also in a post-apartheid future, it will be necessary to challenge technocratic logic and struggle to make the experts (who will be desperately needed and thus in a strong bargaining position) more accountable, and to maximise popular participation in the planning process.

A further consequence of technocratic ideology is that it masks the extent to which economic development strategies involve political, and not exclusively technical, choices, thereby allowing particular policy decisions to be presented as the only technically possible ones. Not only does this serve to confer legitimacy on ruling groups which may seek to bar the masses from the planning process; it also generates a conservative bias in development planning by preventing — even where ruling groups may desire it — an exploration of those genuinely transformative policy options which technocrats may relegate to the realm of impractical utopias. That some options may *in fact* be impractical, and utopian, is beyond dispute, but this should not preclude open and wide-ranging public discussion of more 'radical' long-term options than those preferred by technocrats; and this discussion in turn requires a tempering of popular deference to 'experts'.

The dangers associated with such deference are likely to grow, rather than recede, with the advent of a post-apartheid regime. Because of its unique and severe problem of illegitimacy, the white minority government in South Africa is unlikely to succeed in legitimising its role or its developmental choices by using technocratic ideology. A future post-apartheid government, overwhelmed by urgent economic difficulties and dependent on the advice of excessively cautious experts, may be tempted to temper its radicalism indefinitely and — moreover — encounter little popular challenge in doing so. The call here is not for an ultra-left programme of socio-economic reconstruction; such a programme, especially when implemented from the top down and by coercive methods, leads to tragic disasters like China's 'cultural revolution'. What is being stressed here, rather, is the need for a full unmasking and open public discussion of the short, medium and long-term *choices* facing societies and governments. Planning must, within reasonable limits, be politicised, not in the sense of being subordinated to a utopian and authoritarian 'mass line' determined by an entrenched 'leading party', but in the sense of being self-conscious of its political premises and subjected, where it is amenable, to political scrutiny and decision. And it must, if it is to enjoy popular legitimacy and remain in touch with popular needs, be subjected to a politics that is democratic in its essentials. This entails, at least, an unfettered public contestation of macro-development plans at the national level; and continuous input from representatives of localities, regions and popular classes likely to be affected by the consequences of whatever plans may finally be adopted.

REGIONAL PLANNING AND SOCIALISM

In these conditions of post-apartheid democratisation, the question will arise whether it is politically feasible and economically viable to pursue a socialist path of economic development, both in general and with specific reference to regional planning. Socialists will have to demonstrate, through a critical examination of other post-liberation and 'actual socialist' experiences, and with reference to the specific features of South Africa's own spatial development, both the possibility and the desirability of a socialist approach to regional planning in our country.

This will be no simple matter. It is no longer possible, as it was only a decade or so ago, to be securely sanguine about the benefits of socialist development. In the early 1970s, dependency theory held sway on the Left with its insistence that capitalist development in the Third World was at an impasse; and socialism appeared to offer its own, seemingly clearcut alternatives, most famously the 'Chinese model' of participatory egalitarian and self-reliant development. Since then, bemused socialists have witnessed the popular repudiation of radical Maoism in China; the slowing growth rates of the USSR and eastern Europe; the catastrophic failure of Africa's various (more or less orthodox) socialisms; the ascendancy of 'market socialism' as a 'reform' model in parts of eastern Europe and China; and the increased adoption of material in place of moral incentives in most actual socialist countries. At the same time the spectacular growth of the capitalist NICs during the 1960s and 1970s, together with the growing sophistication of their economies and class structures, 'drove a gaping hole' through dependency theory.[13]

Yet if dependency theory prematurely proclaimed capitalism's incapacity to bring about development in the Third World — at precisely the time, the 1970s, when many of the NICs were doing exceptionally well — then the 1980s may be a peculiarly bad time to herald capitalism once again as the last, best hope of underdeveloped countries. Much of the capitalist Third World is facing an unprecedented crisis of capital export to advanced countries, and the performance of many NIC 'miracles' is losing its sheen.[14] Moreover, socialism's balance sheet over the last few decades has not been completely negative: it has continued to notch up solid developmental achievements, both in terms of growth and equity, in some underdeveloped countries.

There remains, then, room to agree with the cautious judgement of Gordon White that

'Proto-socialist' development in Third World countries is neither historically inappropriate, nor is it the only path to development. The experience of Third World socialist countries suggests, on the contrary, that they constitute a *distinctive* and *viable* mode of development, in terms of certain key social, economic and political indices, and — though this may be true to lesser or greater degrees — *preferable* to hypothetical capitalist alternatives in so far as the interests of the mass of the population are concerned.[15]

In capitalist South Africa — now facing chronic economic stagnation and scarred by extremely uneven development — the prospects for an effective socialist development strategy, one capable of realising in reasonable measure the objectives of equity, democracy and efficiency, are better than in other African countries for a variety of reasons, among them this country's level of utilisable industrial capacity, its developed social and human infrastructure, the disintegration of the independent peasantry and — perhaps above all — the presence of a large, increasingly organised and assertive working class. Work and discussion is only now beginning on what the outlines of an alternative socialist economic strategy in South Africa might look like.[16] The following comments on regional development policy are intended as a brief and very preliminary contribution to this discussion.

A post-apartheid society will be able to alleviate certain kinds of spatial economic and demographic imbalances without necessarily committing itself to a socialist programme. The dismantling of influx controls will result in steady out-migration from some deeply underdeveloped areas, expanding the scope for development in areas of subsistence agriculture and reducing the unemployment problem in some particularly poor areas. Apartheid's regional development programme has focussed inordinately on industrial decentralisation around growth poles, an approach which, in the absence of effective agricultural development, may partly ameliorate certain quantitative inter-regional inequalities but exacerbates intra-regional ones; the solution of spatial inequalities is necessarily bound up with the solution of inter-sectoral inequalities, as for example between industrial and agricultural incomes. At the same time agricultural development and out-migration displace a good deal of the problem to the sphere of urban planning — and the decentralisation of industry to developing growth and urbanisation poles will, in this respect, continue to be important, given the growing case for deconcentrating the PWV and the need to provide urbanising opportunities for relatively immobile populations trapped in depressed regions like the eastern Cape. All this points to the need for national physical planning: the identification of potential growth centres and of regions (and sub-regions) with particularly acute poverty, of potentials for sectoral growth and specialisation. This work has begun under the minority regime whose planners have correctly identified a number of 'technical' deficiencies in the existing plans — an excessive preoccupation with industry, a superfluity of widely dispersed growth poles, an excessive pandering to the political requirements of Bantustan elites, rudimentary financial and institutional structures — but their ability to tackle these obstacles is constrained by the basic power relations and priorities of 'neo-apartheid'.

There will, however, be some good reasons for going beyond a minimalistic redistributive approach to regional planning in the post-apartheid period, and for making full use of the regional planning instruments which socialism offers. Here our argument necessarily becomes more abstract, and calls for a reflection on the experience of capitalist and 'actual socialist' developmental experiences.

The first reason for opting for a socialist approach is a negative one: the record of regional planning in capitalist economies is (as we have already indicated) less than impressive: despite some quantitative successes it has frequently failed to reduce high unemployment or markedly raise wage and skill levels in under-developed areas; it has often replaced inter-regional with intra-regional inequalities; and it has failed to generate 'multiplier effects' or prevent leakage of capital and purchasing power from peripheral to core areas. One result has been a growing restiveness in (often ethnically defined) regional communities. The general slowdown in economic growth rates in the 1970s and 1980s is, in some cases at least, exacerbating the absolute size of the regional problem.[17]

The record of regional planning in 'actual socialist' economies in the advanced and Third worlds is not uniformly good (or even always better than that of capitalist economies). Socialist development strategies do not eliminate all the irrationalities of 'market anarchy': they can themselves often be deeply irrational, especially where information available to planners is poor and goals are too ambitious. The record of regional planning under 'actual socialism' fully confirms this: the East European iron and steel industry, where plants were sometimes located in areas lacking the quantities and qualities of iron ore or coal, infrastructure and skilled labour needed to support them efficiently, is a case in point.[18] Moreover, inter-regional inequalities, and the 'town-countryside contradiction' remain real — and in some instances appear to pose intractable problems for many 'actual socialist' countries. Nonetheless, socialism *does* open up the possibility of a regional planning strategy that is more coordinated, predictable and effective than its capitalist counterpart. Premised on public ownership of principle means of production and (at least a substantial degree of) central direction, socialism facilitates directive, rather than simply indicative regional planning; and it potentially makes possible a high degree of coordination between economic, social and physical plans, so that regional plans can 'contain most of the information needed to assess a substantial part of external economies and diseconomies connected with particular locations'.[19] And for all the unevenness of their record, actual socialist countries have exhibited a capacity for comprehensive, long-range attacks on spatial problems perceived by politically dominant groups to be particularly demanding (whether it be excessive economic concentration in a single urban centre, as in Cuba or Hungary; or uplifting underdeveloped, ethnically defined regions, as in Yugoslavia and Czecho-slovakia; or developed backward sub-regions, as in Poland). In some cases quite impressive results have been achieved.[20]

Under socialist regional development strategies, furthermore, it is easier to target income distribution to particular social groups and regions, and thus to make possible a substantial narrowing of the difference in inter-regional living standards (as is the case, for example, in Cuba). This can occur even where — as in Romania, Yugoslavia and Bulgaria — spatial disparities in per capita income have actually widened. This has been achieved by, inter alia, standardising wages and salaries across regions (except in Yugoslavia) and concertedly extending social services to underdeveloped areas.[21] While a deliberate disproportion between regional income production and living levels can be promoted only within reasonable limits — at a certain point it must take its toll on national economic efficiency — it offers a not unimportant advantage for a post-apartheid government likely to be faced with an immediate problem of ameliorating acute poverty in areas where rapid and immediate expansion in productivity is not feasible.

In fact the regional development experiences of actual socialist countries have been very diverse. They have been most successful where general levels of economic development have been higher (as in the GDR and Czechoslovakia);[22] where sectoral policies have been followed which allow inter-regional specialisation and do not burden underdeveloped areas with inappropriate heavy industries or neglect agriculture (this is, indeed, crucial to economic development in national economies as a whole);[23] where excessive weight has not been attached to heavy industrialisation and the maintenance of high rates of investment at all costs (policies which initially widened, rather than narrowed, eastern Europe's spatial disparities);[24] and where the fixing of wages and other prices, and the structure of capital provision, have not been left too fully or indiscriminately to the marketplace (as happened in Yugoslavia, where a strong form of 'market socialism' has exacerbated, rather than relieved, regional inequalities).[25]

These brief observations do not amount to an analysis of the record of regional policies in planned economies, still less of their prospects in South Africa's specific conditions: but they may contain some pointers, including some fairly optimistic ones. South Africa's high level of industrialisation and agricultural development will allow greater attention to be paid to sectoral needs and specialisation and to regional upliftment than was the case in, for example, post-war south-eastern Europe, or is presently the case in most 'Third World' socialisms. Post-apartheid South Africa will, of course, face a serious capital shortage, but the record of regional development under 'actual socialism' does provide some grounds for arguing that a planned approach will fare better in such circumstances than a market-oriented one. (It should be added — and this was true of eastern Europe — that the question of regional development and specialisation will not be purely an intra-national one; there will, in southern Africa, have to be an approach that encompasses the entire subcontinent. This important issue is not, however, taken up here).

A further reason to opt for a socialist approach is that it allows for a fuller democratisation of regional planning. Instead of the domination of experts and capitalist lobbies, socialist planning promises a real participatory role for organised labour and other mass representatives. Some may argue that the planning experiences described above — whether Cuba or USSR or eastern Europe — hardly provide grounds for optimism about the democratic potential of socialist planning. Indeed, some may wish to question whether the 'actual socialisms' contain any lessons at all, except negative ones, for those concerned to build a democratic planning apparatus. While there can be little doubting the undemocratic character of actual socialist planning, such a position assumes, firstly, that the path of economic reconstruction pursued by these countries bears no significant resemblance to some hypothetically 'ideal' path of socialist development. However, I think it has been sufficiently demonstrated by Kornai, Brus and others that the actual socialist economies obey (in important respects at least) 'laws of motion' quite distinct from those of capitalism. And in the sphere of regional planning itself, the policy instruments employed in actual socialist countries appear to include many which would be essential to *any* meaningfully socialist regional development policy (the pursuit, in most cases, of full employment and spatial equalisation of living levels; the coordination of sectoral and regional plans; the adoption of long-term planning perspectives of ten to twenty or more years, etcetera). I think that it is mistaken to invest socialism 'with fundamentally immaculate features' *in advance*, disqualifying the actual socialist countries from the socialist label 'by definition'.[26] The task of effective critique, and of democratising socialist planning in a future South Africa, requires that we draw a wide range of lessons — both negative *and* positive ones — from established post-capitalist experiences.

I also have reservations about the arguments of those who, in their search for democratic alternatives to the inefficiencies and repressive centralism of actual socialism, advocate an unqualified adoption of 'market socialism'. In the first place, any excessively enthusiastic or uncautious resort to market socialism threatens many of the social gains — like full employment — which underpin the case for socialism. This is illustrated by the regional planning experience of Yugoslavia. Secondly, marketisation of the economy does not necessarily bring in its tow democratisation of the polity — a point starkly demonstrated by Hungary, China, Poland and even, with some qualification, by Yugoslavia.

It is widely assumed that socialist democracy can be realised fully only where market regulation replaces central planning. Marketisation does extend the scope of self-management within enterprises; however, it may also replace the visible external regulation of the state with the less visible external regulation of the market and profit, thereby heavily restricting the range of effective choices open to worker collectivities, and committing self-management to performing the function of the market. Moreover, self-management, while constituting an essential ingredient of socialist democracy, does not exhaust its meaning. If one accepts that such a democracy should represent more than just producers, and that, moreover, central state organs will inevitably constitute a focal point of representation and intervention into the foreseeable future, especially in an area like macro-regional planning, the question is raised as to whether, and how, central state structures can themselves be democratised. And the possibility or otherwise of democratic central planning, in turn, can be assessed fully only if this question is answered. If central plans drew meaningfully on inputs from genuinely representative bodies in localities and regions; if they were contested publicly by independent political parties and tendencies (both socialist and non-socialist) at the national and other levels, and if they were subjected to popular electoral arbitration, many of the authoritarian and arbitrary features presently associated with central planning would be mitigated substantially. One of the chief economic deficiencies of existing central planning continues to be its inability to obtain accurate information and correct signals about economic conditions on the ground. This problem can manifest itself as fully in regional planning as in any other sphere. A pluralistic, contested central planning process would at least partly obviate this difficulty.

Indeed, it is the unwillingness of actual socialist regimes to contemplate such pluralism which drives them (however reluctantly) to employ devices like opinion surveys, encouraging public letter writing and extending the sway of the market in their search for the economic information they need. Brus has captured this paradox: he calls it 'marketization of the socialist economy as a substitute for pluralization of its polity'.[27] It threatens the worst of all possible outcomes: authoritarian rule in the name of socialism propped up by a marketising economy. By contrast a democratic centrally planned economy, incorporating as much direct democracy (and economic decentralisation) as is feasible and compatible, promises fuller operation of a 'visible hand', one capable of puncturing through the invisibility of market mechanism and bureaucratic planning alike.

NOTES

1. I review some of this evidence in D. Glaser, 'A periodisation of South Africa's industrial decentralisation policies', forthcoming. Much of the commentary in Section 3 is drawn from that paper.
2. R. Tomlinson, M. Addleson and F. Pretorius, 'The institutional and financial arrangements for industrial decentralisation', mimeo, unpublished, 1984 or 1985, p.24.
3. *Financial Mail (FM)*, 11 Sept. 1981.
4. S. van der Horst, 'The economics of decentralisation of industry' in *South African Journal of Economics*, 1 March 1965.
5. *FM*, 11 Sept. 1981.
6. *Sunday Times*, 15 Nov. 1981.
7. On these issues see C. Simpkins, 'What has been happening to income distribution and poverty in the Homelands' in *Development Southern Africa*, Vol. 1, No. 2, 1984; and S. van der Berg, 'An overview of development in the homelands' in H. Giliomee and L. Schlemmer (ed.), *Up Against the Fences* (David Philip, Cape Town, 1985).
8. T. Bell, 'Is industrial decentralisation a thing of the past?', mimeo, unpublished, 1985.
9. J. Friedmann, *Regional Development Policy* (MIT Press, Cambridge, 1966), p.14.
10. See for example A. Foster-Carter's 'Korea and dependency theory' in *Monthly Review*, Vol. 37, No. 5, October 1985.
11. W. Stöhr and F. Tödtling, 'An evaluation of regional policies — experiences in mixed and market economies' in N.M. Hansen (ed.), *Human Settlement Systems: International Perspectives on Structure, Change and Public Policy* (Ballinger,

Cambridge, Mass., 1978), pp.86, 96.
12. Buthelezi Commission Report, 1982, Vol. 2, pp.95-98.
13. A. Lipietz, 'How monetarism choked off Third World industrialisation' in *New Left Review*, No. 145, May-June 1984, p.76.
14. *Ibid.*, pp.80-87.
15. G. White, 'Revolutionary socialist development in the Third World: an overview' in G. White, R. Murray and C. White (eds.), *Revolutionary Socialist Development in the Third World* (Harvester Press, Brighton, 1983), p.9.
16. See for example S. Gelb and D. Innes, 'Towards a democratic economy in South Africa', unpublished, July 1985.
17. W. Stöhr and F. Tödtling, 'An evaluation'.
18. F.E.I. Hamilton, 'Decision-making and industrial location in eastern Europe' in J. Blunder, C. Brook, G. Edge and A. Hay (eds.), *Regional Analysis and Development* (Open University, London, 1973), p.239.
19. On this see B. Gruchman, 'Key features of regional development and planning in eastern Europe' in A. Kuklinski (ed.), *Regional Development and Planning: International Prospectives* (Sijthoff, Leyden, 1975), especially pp.259-262. The quotation is from p.262.
20. K. Mihaelovic, *Regional Development: Experiences and Prospects in Eastern Europe* (Mouton, Paris, 1972), pp.43-46, 50-53.
21. On this see K. Mihaelovic, *ibid.*, pp.74-77; B. Gruchman, 'Key features', pp.263-265; G. Milagros de Gonzales, *Regional Planning Under the Transition to Socialism*, pp.31-32 (on Cuba) and p.40 (where Lardy is quoted on China).
22. K. Mihaelovic, *Regional Development*, pp.30-35.
23. See D. Flaherty, 'Regional policy and the reform of central planning: an assessment of the G.D.R., Hungarian and Yugoslav approaches' in *Contributions to Political Economy*, No. 3, 1984.
24. See for example F.E.I. Hamilton, 'Decision-making', pp.240-241; A.H. Dawson, 'The changing distribution of Polish industry, 1949-65: a general picture' in J. Blunden, C. Brook, G. Edge and A. Hay (eds.), *Regional Analysis*, especially pp.250-252.
25. On this see especially D. Flaherty, 'Regional policy', pp45-50.
26. W. Brus, 'Socialism — feasible or viable?' in *New Left Review*, No. 153, September-October 1985, p.45.
27. *Ibid.*, p.61.

7. The Incorporation of African Women into the Industrial Workforce: Its Implications for the Women's Question in South Africa

GEORGINA JAFFEE AND COLLETTE CAINE

INTRODUCTION

Since 1960, increasing numbers of African women have been incorporated into the manufacturing, commercial and service sectors of the South African economy. This participation in the economy provides, for the first time, the potential for large-scale collective organisation of African working-class women. In recent years they have contributed actively to trade union growth and militancy despite their tremendous reproductive responsibilities.[1]

African women workers have to struggle for equality on at least three levels:
• on the factory floor they are employed in the lowest-paid jobs with unhealthy working conditions and an absence of job security, maternity rights and childcare facilities;
• in the trade union movement and amongst their fellow male workers, women have to fight for equality against well-entrenched patriarchal traditions;
• at home they have to carry the burden of domestic and childcare responsibilities. Involvement in trade union activities has brought them into confrontation with their fathers or partners who often view their activities with suspicion.

Walker has argued that the history of women's resistance in South Africa has 'combined an overriding commitment to liberation for blacks from white oppression and exploitation with a more muted, inconsistent but nevertheless oft-expressed commitment for full equality for women with men'.[2] During the last wave of popular resistance in the 1950s, women's organisations were committed in principle to both the aims of national liberation and the emancipation of women. There were exceptionally advanced demands set out in the Women's Charter of 1954. In practice, however, the material conditions of the times prevented the full integration of women's specific interests into the politics of mass mobilisation and national liberation.[3]

Over the last few years, as popular resistance has intensified, working-class women have increasingly formed and participated in women's organisations which have played a major role in progressive politics. From 1980 onwards, women's political organisations re-emerged in most South African black communities. Local women's groups have initiated projects around childcare, adult literacy and cooperative buying.[4] Women have also participated in campaigns against the rise in General Sales Tax (GST), struggles around education, consumer boycotts and rent boycotts, and demands for troops to get out of the townships. But they have done so more as members of a community than as women with specific interests. Meanwhile, increased repression of black communities over the last three years has disrupted popular organisation, and worked against the emergence of the sorts of grassroots organisation necessary to advance the specific interests of working-class women. 'It is difficult to organise crèches when our children are being shot by the soldier boys', explained one woman.[5]

The growth of the trade union movement has provided the impetus for increasing organisation of women in previously non-unionised sectors of employment. Domestic workers, who number 800,000,[6] have started organising along trade union lines. They are affiliated to the Congress of South African Trade Unions (COSATU) with 60,000 members.[7] COSATU has committed itself to the organisation of agricultural workers, where 16% of economically active African women are employed.[8] In this chapter, we argue that the changing economic location of women and their incorporation into trade unions increases their potential to influence the direction the 'women's question' takes as it emeges in the popular-democratic movement. Women organised into trade unions have the potential to inject the struggle for women's emancipation with a solid working-class base.

Working-class women occupy a unique position as a fraction of the exploited social class. As workers, they have a structurally determined interest in the eradication of capitalist relations of production. As women they are, by their position, opposed to all forms of patriarchal domination. And as black women under apartheid, a racially oppressed group, they have a material interest in national liberation. As such, the female section of the African working class occupies an antagonistic relationship to capitalism, apartheid and male domination. This potentially places them in a unique position to be carriers of relations and structures which aim at the social, economic and political transformation of society post-apartheid.

There has been a general absence of intellectual debate and analysis of the 'women's question' and how it fits into the politics of national liberation. Debates on the relationship between working-class hegemony and national liberation have not seen women's oppression as central to the distinctions between the 'politics of liberation' and the 'politics of transformation'.[9] In this distinction, the latter secures the interests of the working class and changes in the relations of production, while the former serves to end apartheid.

In contrast, a younger generation of women activists is articulating the need to address the oppression of women as part and parcel of the struggle for national liberation. They have started a debate about the relationship between the affiliates of the United Democratic Front (UDF) and the newly-constituted women's organisations. Questions are being asked about the lack of women in leadership positions in the UDF; how women's issues can be taken up within its affiliates; and the special problems faced by women workers in the factory and in their relationships with men. Women in both the trade unions and community organisations are beginning to address the question of women's oppression as integral to the struggle for national liberation. According to the Federation of Transvaal Women's education officer, speaking at a recent workshop,

Our understanding of the special disabilities faced by women is that they are rooted in exploitation, racial oppression and sexism. The battle against capitalism, racism and sexism cannot be fought as part of a three stage plan — the struggle must be waged simultaneously at all these levels. We are committed to building women's organisations; to uniting women; to raising the voice of women in the national-democratic struggle led by the working class. It is our task to develop working-class leadership amongst women and to allow working-class interests to dominate our women's organisations.[10]

Although embryonic, the struggle that working-class women are beginning to wage both on the shop floor and within communities opens up a crucial area for debate on the politics of transformation. The struggle to change patriarchal attitudes, share the double shift, and achieve higher wages and better working conditions opens up questions about economic transformation and social policy in post-apartheid society.

WOMEN IN THE ECONOMY:
CHANGES IN THE POSITION OF AFRICAN WOMEN

An analysis of the position of women in the South African labour market has to take into consideration the segmentation of the occupational structure along lines of race and gender. The overall occupational hierarchy follows a specific pattern where white men occupy the most highly specialised positions, followed by white women. At the bottom of the hierarchy are African men, followed by African women, with coloureds and Indians occupying the intermediate positions. African women were the last to enter the industrial sector, after white, coloured and Indian women. This late incorporation of African women into industry has been attributed to both racist legislation and labour controls and the fact that white and coloured women met the needs of the economy in the early periods of industrialisation.[11]

Martin and Rogerson have identified three broad phases of the incorporation of women into industry.[12] The first phase (1915-1945) is characterised by the employment of white, predominantly Afrikaans women who remained in the workforce up until the Second World War. In the second period (1945-1960) coloured women took the places vacated by white women who moved into public service, commerce and finance. After 1965 African women moved rapidly into industry and commerce and by 1980 formed almost two-thirds of all economically active women. By 1980 African women formed 58% of the female workforce in production; whites 5.5%, coloureds 28.5% and Indians 8%.[13] Coloured women have been moving out of production and into sales and clerical occupations in the commercial sector.

The incorporation of African women into industry accelerated in the 1960s, during a period of heightened economic expansion. As part of a reserve army of labour they could easily be absorbed into a growing economy with their low wages contributing to this expansion. Their vulnerable position in the labour market made them an ideal workforce to be incorporated into the production process at a time when industry was becoming more mechanised.[14] In addition to this, the 1960s saw the beginning of the state's policy of industrial decentralisation. Increasing numbers of women have been incorporated into industries in the eight regions which are part of the decentralisation programme. This will be dealt with in more detail below.

This paper focusses on African women because they form the majority of women workers in wage labour. The interests of this strata of the working class will have to be incorporated in any post-apartheid programme for economic and social restructuring.

This is not to deny the fact that both coloured and Indian women play an important part in industry. In the western and eastern Cape coloured women occupy similar job categories to Africans in the Transvaal and Natal. However, the withdrawal of coloured labour preference policies in the western Cape (1985) meant that Africans could compete with coloureds in the job market. This may lead to the replacement of coloured women workers by Africans. There is also evidence to show that in the western and eastern Cape employment of women is declining with the overall decline of these industrial regions. The only areas which show an increasing number of women in employment are the areas of industrial expansion — southern Transvaal and Natal, where the workforce is predominantly made up of Africans.[15] In Natal, Indian women also occupy similar job categories to their African counterparts, having moved into the workforce at about the same time. Indian women workers are predominantly located in the textile industry in Natal, making up about 43% of the female workforce. But African women constitute the majority of the workforce in textile production in Natal.[16]

These regional differences in the composition of the workforce, the hierarchical segmentation of the workforce along racial lines, and the different political traditions of racial groupings make the working class extremely heterogeneous and complicate the possibility of racial alliances. Racial discrimination has affected racial groups in different ways and the racial hierarchy of the female workforce has created real divisions amongst women workers which strategies on the women's question will have to consider.

Table 7.1: Percentage of Economically Active Women aged 15-59 in the South African Labour Force by Racial Group

Year	Female	African	Coloured	Indian	White
1951	20	—	—	—	—
1960	23	22	32	9	26
1970	32	31	35	19	30
1980	33	32	38	26	33
Percentage Distribution of Economically Active Women by Race					
1980	100	65	12	2	21

Table 7.1[17] shows that between 1960 and 1980 there was an overall increase in the number of economically active women in all racial categories in the economy. There was a rapid increase in African and Indian female employment after 1960 and a steady increase in the other three racial categories between 1960 and 1980. African women currently constitute almost two-thirds (65%) of the economically active female workforce. Coloured women form 12%, Indians 2% and whites 21%.

• Table 7.2[18] shows that from 1960 women have been concentrated in agriculture,[19] manufacturing, commerce, finance and services. Over the last twenty years there has been an enormous increase of women employed in manufacturing, commerce and finance. The increase from 15% to 25% in manufacturing and 24% to 34% in commerce reflects the incorporation of African women into these sectors (Table 7.3).

Table 7.2: Women as a Percentage of the Labour Force by Industrial Sector

Sector	1960	1970	1980
Agriculture	12.0	35.8	24.1
Mining	0.7	1.0	1.9
Manufacturing	15.0	21.0	24.5
Electricity/Gas/Water	2.2	3.7	7.5
Construction	0.9	2.4	4.4
Commerce	23.6	27.6	38.6
Transport and Communications	8.1	9.2	11.5
Finance	31.9	39.3	44.1
Services	60.5	63.4	56.8

• The decline of women in the service sector from 61% in 1960 to 57% in 1980, reflects the movement of coloured women out of this sector into clerical and sales positions in the commerical sectors.

• The service sector includes African women in domestic service which has been steadily shrinking over the last twenty years. By 1980, one-third of economically active African women were in the service sector.[20]

• The increase of African women in this sector occurred between 1970 and 1980, a decade in which their presence increased by 79%.[21] African women in the service sector occupy the most menial job categories which include labouring, cleaning, waitressing, laundry work, kitchen work and tea service.

• The majority of women in finance are white. In 1980 they constituted 80% of the female employment in this sector.[22]

Table 7.3: Percentage of African Female Workforce in Selected Occupations[23]

Occupation	1970	1980
Sales	20	47
Services	84	83
Agriculture and Fisheries[24]	98	89
Production	45	58

Table 7.3[25] shows changes in African female employment in four occupational categories — sales, service, agriculture and production — which comprise 74% of the female workforce. Sales comprises 5%; service 43%; agriculture 16%; and manufaturing 11%.[26]

Comparing the changes in occupation from 1970 to 1980 in the occupational categories where most women are concentrated, there is an enormous increase in the sales (20-47%) and manufacturing sectors (45-58%). This indicates the point of entry of African women into the economy and accounts for the increases revealed in the manufacturing and commercial sectors of the economy in Table 7.1

The increase of African women in the occupational category of sales reflects their participation in the retail and wholesale subsectors of the economy. A breakdown of women in production shows that 55% of all women are concentrated in food, textiles and clothing, and that 64% of African women are concentrated in these sub-sectors.[27]

Table 7.4:[28] *Percentage of Women by Racial Group in Food, Textiles and Clothing, 1980, and Average Monthly Wage*

Industry	White	Coloured	Indian	African
Food	18%	29%	2%	51%
	R837	R199	R323	R175
Textile	7%	22%	5%	66%
	R917	R217	R291	R173
Clothing	5%	38%	21%	38%
	R815	R172	R189	R107

Table 7.4 shows that African women are located in the lowest paid and least-skilled jobs in the food, clothing and textile sub-sectors, and are concentrated in the manufacturing, service, and commercial sectors. It is here that women are becoming increasingly unionised and that women-specific demands are emerging. This will be discussed below.

WOMEN IN DECENTRALISED INDUSTRIES

The government's policy of industrial decentralisation which was first implemented in the 1960s has led to the incorporation of women into industrial production both within the Bantustans and in industries located on their borders. In the latter case workers commute on a daily basis from their place of residence in the Bantustan to their place of work in 'white' South Africa. In 1982 it was estimated that there were 773,000 commuters.[29] This form of industrialisation was set up to curb the influx of Africans into urban areas and as an attempt to give both political and economic credibility to the Bantustans.[30]

Industrial expansion in peripheral areas was encouraged by the state in two distinct ways: firstly by placing a limit on the expansion of industries in metropolitan centres through legislative controls such as the 1967 Physical Planning Act; and secondly by providing incentives to capital to relocate. The decreasing demand for domestic labour and the low wages paid in this sector, the increasing impoverishment of the rural areas, and the collapse of subsistence agriculture provided a ready-made cheap labour force for the expansion of industry. Women were drawn into the labour force from newly developed townships set up adjacent to industry or from pre-existing landless rural villages. In Transkei, for example, women's employment in manufacturing increased from 6% in 1980 to 13% in 1985, compared to only a 2% increase in male employment. The total increase in private sector employment over the same period for males was 69,938 to 70,544, and for females from 36,611 to 51,388.[31] Martin and Rogerson have shown that in Lebowa and Bophuthatswana females make up 50% of the workforce in manufacturing and in Venda and the Ciskei 64%.[32] In the Bantustans, the female percentage of the workforce increased from 8.1% in 1970 to 16.6% in 1980 in the occupational categories of production and transport. Over the same period women employed in sales increased from 25.35% to 50.5%.[33]

The conditions of work of South African women in decentralised industrial areas are very similar to those in the new labour intensive export-processing industries run by multinationals in the Third World. Women are concentrated in the least-skilled jobs and are paid the lowest wages.[34] In addition to being cheap, women's labour is attractive because sexual stereotyping maintains that women are industrious, nimble-fingered and subordinate. An interview with the management of Alfa before they withdrew (for economic reasons) from a decentralised zone in Brits (western Transvaal) revealed that 20% of its workforce was female. All the women worked on the seats of the cars as cutters and trimmers. These jobs were specifically reserved for women because, as the manager put it, 'the female is a natural machinist handyman [sic]'.[35]

Another similarity between these areas in South Africa and those in other Third World countries is that the workforce lives in areas of high unemployment characterised by rural poverty. In South Africa these zones are exempt from minimum wage regulations and have been the most difficult for trade unions to organise. Legislation preventing South African unions from operating in Bantustans and the excessive repression meted out to the residents of Bantustans who join unions works in capital's interest, helping to maintain a disciplined and cheap labour force.

In some decentralised zones, for example those on the borders of Bophuthatswana, unions have been successful in winning wage increases. An example of this is the Brits industrial complex which was established in the late 1960s. A survey conducted by one of the authors shows that a third of the workforce in this zone is made up of women.[36] They are concentrated in factories making electrical plugs, motor components, furniture and chemical products. In some of these industries women comprise over 50% of the workforce. However, in other areas such as farming implements, tyre production and engineering their presence is negligible.

Unions have been organising in this area since the early 1980s. Bad conditions at work, low wages and the politics of Bantustanisation have created a militant unionised labour force of which many women are a part. This may have to do with the existence of a number of foreign companies which have been forced to change many of their labour relations practices. Other factories have displayed great antagonism towards unionisation by dismissing entire workforces or moving out of the area. Obviously the recession has had an impact on employment patterns but there is no indication that women are being retrenched before men.

Women workers in these areas face untold hardships. They live in dwellings located in impoverished landless villages. Their homes range from corrugated iron shacks to small brick houses. There is no electricity or running water in any of the villages. Workers are forced to spend a large percentage of income on transport, often living up to 80 kilometres from where they work, and thus spending up to three hours in transit. Working women are faced with the responsibilities associated with the reproduction of their households. As there is no infrastructural development in these villages domestic tasks include collection of water and firewood. Research in progress[37] reveals that the majority of the workforce is made up of younger women, many of whom are supporting their parents and other members of the family in large extended family households. The other household type is smaller where the women remain head and do not form any permanent attachments to men.

The reasons for the emergence of these household types have not yet been established in this study, but research on women in Third World countries[38] working in 'runaway shops' suggests some answers. Studies done in Asia, Jamaica and Mexico show that younger women who supplement the family income do not threaten the male head of household nor challenge the sexual division of labour; but single-headed households develop out of a sense of economic autonomy and allow women the choice to accept or reject marital partnership. In South Africa the very different conditions under which these women live and work and the deep patriarchal values of male workers may also contribute to the desire of women to remain single and independent.

It has not been possible to calculate the exact numbers of women involved in production in all the decentralised areas. But if decentralisation continues as an industrial strategy, it is likely that more and more women will form part of the workforce in these areas. The experiences of these women within their communities as well as within their work and union activities could provide important input to women's organisation.

DEMANDS FROM THE SHOP FLOOR

Women's demands from the factory floor reflect the increasing strength of the organised working class in the post-Wiehahn period. The achievement of enforceable rights in the workplace has allowed trade unions to enter negotiations on all aspects of work conditions, including women's rights, health and safety, etc. Gains made on the factory floor allowed for greater organisational initiatives, and over the last seven years the independent trade union movement has grown significantly: it now comprises over 800,000 members.[39]

Unions which have large numbers of women are faced with a set of demands linked to, but different from, the demands of African male members. These include the rejection of low pay for 'women's work' and unequal pay for the same job, the inclusion of demands for maternity rights and childcare facilities in negotiations, the taking up of occupational health problems specific to women, and ending incidents of sexual harassment.

Unequal pay

Although it is now illegal to set separate wage rates for women,[40] this is unlikely to make any substantial difference to the income of African women in general as most are segregated into the lowest-paid, least skilled 'women's jobs'. Since many African women workers are the sole breadwinners or support extended families, the fight against low wages and 'women's work' is a central issue around which unions have organised. The unions have resisted attempts by management to impose percentage increases which widened the wage differential between low and high grades. Instead unions have attempted to negotiate for flat-rate increases in an attempt to narrow the gap between low and high grades. Furthermore, there has been an attempt to fight for a 'living wage' for all workers rather than a 'family wage' which tends to regard women's wages as supplementary. A recent example of the success in equalising wages is reflected in negotiations between the Chemical Workers Industrial Union and the Vulco Latex rubber company which resulted in a R30-a-week rise for women. Male workers on a higher grade received a R20 per week increase.[41]

Equal pay for equal work is only effective if combined with the same access to promotion. Trade unions are also fighting the tendency for management to invent new titles for women which have lower status and benefits compared to men who perform the same duties.

Overtime

In 1985, legislation was changed to allow women to work the same amount of overtime as men.[42] This equalisation in legislation has placed an extra burden on women workers. Women start a second shift — cooking, cleaning and childcare — at the end of the work day. Overtime means a triple shift. The removal of the protective clause for women workers has placed the issue of overtime firmly on the agenda of unions which have large numbers of women workers. While women workers suffer most from overtime they are also most in need of the extra money. Overtime is presently being dealt with through the demand for the overall reduction of the working week to 40 hours for all workers. Fighting overtime will only be viable once a living wage is won for all workers in the country.

Job security

Job security is a crucial demand for women in the unions. As mothers and workers, their job security is further threatened by lack of paid maternity leave. Bird argues that 'without job protection, women can find that maternity leave becomes retrenchment'.[44] The struggle for maternity benefits has been at the centre of women's demands and has met with widespread success in unions such as the Commercial, Catering and Allied Workers Union (CCAWUSA).

The growth of CCAWUSA is an example of the expansion of women into the retail sub-sector. Seventy per cent of the 40,000 paid-up members of CCAWUSA are women. In 1985 CCAWUSA signed the most comprehensive maternity agreement yet with a national retailer, Metro Cash and Carry. This agreement allows for twelve months maternity leave with a guaranteed right to return to work; seven of the twelve months are on paid leave at 33% of salary. With Unemployment Insurance Fund (UIF) payments, this amounts to 78% of salary for six months and one month at 33%; paid paternity leave of three days for the biological father; and time off to facilitate breast-feeding and to attend antenatal and postnatal clinics. Other clauses in the agreement include a health and safety section, the prevention of discrimination against pregnant job applicants and flexibility in terms of leave.

A number of other maternity agreements have been signed in affiliates of both the Confederation of South African Trade Unions (COSATU) and the Council of Unions of South Africa (CUSA). Although they are not as comprehensive or as far-reaching as the Metro agreement, they generally include twelve months leave, six months paid leave, and job security.

The recession has focussed attention on women's job security as companies have retrenched large numbers of workers. Unions have adopted the LIFO (last in, first out) principle and forced employers to investigate alternatives to retrenchment in consultation with workers' representatives. Although the battle to save jobs has been a difficult one, where attempts to negotiate have met with success, these have also contributed towards preventing women from bearing more of the burden of job loss.

Health and childcare

Health and safety has become a very important component of worker demands. In most recognition agreements, clauses are being included on health and safety which consider the special conditions required for women workers, particularly when they are pregnant. Education and information on health and safety has also limited managements' attempts to impose certain forms of family planning on female workers.

With increasing numbers of African women entering the labour market, there is a growing need for childcare services either in the townships or at their places of work. But this has not been met by the state or capital. Recent studies have shown that black working class women have to rely on family members or informal childminders to look after their children[45] and that of a population of four million pre-school African children only 0.3% were looked after in crèches. These crèches are predominantly funded by fees and subsidies from private welfare groups rather than the state.[46]

The demand for childcare has started to feature in negotiations. BMW has agreed to finance a crèche based at its factory in Rosslyn. This will be jointly administered by management and the union, the National Automobile and Allied Workers Union (NAAWU). In the Programme for Women developed by CUSA in 1984, there is a demand for the establishment of crèches, nurseries and after-school centres (see Appendix A). The demand for childcare will certainly feature in the near future. Unions intend forcing the private sector and the state to provide childcare facilities in the townships and, when convenient, at the place of work. The fact that most workers in South Africa live a long way from their homes makes childcare at the point of production impractical.

Sexual harassment

Sexual harassment is another of the problems specific to women workers, one which they are organising to fight. Over the last few years there have been several strikes over this issue, with men responsible being dismissed. At Unilever in 1983, a white employee was sexually harassed by a manager and this led to a one-day stoppage by the black workforce. They demanded that the man be fired. The final result was his transferral to another plant.[47]

WOMEN'S RIGHTS ON THE AGENDA

COSATU believes that women workers should take first place in our struggle. Women workers suffer the most under the bosses and the system.[48]

The December 1985 launch of the Congress of South African Trade Unions (COSATU) saw women's rights placed firmly on the agenda of the country's major trade union federation. COSATU, representing more than half a million workers, has written into its constitution a resolution on women which commits it to fight for women's rights at work, in society and in the Federation.[49] The constitution also commits COSATU to finance and set up a sub-committee to monitor progress made in implementing these resolutions and to promote the understanding of specific discrimination suffered by women workers. The acceptance of this resolution signifies a clear advance in formal recognition of the needs of working-class women, though for many women the fight for equality within the trade union movement is likely to be long and hard. These policies are yet to be applied. But now that increasing numbers of women have become active in the trade union movement, there is a material basis for their implementation.

The COSATU resolution developed from a growing awareness within a small women's group in the Federation of South African Trade Unions (FOSATU).[50] One of the group's aims was to achieve equal rights for women within FOSATU. 'We wanted our presence to be felt. There are just about no women in union leadership — men are in control and we felt our silence within the Federation was proving the inferiority of women. It proved the thinking in traditional African society that the dignity of women is lower than that of men'.[51]

CUSA has twelve union affiliates and a total membership of 200,000, 30% of which is female. It passed a resolution in 1982 to establish a Women's Unit; redouble efforts to stamp out discrimination in all aspects of employment; increase the number of childcare services in the community; and encourage the full participation of women in the union and political processes. In 1984 this unit was set up with the objectives of investigating all issues of concern to women workers in CUSA. The unit has a very active educational component, producing documents on health and safety, equal pay, maternity and paternity leave, and sexual harassment. The unit also publishes a women's news digest which contains articles on women in South Africa and other parts of the world.

Recently the unit has run a number of seminars for women shop stewards and women members and has adopted a programme for women (See Appendix A). This unit is drawing attention to the specific plight of working women and making far-reaching demands on both capital and the state regarding the specific burden carried by women workers. Referring to the rich tradition of women in resistance in South Africa, CUSA's information officer argues that 'it is now incumbent on women in the trade union movement to organise and mobilise themselves to press for their own special interests and thereby contribute to the struggle to fight for the rights of all workers'.[52] Amid state repression and the demands of other union business, it is a struggle in itself to add women's issues to the exhausting list of things to be done. Despite this, officials are confident that women's issues will continue to be taken up and given due recognition at all levels in the future.

WOMEN IN COMMUNITY AND POLITICAL ORGANISATIONS

Demands made by the organised working class and the heightened awareness of the link between class oppression and gender subordination is starting to influence community and political organisation.

The first major mass mobilisation of women occurred in the 1950s when the Federation of South African Women (FSAW) organised against the extension of passes to African women. FSAW organised women nationally, across class and ethnic divisions, and was the first organisation seriously to address the independent political role of women in resistance. Dismantled in 1964, after the banning of its major affiliate, the African National Congress Women's League (ANCWL), FSAW left a legacy of commitment to both national liberation and the emancipation of women.[53]

South African Women's Day, 9 August 1986, marked the 30th anniversary of the FSAW march by 20,000 women to Pretoria to protest the extension of passes. It was to have been celebrated by the rebirth of a national women's organisation, but disruption of progressive organisation by the current state of emergency forced a postponement of the launch. This new federation would have brought together the regional organisations formed since 1980 — the United Women's Congress (UWC) in the western Cape, the Federation of Transvaal Women (FEDTRAW), and the Natal Organisation of Women (NOW), as well as many local women's groups, most of which are linked to the UDF.[54]

The massive impact of the 1976 student rebellion, and the generalised resistance it brought in its wake, set the stage for the mobilisation and organisation of African women. This has its roots in spontaneous localised protest at the harshest manifestations of crises in the apartheid state and the South African economy — the fight against Bantu Education, housing shortages, high rents, the soaring cost of living and the lack of social services.

In the western Cape, the United Women's Organisation (UWO) was initially formed to support students in the education struggle. As a UWO executive member explained,

> 1976 showed parents that they were not able to support their children and that there was something wrong in our society. We had fought Bantu Education when it was started in 1954, yet many parents became their children's enemy when they stood up against that education in 1976. We saw that we had no voice to speak for us or our children. We knew that as women we were oppressed both in our houses and at work, and that we needed to work towards changing things as women with both short- and long-term goals.[55]

In the Vaal industrial complex, the initial impetus was similar. The Vaal Women's Organisation (VWO), a FEDTRAW affiliate, became very active in 1984 in those townships where current nation-wide revolt flared. A small group of women came together to discuss problems in education and childcare. Once established the group's involvement quickly broadened to embrace high rents, inadequate housing and low wages. Boycotts against high rents, and the government-sanctioned community councils which administer them, have been one of the major campaigns in the current phase of mass resistance. According to a VWO member,

> The problem is that people in the Vaal get low wages and can't afford a rent of R65 or R78. As mothers we cannot afford the rent. When a child is hungry, the mother is affected and she cannot afford to educate her children because the rent is high.[56]

Townships all over the country have boycotted rents in the last year. Women have faced harsh state repression by sustaining the boycotts. Recently, troops and council staff have started to evict rent defaulters. In at least two cases, hundreds of women marched in protest against these evictions, only to be met with army and police violence.[57] Brutal attempts by the state to crush these campaigns have brought more women into organisations. According to one woman, 'mothers see their children shot outside their home; troops patrol the streets day in and day out'. This has mobilised women to participate in one of the campaigns undertaken since the 1985 Emergency, the demand for troops to get out of the townships.

Earlier this year, in the wake of attacks on residents of Durban's Chesterville township by police-backed vigilantes known as the 'A Team', local women formed a township watch. They guard the two entrances to the township every night. Unarmed and with no support from the authorities, they have succeeded in preventing further 'A Team' attacks.[58]

Despite the substantial increase in numbers of women active in resistance groups, in general they have been unable to break into the male-dominated hierarchies of popular organisations. Just as women are largely excluded from union leadership, so they are largely absent from decision-making positions in the political movement. It is interesting that in the western Cape, within the community organisations which UWO pre-dated and helped to initiate during the current phase of resistance, women have maintained a strong representative presence. On the whole, however, women still find themselves excluded from leadership. In the words of one woman activist: 'Even when you have worked twelve or fourteen hours a day for the struggle and earned your place within it, you still have to continue fighting for affirmation'.[59]

This exclusion has weakened a number of the recent consumer boycotts used as tactics to enforce political demands. In those areas where women were under- or unrepresented in local boycott committees, tensions developed between the mainly male organisers and the largely female boycotters.[60] For it is women who do the shopping and cooking to feed families. Excluding women from the decision-making process, in a situation where they are primarily responsible for sustaining a campaign, further alienates them from political and community organisation. While there is no suggestion that any of the boycotts actually broke down under this tension, it can be argued that the exclusion of women did not promote democratic grassroots organisation. The exclusion and alienation of women also increases the tendency to use violence in enforcing such campaigns and has an overall disorganising effect on the politics of the community. By contrast, women activists point to a clear link between women's representation on local boycott committees and a stronger sense of unity within the community.

Women's participation is important for the success of broad political campaigns. However, although these campaigns address issues of vital importance to women, they do not confront the oppression of women. Women are appealed to and mobilised as mothers, although the issues around which they are being mobilised concern everyone in the community. This stereotyping of women in the course of mass mobilisation is double-edged. On the one hand it is a real rallying point reflecting the genuine concerns of women and mothers; on the other hand it serves to perpetuate the narrow image of women as nurturers rather than workers or activists. This has a tendency to reinforce the subordination of women's interests to the broader struggle, instead of integrating them within it.

In isolated instances some tentative steps have been taken to change the circumstances which exclude women from pursuing more active political lives. In the eastern Cape, where grassroots political organisation is commonly regarded as more developed than elsewhere,[61] where there is a long tradition of community and popular organisation, experiments to release women from domestic labour have been tried. Young comrades are helping run crèches, and in the formation of housework and laundry cooperatives, in order to free women from the tasks which tie them to their homes.[62] In turn, these women are able to participate in street communities and other community programmes.

Port Alfred, a small town between Port Elizabeth and East London, is well known for its high degree of community organisation. Local affairs are run by a civic association; the schools are run by teacher-parent-student committees; students and pensioners are organised into representative bodies. In this small community, women's specific interests have been incorporated into broader political demands and campaigns. The Port Alfred Women's Organisation (PAWO) was formed in March 1986, primarily to discipline and run projects with the youth. Two months after its launch PAWO successfully organised a stayaway by the township's entire female workforce. This was in protest at the rape of an elderly resident and the police refusal to charge the rapist. Every African woman worker in Port Alfred stayed away for a week. The vast majority are domestic workers, and they demanded that their white women employers help in the prosecution of the rapist. The rest of the community supported this initiative by the women and helped enforce their decision to banish the rapist from the township. Domestic workers' action around this incident has also enabled them to open up communication with employers through PAWO.[63]

Already women have been mobilised in support of worker conflicts with employers. In a recent wave of sit-in strikes, support from women made it possible for workers to sit it out until their demands were met. At the Bosch factory in Brits in the Transvaal, 300 male and female Metal and Allied Workers Union members staged a sit-in after they were dismissed during a wage strike. Women (and men) in the communities organised to bring food and blankets to the factory for the striking workers.

CONCLUSION

This chapter has shown that women are participating in organisations which are beginning to address their triple oppression as blacks, women and workers. The incorporation of African women into important unionised sectors of the economy and the commitment of the trade union movement and women's organisations to women's equality, provides the potential for addressing the interests and needs of working-class women in a post-apartheid society.

The oppressive conditions under which women live and work have led to the emergence of specific demands from the shop floor, while in the trade union movement women are struggling for the principle of representation in leadership positions. Women workers are beginning to develop a consciousness which identifies the link between economic exploitation and gender oppression. This consciousness is slowly beginning to affect the views of male workers too. Some recognise the divisive impact of women's inequality on the working class as a whole. For example, at a FOSATU workshop on women workers in 1983, a male shop steward said:

> It's high time that we surrendered brothers. ... This is the struggle and for the sake of the struggle we should be hand in hand [with the women]. If we are both in the struggle — my wife and I — and we are both working, then when I get home I must not rest while my wife carries on for 24 hours.
> Women are doing a double job. We say we are the oppressed nation, but women are more oppressed. They go to work and then start again at home. We should put aside the whisky and make the fire if the wife is not yet home. And also carry the child. After all it is the man's child also. We must appeal to our bosses. Pregnant women's jobs must be protected. If not, we are oppressing our women. And bosses will see to it that they can pay low wages to women — and some time they will chuck us out. Then we will cry! So it is high time that we showed the bosses we're equal.[64]

There is a growing awareness that women do not win their conditions of emancipation from concessions or from the politics of mass mobilisation. They struggle for them within organisations which are simultaneously struggling for national liberation. 'After we have thrown in our lot with the struggle for democracy, we may find that on the day when freedom comes we are in fact not so free. ... This is precisely why we struggle today, and why we need to plant the seeds of the new society in the womb of the old so that it grows and develops in the direction we would like it to go'.[65]

Despite many of the shortcomings of existing socialist societies, they appear to provide the necessary conditions for the formal emancipation of women. Women in these societies have achieved a degree of equality in education and law, and have benefitted from the extension of social services. These formal equalities can provide the basis to extend the struggle against women's oppression into other spheres of inequality. If changes are made to accommodate the specific needs of working-class women at all levels, they will benefit all women in South African society.

If a post-apartheid state is committed to addressing inequality in all parts of South Africa, the question of working-class interests in general, and the needs of women workers in particular, becomes central. The degree to which women's demands are integrated and accepted will test the depth of the transformation of South African society.

APPENDIX A

Programme for Women

Believing that trade unions should be geared to meet the needs of women workers.
Agreeing that facilities must be provided so women can participate fully in all activities.
Rejecting the idea that women play only a supportive role.

We acknowledge
• that women must play a full role in their own right;
• that union activities is a crucial issue for women;
• that women need to assume leadership positions as representatives elected on their record and policies;
• that sexist attitudes and other prejudices will only be broken down through involvement of women in the worker struggle.

We commend therefore that the J.E. adopts the following Programme for Women:

1. Fight all forms of discrimination on the basis of sex.
2. Ensure equal pay for work of equal value.
3. Jobs for every woman seeking employment.
4. Living wages for all women including pregnancy leave, pregnancy pay, sick pay, disability pay and equal pensions.
5. Implementation of a 40 hour working week.
6. Full rights for all temporary and casual workers with equal rates and full entitlement to all benefits.
7. Full pregnancy leave of at least six months, with a guaranteed return to the company with no loss of employment rights or benefit entitlements.
8. Crèche and nursery facilities near to homes, combining health care and safe environments to ensure fullest development.
9. After school centres and assisted homework activities for school aged children and young people.

10. Resist violence against women.

11. Adequate access to educational and vocational facilities for women with the right to time off on full pay to attend such courses.

12. Establishment of low cost community services such as eating, laundry and other communal services to eliminate domestic labour in the home.

13. Implementation of housing schemes to provide adequate low payment homes with total ownership for single parents and individuals.

14. Launch a massive programme of public works to build roads, improve transport, provide and improve street lighting, build nurseries, schools, clinics, sport and social amenities.

15. Provide health education and services through community based health clinics to provide education and concentrate on preventive rather than curative medicine.

16. Provide in nationalised industries full participation of workers on management boards through trade union worker representation to ensure the provision of low-cost necessities.

17. Improve immediate price controls over all monopolies which dominate the manufacture, wholesale or retail of food and consumer goods.

18. Fight for a massive cut in defence expenditure to ensure payment of community services.

19. Fight to defend trade union rights and campaign to organise women into trade unions to defend job and living standards and to eliminate influx control and all its evils.

NOTES

1. Iris Berger, 'Sources of class consciousness: the experience of women workers in South Africa, 1973-1980', Working Papers, No. 55, African Studies Center, Boston University, 1982, shows that women workers in South Africa have been particularly militant in the trade unions from 1973 onwards.

2. Cherryl Walker, 'In search of a South African feminism', Work in Progress, No. 34, October 1984, p.25.

3. Cherryl Walker, Women and Resistance in South Africa (Onyx Press, London, 1982), pp.176-179.

4. Aneene Dawber, 'Transvaal women organise', Work in Progress, No. 34, October 1984, p.31.

5. Author's interview with women worker, Brits location, 1986.

6. Pundy Pillay, 'Women in employment in South Africa: some important trends and issues', Social Dynamics, Vol. 11, No. 2, December 1985, p.28.

7. Author's communication with Mrs. Margaret Nhlapo, chairperson of the South African Domestic Workers Association (SADWA).

8. Jane Barrett et al, Vukani Makhosikazi. South African Women Speak (CIIR, London, 1985), p.20.

9. This distinction was first made by Alec Erwin, 'The question of unity in the struggle', South African Labour Bulletin, Vol. 11, No. 1, September 1985. Erwin's article gave rise to an extensive debate. See Jeremy Cronin, 'The question of unity', South African Labour Bulletin, Vol. 11, No. 3, January 1986; Duncan Innes, 'Unity and the Freedom Charter: worker politics and the popular movement', Work in Progress, No. 41, April 1986; and Tony Karon and Max Ozinsky, 'The working class in national-democratic struggle', Work in Progress, No. 42, May 1986.

The annual conference of the Association of Sociologists of Southern Africa in Natal in

1986 was one of the first times that there were a number of papers which addressed the 'women's question'.

10. Leila Patel, speech given at United Democratic Front workshop on women, Johannesburg, February 1985.

11. A. Mariotti, 'The incorporation of African women into wage employment in South Africa, 1920-1970', unpublished Ph.D. thesis, University of Connecticut, 1979; Caroline Stone, 'Industrialisation and female labour-force participation', *South African Labour Bulletin*, Vol. 2, No. 4, 1975; Joanne Yawitch, 'African women and labour-force participation', *Work in Progress*, No. 9, 1979.

12. V. W. Martin and C. M. Rogerson, 'Women and industrial change: the South African experience', *The South African Geographical Journal*, Vol. 66, No. 1, April 1984.

13. Pillay, 'Women in employment', p.27.

14. Joanne Yawitch, 'The incorporation of African women into wage labour, 1950-1980', *South African Labour Bulletin*, Vol. 9, No. 3, December 1983.

15. Martin and Rogerson, 'Women and industrial change', p.41.

16. Pillay, 'Women in employment', p.27.

17. Calculated from *South African Statistics*, 1968, 1980, 1982; and Development Bank of Southern Africa, *1980 Census Reports on Transkei, Bophuthatswana and Venda*, reproduced in Pillay, 'Women and employment', p.23.

18. *Population Census Reports 1980*; and Development Bank of Southern Africa, *1980 Census Reports*, reproduced in Pillay, 'Women and employment', p.25.

19. Figures on women in agriculture should be treated with extreme caution. The 1970 census included women in subsistence agriculture, but this category was excluded in 1980. The definition of agricultural workers has also changed in the last 20 years.

20. Yawitch, 'The incorporation of African women', p.83.

21. Merle Favis, 'Black women in the South African economy', unpublished paper, Durban, January 1983.

22. Pillay, 'Women in employment', p.25.

23. Calculated from *South African Labour Statistics*, 1986; and Pillay, 'Women in employment', Table 9.

24. Once again, figures on agricultural employment are problematic. See Note 19 above.

25. Data calculated from Pillay, 'Women in employment', Table 9; and from *South African Labour Statistics*, Central Statistics Services, 1986.

26. Calculated from *South African Labour Statistics*, 1986.

27. Pillay, 'Women in employment', p.28.

28. *Population Census Report, 1980* and *South African Statistics, 1982*, in Pillay, 'Women in employment', Tables 11 and 12.

29. South African Institute of Race Relations, *Race Relations Survey, 1984* (Johannesburg, 1984), p.259.

30. William Cobbett *et al*, 'South Africa's regional political economy: a critical analysis of reform strategy in the 1980s', Southern African Research Service, *South African Review 3* (Ravan Press, Johannesburg, 1986).

31. Authors' communication with Southern African Development Bank research department.

32. Martin and Rogerson, 'Women and industrial change', p.44.

33. Data from forthcoming publication, South African Labour and Development Research Unit, University of Cape Town.

34. H. Safa, 'Runaway shops and female employment: the search for cheap labour', *Signs*, No. 7, 1981.

35. Authors' interview with Alfa management, Brits, March 1986.

36. Georgina Jaffee, unpublished survey conducted in Brits, 1985.

37. Georgina Jaffee, research in progress.

38. Safa, 'Runaway shops'.

39. J. Lewis and E. Randall, 'Focus: state of the unions', *South African Labour Bulletin*, Vol. 11, No. 2, December 1985, p.75.

40. The 1981 Labour Relations and Wage Acts, following on the recommendations of the Wiehahn Commission, abolished discrimination based on sex in minimum wage agreements.
41. Authors' communication with Chris Bonner, Transvaal secretary of the Chemical Workers Industrial Union.
42. See the Basic Conditions of Employment Act, 1983, discussed in Jonny Myers and Malcolm Steinberg, 'Health and safety: an emerging issue on the shop floor', *Southern African Reserch Service* (eds.), *South African Review 2* (Ravan Press, Johannesburg, 1984), p.146.
43. Adrienne Bird, 'Organising women workers', *South African Labour Bulletin*, Vol. 19, No. 8, August 1985, p.86.
44. *Ibid.*, p.82.
45. J. Cock *et al*, 'Childcare and the working mother: a sociological investigation of a sample of urban African women', Carnegie Conference Paper No. 115, Cape Town, 1984.
46. CUSA, 'Women's unit paper', 1985, p.11.
47. Personal communication with Dale Tifflin, CUSA's information officer, August 1986.
48. *COSATU News*, Vol. 1, No. 1, August 1986.
49. The COSATU resolution on women states that the federation is

1. against all unequal and discriminatory treatment of women at work, in society and in the federation;
2. for the equal rights of women and men to paid work as an important part of the broader aim to achieve full and freely chosen employment;
3. for equal pay for all work of equal value — the value of work must be determined by organised women and men workers themselves;
4. for the restructuring of employment so as to allow women and men the opportunity of qualifying for jobs of equal value;
5. for childcare and family facilities to meet workers' needs and make it easier for workers to combine work and family responsibilities;
6. for full maternity rights, including paid maternity and paternity leave and job security;
7. for the protection of women and men from all types of work proved to be harmful to them including work which interferes with their ability to have children;
8. against sexual harassment in whatever form it occurs;
9. for adequate and safe transport for workers doing overtime and night work.

50. After two years of unity talks, FOSATU and other unions joined to launch COSATU in December 1985.
51. Authors' interview with ex-member of FOSATU women's group, 1986.
52. D. Tifflin in the CUSA newspaper *Izwilethu*, October 1984.
53. The Women's Charter, drawn up by FSAW in 1954, articulated women's demands for inclusion in the Freedom Charter. It deals with demands such as the right to vote, full opportunities for employment and equal pay, equal rights with men in relation to property and marriage, maternity benefits, welfare, clinics and crèches. It demanded the removal of all laws restricting free movement of women and committed itself to build and strengthen the women's section of the national liberation movement.
54. The United Women's Congress (UWC) was formed in the Western Cape in March 1986. It brought together the United Women's Organisation (UWO) and the Women's Front (WF). The UWO and WF were both formed in 1980, but organised and campaigned separately until 1986.

The Federation of Transvaal Women (FEDTRAW) was established in December 1984 with the purpose of uniting women in common action for the removal of political, legal, social and economic disabilities. FEDTRAW claims to be active in 22 areas in the Transvaal. It has participated in campaigns to end military conscription, for the withdrawal of troops from the townships, for a free and equal education for all in South Africa, and the abolition of apartheid. FEDTRAW sees itself following in the tradition of women's organisation in the 1950s under the leadership of FSAW.

The Natal Women's Organisation (NOW) was formed in 1983. It has about 20 branches in the Durban area, and is expanding to the rural areas. Its aim is to organise women around issues that most affect their lives — the high cost of living, poor housing, maternity benefits and childcare. NOW sees the participation of women in trade unions and community organisations as important.

There are many other women's organisations. Not all of these have progressive potential, in particular those linked to Bantustan structures of administration.

There are also a number of women's service organisations which provide resource material. *Speak* is a women's magazine which started in 1982 in an attempt to expose the problems that face women. It is widely used in trade union education. In 1983 the Women's Centre was set up in Durban and is mainly involved in providing literacy seminars, resource material and other educational services for women. In Johannesburg the Johannesburg Democratic Action Committee Women's Group is presently involved in issuing a booklet for working women.

55. According to the Bureau of Market Research the average monthly wage in the Vaal in 1983 was R296.23.

56. Barrett *et al, Vukani Makhosikazi*, p.242.

57. In Naledi, Soweto, more than a thousand women and youths marched on the administration board offices in early July 1986 in protest against these raids (*Star*, 17 July 1986). In Tembisa, near Johannesburg, scores of mothers, some carrying their babies, were severely beaten by police while protesting against police raids, troops in the township, and restrictions placed on funerals (*Sowetan*, 29 May 1986).

58. *Weekly Mail*, 6 June 1986.

59. Authors' interview with Leila Patel, FEDTRAW's education officer, July 1986.

60. Interview with Jessie Duarte, FEDTRAW's public relations officer, July 1986.

61. Tom Lodge, *Black Politics in South Africa since 1945* (Ravan Press, Johannesburg, 1983).

62. Authors' interview with FEDTRAW spokesperson, May 1986.

63. Kally Forrest and Karen Jochelson, 'Uniting against rape: the Port Alfred women's stayaway', *Work in Progress*, No. 43, August 1986; Franz Kruger, 'Women's stayaway in Port Alfred', *South African Labour Bulletin*, Vol. 11, No. 6, June-July 1986.

64. 'Workshop on women', *South African Labour Bulletin*, Vol. 9, No. 3, December 1983, p.14.

65. Leila Patel, speech given at United Democratic Front Workshop on women, Johannesburg, February 1985.

The authors express appreciation to all those who gave up time to be interviewed.

8. Investment, Savings and the Capital Market in South Africa[1]

JESMOND BLUMENFELD

INTRODUCTION

It is common cause on all sides of the political divide in South Africa that there is an urgent need to improve the access of blacks, particularly in the urban areas, to social overhead capital — housing, education and training, health care, public utilities and other economic infrastructure — as a direct contribution to redressing the existing severe racially-based imbalances in living standards.

Implicit in some political positions, however, is the assumption that the abolition of racial discrimination will, in itself, resolve these imbalances. In addition, if only as a reaction against the earlier experiences of poverty and deprivation, expectations are bound to be high in post-apartheid South Africa.

It is undeniable that a major reason for the highly skewed distribution of income and wealth is to be found in the system and policies of apartheid. It follows that the dismantling of apartheid will indeed remove one major set of political and economic constraints on the raising of black living standards. Furthermore, it is to be hoped that this removal will be coupled with the pursuit of more development-oriented policies in general, and that the transition will be achieved without substantial damage to the physical fabric and operational quality of the economy and its existing infrastructure.

It is also true that, with its varied and favourable resource endowments, and with its relatively diversified economy and mature infrastructure in which modern technologies play a predominant role, South Africa is a country of considerable development potential. Indeed, on account of these factors, and perhaps also on account of the exceptionally high standard of living enjoyed by whites, South Africa has long been regarded in some quarters as a relatively developed, high-income country.

In truth, however, per capita income in South Africa still lags far behind that in the industrialised countries. Moreover, the other countries which have comparable income levels are predominantly Third World countries which, though not subject to the distortions and constraints imposed by apartheid, are also characterised by endemic poverty, illiteracy, inequality and unemployment.

In short, whilst the abolition of apartheid is undoubtedly a necessary condition for removing the barriers to higher living standards for blacks, it is unlikely to be a sufficient condition. Attainment of this objective will, at the minimum, also require the generation of large increases in the volume of investible resources.

In this sense, therefore, the problem is one of securing substantial increases in the supply of scarce real resources and of ensuring the appropriate division of output between the competing claims of consumption and investment.[2] In particular, it is a problem of producing enough new investment goods to increase the stock of capital and so sustain the growth of output over time.

But the problem is also a financial one in that most capital formation in a modern economy takes place via the creation of financial assets. Achievement of the desired level of real investment therefore requires that savings be mobilised into the appropriate forms and volumes of financial assets. This, in turn, depends upon the efficiency and capacity of the (financial) capital market.

The purpose of this chapter is to raise some questions about the capacity of the South African economy and of the capital market to generate, mobilise and allocate savings on a scale large enough to make significant inroads into the backlog of provision of basic facilities for the black population. The objective is more to establish an agenda for further research than to provide detailed and definitive answers at this early stage. A broad-brush approach has therefore been adopted.

The bulk of the chapter addresses the following issues: the determination of a target growth rate for bringing about rapid increases in black living standards; the consequent scale of investment demand; the potential sources of savings, both domestic and foreign, to finance this investment demand; and some relevant characteristics of the domestic capital market. The discussion is preceded by some comments on the political and ideological framework within which future economic and social policy will be conducted.

THE CONTEXT FOR RESOURCE ALLOCATION DECISIONS

The assumption in this chapter is that the broad framework within which future economic and social policy will be conducted will not be unrecognisably different from that which currently exists. It may be objected that this assumption is rendered invalid by the possibility of a major shift in the balance between market forces and state intervention in resource allocation decisions. Leaving aside punitive confiscations of wealth, at least some redistribution of agricultural land from white to black ownership and some nationalisation of mining enterprises and financial institutions can reasonably be anticipated, in the event of black majority rule.

The probable extent of such a shift can, however, be overstated, notwithstanding the understandable and rising antipathy amongst many blacks towards the capitalist system. There are at least five reasons for this.

First, the public policy stances of most representative black organisations, both internal and external, remain conciliatory rather than firmly committed on this question. Second, the disastrous economic performance of neighbouring Mozambique and Tanzania will provide sobering reminders to any future black nationalist government that wholesale rejection of market-based resource allocation mechanisms offers no panacea for economic ills. Third, the 'pragmatic' approach adopted by post-independence Zimbabwe renders the complete socialisation of the economy a less likely outcome than many might presently believe.

Fourth, apart from the excessive weight of the bureaucracy, especially in the administration of apartheid structures, economic policy in South Africa has long been highly interventionist. Many major industrial enterprises and much marketing (and even some production) of agricultural produce are subject to substantial state influence or even control. This remains true today, notwithstanding the present government's espousal of more market-oriented policies.

Finally, if major increases in expenditure on urban infrastructures are to be achieved, it will almost certainly be necessary to expand the available pool of uncommitted government revenues. Since higher tax rates and restraints on public sector consumption expenditures could prove inadequate (not to say inappropriate) in this respect, the understandable temptation to eschew market-based provision of services may well need to be more strongly resisted than currently seems likely.

Naturally, much of the detailed structure of the future economy will be determined by the particular forms of constitutional and governmental systems and institutions which have yet to be determined. Even so, economic structures, systems, values and institutions, not to mention production technologies, are often far more durable in the face of changing political dispensations than is sometimes recognised.

OUTPUT GROWTH: SETTING A TARGET

The starting point for any analysis of future investment demand must be growth of output, since no conceivable reallocation of existing outputs and income, or even of wealth, could make anything more than a marginal impact upon the present lack of access of blacks to economic facilities and opportunities.[3]

In seeking to throw some light on the financing implications of a higher growth rate, my approach will be to work back from a 'target' growth rate to the requirements for investment and savings. In doing this, I fully recognise that I am oversimplifying, since the relationship between growth on the one hand and investment and savings on the other hand is not one-way. But, as a means for establishing the future demand for investible resources, it represents a satisfactory first approximation.

Although South Africa's recent growth performance has been relatively poor, the long-term track record has been rather more impressive. GDP growth has averaged 3.8% per annum since 1911, 4.6% since 1920 and 4.1% since 1950.[4] The economy has also shown itself capable of even faster bursts of growth over short periods of time. During the 1960s, for example, South Africa's real output growth averaged almost 6% per annum, implying substantial increases in per capita incomes of around 3% per annum, or almost 35% in a decade. In the 1970s, however, output growth slowed to only 3.1% — barely ahead of population growth. In the 1980s, per capita incomes have actually declined.

Looking to the future, provided the economy can be freed from at least some of the current internal and external constraints upon growth, it should be well capable of achieving growth in excess of the rate of population increase and hence of generating continuing increases in incomes per head. As mentioned above, however, there are likely to be high expectations that the post-apartheid economy should achieve more than its predecessor. To deliver on any such expectations, it will have to grow significantly faster than the 4 to 4.5% long run annual rate hitherto achieved.

It has long been a commonplace that an output increase of at least 6% per annum will be necessary to make substantial inroads into existing levels of unemployment in addition to absorbing the anticipated growth in the labour force. In the longer-term, it is hoped that more employment-oriented industrialisation and urbanisation strategies (including reductions in the price of labour relative to the price of capital) will permit larger and quicker reductions in unemployment at slightly lower rates of growth. Even so, a growth rate well in excess of the long-term average will still be required. The experience of the 1960s indicates that when both internal and external conditions are favourable, rates of this magnitude are, or at any rate previously have been, attainable and sustainable for extended periods.

However, one recent estimate of the long-term growth rate of potential output — namely, the output which the economy would be capable of producing under conditions of full employment of productive resources — puts the maximum attainable rate at only 3.6% per annum given current internal and external constraints.[5] According to this source, only under decidedly optimistic assumptions about the growth in world — and especially industrialised country — economic activity, as well as about the internal availability of capital and the training of labour, can faster growth in production capacity be postulated.

The above data provide some rough yardsticks for the otherwise arbitrary process of selecting a realistic 'target' growth rate for illustrating the economic implications of seeking to raise average living standards in a post-apartheid South Africa. At the minimum, they imply that the target rate needs to be markedly higher than the existing long run average. In principle, this should not be beyond the realms of possibility: admittedly, the removal of apartheid cannot alter the various exogenous factors (like the growth of world demand) upon which the actual growth rate partly depends: but without apartheid, significant relaxations both in the current internal political and economic constraints upon growth and in the existing constraints on the availability of external finance should be possible. On the other hand, it would probably be wishful thinking to hope for any prolonged repetition of the heady conditions of the 1960s. For these reasons, I propose to assume a target growth rate of 5.5% per annum.

THE DEMAND FOR INVESTIBLE RESOURCES

Achievement of any target rate of growth is crucially dependent upon the capacity to generate the requisite level of investment in order to maintain and increase the capital stock.

Between 1977 and 1984 the capital : output ratio, i.e. the relationship between the size of the capital stock and the volume of output it is capable of producing, averaged 2.8, implying that it required R2.8 of capital stock to produce every one rand's worth of output.[6]

If the ratio were to be projected forward at a value of 2.8, a 5.5% annual increase in output in future years would be dependent upon an equivalent percentage increase in the capital stock. This requirement, in turn, would imply that net investment (i.e. after allowing for depreciation), would have to be some 15.4% of GDP.[7]

Apart from the *prima facie* evidence of a secularly rising trend in recent years, there are three reasons to believe that the capital : output ratio may continue to rise.[8]

First, despite some conflicting trends, the balance of compositional shifts in output is likely to give an upward bias to the aggregate ratio. The productivity of capital is highest in manufacturing (capital : output ratio of approximately 1.0) and progressively lower in mining (1.7), in agriculture (2.3), and in transport and communication (4.7).[9] It is also low in both private and public services, the latter including education, health and government administration.

On the one hand, therefore, the fact that the share of manufacturing industry in GDP has increased from 16% to 26% since 1960 would have acted to reduce the aggregate ratio. On the other hand, the contributions to GDP of agriculture and mining, both of which also have lower-than-average capital : output ratios, have fallen from 12% to 8% and from 21% to 11% respectively in the same period. In addition, the proportion of output contributed by the less productive infrastructural and service activities has risen, thereby increasing their weight in the overall ratio. The directions of these compositional changes can be expected to persist in the future, especially if investment in housing and urban infrastructure is given priority. Consequently, their overall influence on the aggregate ratio is likely to be upwards.

Second, the changing sectoral allocation of new capital expenditure itself is similarly likely to raise the aggregate ratio. In particular, the rate of capital accumulation in the public sector has significantly outstripped that of the private sector. The latter's share in the total fixed capital stock fell from 51% in 1946-50 to only 42% in 1979 and undoubtedly has declined further subsequently. This shift will have reinforced the recent upward trend in the aggregate capital : output ratio, and here too it is a reasonable assumption that a further upward bias can be anticipated in the years ahead.

Third, the aggregate capital : output ratio is also sensitive to changes in emphasis between capital widening (which, broadly speaking, increases employment via the replication of existing methods of production) and capital deepening (which increases productivity via the introduction of more sophisticated production techniques). The evidence suggests that, particularly in manufacturing industry and in agriculture, investment has become more capital intensive in recent years; and increasing capital intensity also has the effect of (temporarily) increasing the capital : output ratio. Unless this trend is offset by extensive capital widening in other sectors, it too will tend to raise the future capital : output ratio.

It was noted above that, with the capital : output ratio assumed constant at 2.8, over 15% of total output would have to be devoted to net investment. But if we allow for an increase in the ratio to only 3.0, the net investment requirement would rise to 16.5% of income.[10] To translate this into a gross investment requirement we have to look at the rate of depreciation of the capital stock. This rate has typically been very volatile, but in recent years, on average, depreciation has been approximately 55% of gross investment. Thus, on the assumption made, a net investment requirement of 16.5% would imply a gross investment : income ratio of no less than 36.6%.[11]

The South African economy has hitherto seldom proved capable of devoting more than 30% of total output to investment, and certainly not for a sustained period.[12] If the investment : income ratio is to be raised to over one third a correspondingly reduced share for either private consumption expenditure or public consumption expenditure (or both) will have to be accepted. Even with output growing rapidly, this is likely to prove politically difficult to achieve in the face of demands for rapid increases in living standards.

THE SUPPLY OF SAVINGS

Investment must, of course, be financed either from domestic savings or by borrowing from abroad. Consequently, if the historical record on investment is to be improved upon, substantial increases in funding will have to be forthcoming from either or both of these sources.

Since the mid-1950s, South Africa has demonstrated a capacity to generate domestic savings rates which, on average, have proved sufficient to finance most domestic investment. Since 1970, for example, the ratio of gross domestic savings to gross domestic investment has averaged almost 95%. This implies that, on average, the savings : income ratio has lagged only slightly behind the investment : income ratio.[13] The sources of domestic savings are threefold: personal savings, corporate savings, and general government savings. Data on these are generally available only after allowance for depreciation, i.e. they refer to net savings, rather than gross savings. What, then, are the prospects for increasing the supply of net savings from these sources?

The contribution of personal savings to total net savings has declined slightly from an average of about 42% in 1955-72 to about 36% in subsequent years. More importantly, the personal savings ratio, i.e. the ratio of personal savings to personal disposable income, has declined from 11.3% in the 1960s, to 10.6% in the 1970s and to an astonishingly low 4% in 1981-84. The latter figure will undoubtedly rise again, but a secular downward trend does seem evident, and this will obviously make it more difficult to attain a higher savings ratio in the future.

The reasons for this decline are not immediately apparent. In the 1970s, nominal interest rates were generally below the rate of inflation, with the result that real interest rates were negative. This would naturally have tended to reduce savings. On the other hand, inflation was on a rising trend and this would have acted to raise savings. The fact that the savings ratio fell only slightly suggests that these two effects were largely offsetting.[14] In the early 1980s, however, not only did inflation accelerate, but real interest rates turned very sharply positive. Yet savings fell precipitately. There were some special factors — such as the advance announcement of increases in general sales tax — which undoubtedly induced people to temporarily dissave. The decline may also have had something to do with compositional changes in total income. If, for example, blacks have a lower propensity to save than whites, then the rising share of blacks in total income would have reduced the overall savings ratio.[15]

But even after allowing for these factors, the explanation for the sustained decline in savings may well prove to have been a shift in savers' time preference rates, i.e. a decline in the value which people place on postponing current consumption through saving in order to be able to consume more in the future. A shift of this nature would be explicable in terms of the heightened levels of political and economic uncertainty of the past few years. Even if this trend can be reversed by fundamental political change — and it is far from certain that such changes would significantly lengthen consumers' time horizons again — the prospects for personal savings rising voluntarily above their historical levels cannot be rated very highly.

Corporate savings are by far the largest component of net savings. Since the war, they have grown substantially from almost negligible proportions to a typical contribution of around one half. They are also the most volatile component, since they naturally depend upon profit earnings and upon the proportion of after-tax profits which firms choose not to distribute to shareholders. It goes without saying that fluctuating fortunes of mining — especially gold mining — corporations and, to a lesser extent, of agricultural enterprises, dominate the corporate profits scene. Although the proportion of retained earnings can be influenced by fiscal measures, it clearly cannot be increased substantially without prejudicing the ability of firms to raise new investment capital. In the long run, only growth itself and the continued profitability of new investments can induce further increases in corporate savings.

Government savings arise from the excess of current government income (mainly from taxes and from earnings from government-owned enterprises) over current government expenditure (mainly civil service salaries and wages, purchases of goods and services, production subsidies, pension and other transfer payments, and interest on the public debt). All levels of government are included. In effect, such savings represent a pool of uncommitted resources from which capital and development projects can be financed. The contribution of the government sector to net savings has never been very substantial — it has fluctuated fairly widely around the 20% level. Given the recent proliferation of new levels and departments of government in South Africa, it comes as little surprise to find that government's contribution has recently become negative. Indeed, in 1983 and 1984 net government dissavings completely offset net personal savings.

Current government expenditure has been on a rising, if fluctuating, trend from around 12% of GDP in the early 1970s to almost 18% in 1984. As to the future, there seems little prospect of a significant reduction under almost any scenario. Indeed, the reverse seems likely. The best that can be hoped for is that its rate of growth might be slowed, but even that seems improbable. Any renewed contribution by government to net savings would therefore have to come from increased revenues. Leaving aside one-off contributions from asset sales, this necessarily means higher taxes. No doubt there is always scope for further tax increases. But personal taxation as a proportion of personal income has already doubled in the past 15 years from 6% to 12%, and here one must bear in mind that the vast majority of income earners are liable for very little, if any, income tax, so that the tax base is very narrow. 'Fiscal drag' and 'bracket creep' in times of inflation can always raise the tax above budgeted levels, but there must rapidly come a time when higher personal tax rates become counter-productive. The top marginal tax rate, currently 47.5%, presumably could be raised to punitive levels as part of a redistributive strategy, but that might be difficult to reconcile with a growth strategy. The same constraint is surely also applicable to corporation tax, especially if private investment is to be a driving force in the attainment of a higher growth rate. It must also be remembered that the milch cow provided by the gold mines could begin to run dry if either the dollar price of gold falls or the production costs of the mines rise steeply. In any event, it is apparent that the corporate tax base is also rather narrow.

This leaves only indirect taxes to be considered. Until recently, this source of income was relatively unexploited, but GST was introduced in 1978, and was rapidly escalated from a rate of 4% to 12%. Here, too, further increases are possible but not without significant disadvantages. Although sales taxes do broaden the tax base, they are highly regressive, and even with exemptions for food and other basic commodities, higher rates would soon begin to erode black living standards. Higher property rates and service charges, especially in urban areas, are an obvious alternative (as the present goverment has already recognised), but again there is a risk of raising business costs to levels which might adversely affect profitability and hence the direct tax take.

Taking government revenues as a whole, therefore, these have risen over the years to almost 22% of GDP. They will probably continue to rise under any future administration, but there seems little scope for them to outstrip current expenditures by a margin large enough to permit a significant contribution by government to the financing of higher investment rates. In short, any attempts to increase the aggregate savings ratio will be subject to serious constraints. Leaving aside a programme of forced savings, it follows that major increases in investment demand will probably have to be financed to a significant extent from external sources.

My earlier comments indicated that South Africa has hitherto been relatively self-sufficient in its capital requirements. However, even on an aggregate basis it is clear that a gap has existed between the supply of, and the demand for, investment capital. Recourse to at least some foreign capital has, therefore, always been necessary to bridge this gap. Moreover, the aggregate figures mask two factors which have resulted in a continuing and substantial need for foreign capital.

First, the year-to-year volatility of investment and, to a lesser extent, the volatility of domestic savings, means that in many individual years there is a substantial mismatch between total demand and supply. For example, for eight consecutive years between 1969 and 1976, investment exceeded domestic savings, the average shortfall being no less than 14% of gross investment. Second, the fact that, *ex post*, aggregate domestic savings are seen to be almost sufficient to finance aggregate investment overlooks the fact that, at the disaggregated level, different types of savings are not always perfect substitutes for each other, and hence that some forms of investment demand may be being rationed. Access to appropriate sources of foreign capital can relieve such bottlenecks and permit more rapid growth. Considerations such as this have been responsible for the growing recourse, especially by the parastatals, to the international capital market in recent years. A further factor which sometimes necessitates recourse to foreign capital is that, for either technical or copyright (patent) reasons, the acquisition of foreign technology may be possible only via the importation by foreign corporations themselves of capital goods embodying the relevant technology. In these circumstances, neither domestic savings nor foreign borrowing can substitute for direct foreign investment.

It is obviously to be hoped that a post-apartheid South Africa will regain normal access to international capital markets, and that as a developing country with substantial development potential it will be able to revert to a position of importing capital, rather than being a net exporter, as at present. At the minimum, a major debt rescheduling programme can be anticipated, so that a gap can be opened up between annual net earnings of foreign exchange on current account and debt repayment obligations. This would release at least some resources to finance more foreign borrowing and/or increased imports. But, leaving aside any political considerations, with foreign debts currently still totalling some $22 billion, and an annual interest burden alone of around $2 billion, the judgement of the markets may well be that the capacity to absorb much new foreign finance may be in doubt. In practice, therefore, unless direct foreign investment comes to the rescue — and this will also depend crucially upon the political climate —

reliance on indirect commercial foreign capital may still not provide funds in sufficient quantities to bridge the development gulf between white and black. In that event, concessionary finance will be necessary. There is, of course, no reason in principle why foreign aid should not be a satisfactory substitute for most other forms of foreign resources, but the experience of many other countries suggests that this might not prove to be the case in practice.

THE CAPITAL MARKET[16]

In a monetised economy, with few exceptions, those who save invest not in physical investment goods, but rather in financial assets, such as money, savings deposits, shares and bonds.[17] Likewise, those who create physical capital seldom do so from their own resources. Instead, they borrow or otherwise incur financial liabilities. Moreover, except in the case of so-called direct finance (such as new share issues), lenders and borrowers do not normally trade directly with each other but via the mediation of banks and other financial institutions.[18] Thus, regardless of whether a higher demand for capital is to be met by an increase in domestic or in foreign savings, there is still the problem of mobilising these savings and channelling them, via the appropriate financial assets, towards those economic sectors and units seeking funds for real investment.[19]

Other things equal, the supply of financial savings to the capital market will rise with the real rate of interest, whilst the demand for such savings — in effect, the demand for loanable funds or other investible resources — varies inversely with the price.[20] The equilibrium price is the (real) lending rate of interest which, in order to cover the costs incurred by financial intermediaries and to allow for the risk of default, is normally higher than the deposit rate of interest.[21] It follows that an increase in the demand for financial savings relative to their supply can be expected to raise the equilibrium price. Whether or not post-apartheid South Africa will regain its earlier capacity to attract financial capital and so minimise the necessary rise in real interest rates is clearly a question about which little can be said definitely at this juncture. Apart from the political risk factor for all investors and the exchange risk for foreign investors, financial policies will be crucial in determining whether the future capital market will be characterised by a process of financial deepening or of financial repression.[22]

Moreover, whilst the simple model outlined above is useful for illustrating some of the basic issues regarding the overall demand for and supply of financial savings, a more complex analytical framework is needed to take account of the existence of many different kinds of financial assets, for each of which there likewise exists both a demand and a supply and an equilibrium price. Because of substitutability between assets in the minds of both borrowers and lenders, the price of each asset is interdependent with that of every other asset. Yet, the structure of relative prices of financial assets is by no means the only consideration. At the present time, for example, the heightened state of political uncertainty has not only reduced the demand for investment in growth-generating capital, but has also rendered it difficult to attract savings to long-term investments. Here, too, predictions would necessarily be highly speculative. However, some insight into the problems which will be faced can be gained by consideration of the inter-sectoral financial flows which will be generated by the trade in financial assets which must arise from attempts to meet the economy's increased financial requirements.

By assumption, we are considering large increases in investment demand on the part of the following sectors:
• the private corporate sector, for the purpose of increasing both employment and productivity via modernisation and expansion of the capital stock, especially in industry, in mining, and in the distributive trades;
• the public corporate sector, where, on the assumption of no major expansion in the scope of the sector (with privatisation, a decline in scope is conceivable), the primary purpose would be productivity improvements; however if we assume a major nationalisation programme, the investment would be for the same purposes as in the private sector;
• the general government sector, both central and regional/local, for the purpose of expanding the social — particularly urban — infrastructure, for housing development, and for expanding employment;
• the household sector, mainly for the purpose of house-building.

An examination of the National Financial Accounts since 1970 (see Table 8.1) shows that, of the above-mentioned sectors, only the private corporate sector and the household sector have positive financing balances, i.e. a surplus of gross saving over gross investment (after adjustment for net capital transfers from and to other sectors). The public corporations and general government (both central and local) are consistently financial deficit sectors, i.e. with gross investment exceeding gross saving (again after allowance for capital transfers).[23] Of the remaining sectors, the financial institutions predictably have a collective financial surplus, whilst the foreign sector (the rest of the world) has either a financing surplus or deficit depending respectively upon whether the current account of the balance of payments is in deficit or surplus.[24] It is highly improbable that this general pattern of financing balances will alter in the future. Leaving aside the requirement of the accounting identity that one sector's financing surplus must have with its counterpart in the financing deficits of other sectors, it is certainly to be hoped that the household, financial intermediary and private corporate sectors will continue to generate savings well in excess of their own investment needs!

The public enterprise sector includes SATS, Post and Telecommunications, Escom, Iscor, the Rand Water Board, the Mint, the IDC, other development corporations, the agricultural boards, etc. Although traditionally in financing deficit, this sector could, in principle, also achieve a surplus (or, at least, reflect a reduced deficit), but only at the 'cost' of greatly increased profits and/or greatly reduced real investment. In so far as the latter development would lead to deterioration of the sector's capital stock, it would presumably be deemed undesirable, regardless of arguments about nationalisation or privatisation. The former possibility — more profits — may well appear to conflict with social and political imperatives, not least because the only realistic way of achieving it would be via 'economic' charges for, or even privatisation of, most services. This option may, however, not be without its attractions, even for a socialist-minded administration. If housing and jobs are to be the priority, and if adequate savings cannot be generated from other sources, then higher charges may yet be judged an acceptable, even necessary, price to pay.[25] For the general government sector to achieve a consistent financing surplus would, however, seem to be politically inconceivable. Even if the current capacity — crucially dependent upon the profits of the gold mines — to generate continuing large increases in exchequer revenues was preserved, and even if substantial savings could be made by disbanding redundant apartheid-related administrative structures (such as the homelands administrations), the demands for socially desirable development expenditures are bound to exceed the pool of government revenues not already committed to salaries, debt service, administrative expenses, etc.

A sector which has a financing surplus will, in consequence, reflect a positive net acquisition of financial assets. In contrast, a financing deficit will give rise to net incurment of financial liabilities.[26] Beyond the general inter-sectoral flows, the National Financial Accounts also provide a sector-by-sector breakdown of the sources and uses of funds. The sources of funds indicate the nature of the liabilities incurred by each sector, and the uses the nature of the financial assets acquired by each sector. The difference between the total of sources and uses for each sector is therefore equivalent to its financing balance.[27] A detailed analysis of the pattern of sources and uses is far beyond the scope of this chapter. However, there are some noteworthy features which have implications for any future attempts to extend the depth and scope of operations of the capital markets in the interests of funding more development expenditures.

As Table 8.1 shows, private corporate enterprises generally have the largest financing surpluses and hence are the primary source of funds for other sectors and potentially important for future attempts to mobilise financial capital for housing and infrastructural development. But the vast majority of total asset acquisitions by the sector are devoted to the provision of trade credit and other short-term loans (see Table 8.2), the primary users of which are households, public sector corporate enterprises, other private corporations and, to a varying degree, the foreign sector. Typically, this item represents between 60% and 90% of the sector's asset purchases. Bearing in mind that a substantial proportion of the remaining acquisitions are in the form of cash and demand deposits and other short-term deposits with banks and financial institutions, it is apparent that the bulk of the sector's uses of funds are for its own working capital purposes. It follows not only that relatively little of the sector's resources currently find their way into government bonds and other forms of long-term lending (including mortgages) which might conceivably provide finance for black development, but also that the prospects for inducing a much greater flow into such assets in the future must be relatively slim.[28] Obviously, either an increase in their relative rate of return, or the provision of government subsidies (including fiscal incentives), would assist in bringing about some adjustment in the sector's asset portfolio. But the much-vaunted plan for greatly increased private sector involvement in black housing development is unlikely to come to very much in global terms.

Turning directly to housing finance, it is of course the household sector for which mortgage loans represent a major source of funds. (The only other major sources are consumer credit and bank overdrafts and loans.) The suppliers of mortgage funds are predominantly the building societies and, to a very much smaller extent, local authorities and 'other financial institutions' (amongst which are included the National Housing Fund and participation mortgage bond schemes). Recently there has been considerable discussion of the possibility that the funds available to pension and insurance schemes might be directed towards black housing development.[29] Hitherto, apart from deposits with banks and other financial institutions, the main uses of funds by the pension and insurance schemes have been for ordinary shares, long-term government stock, local authority and public enterprise securities and long-term loans (other than mortgage loans). Much of this investment has, of course, been in accordance with the prescribed asset regulations governing the use of the scheme's funds. In principle, the scope for diverting funds from this source to black housing appears considerable. For example, it has been suggested that investments in black housing projects could also be included in the prescribed assets category. However, the need to protect the interests of the fund's contributors means that this could not be done at the expense of their incomes. Thus, the return on housing investments could not be too far out of line with returns on other long-term assets. In the final analysis, therefore, state guarantees and/or subsidies will almost certainly be necessary.[30]

CONCLUSION

The problems facing any future administration seeking to narrow the development gap between whites and blacks will be formidable. Even allowing for the employment of redistributive policies, an output growth rate well in excess of recent experience will be essential. It is far from certain that either the necessary climate of confidence or the requisite supply of investible resources will be forthcoming. The financial aspects of the problem will also require careful attention. Attempts to divert financial savings from their current uses into assets which can be applied to black development will necessitate changes in the structure of relative rates of return and, even in the case of greater private sector involvement, will generate substantial additional demands on the exchequer. Maintaining a delicate balance between all these requirements will be no easy task.

Table 8.1: Financing Balances,[1] 1970-1984 (R millions)

Year	Foreign Sector [2]	Financial Inter- mediaries	General Government	Public Enterprise	Private Corporate Enterprise	Households etc [3]
1970	868	58	-168	-492	-577	311
1971	1,057	108	-428	-723	-504	490
1972	90	226	-461	-818	134	829
1973	52	95	48	-763	240	328
1974	998	104	125	-1,365	-28	166
1975	1,813	260	-588	-2,029	-228	772
1976	1,671	36	-974	-2,373	1,160	480
1977	-412	218	-859	-2,378	1,833	1,598
1978	-1,330	204	-546	-1,883	2,144	1,411
1979	-2,970	749	-280	-2,628	2,900	2,229
1980	-2,830	362	862	-3,617	3,274	1,948
1981	3,704	673	-587	-5,480	1,267	442
1982	3,210	814	-1,974	-4,497	1,958	489
1983	-265	1,019	-3,436	-3,736	4,540	1,878
1984	1,410	1,308	-5,806	-2,035	3,836	1,287

1. Gross savings (and capital transfers) less gross investment (and capital transfers). Data for Namibia included.
2. A positive value reflects a surplus for the rest of the world vis-à-vis South Africa and hence a deficit on the latter's current account of the balance of payments. A negative value indicates a corresponding current account surplus.
3. Includes unincorporated enterprises and self-employed.

Source: S.A. Reserve Bank Quarterly Bulletin, various issues.

Table 8.2: Private Corporate Enterprises: Uses of Funds (1970-84) (R millions)

	1970	1971	1972	1973	1974	1975	1976	1977	1978	1979	1980	1981	1982	1983	1984
Trade credit and other short-term lending	646	810	713	831	2,012	1,906	2,215	1,794	2,781	1,179	3,313	4,256	7,675	6,600	6,537
(As % of total)	(140)	(83)	(62)	(45)	(80)	(83)	(84)	(59)	(61)	(36)	(63)	(92)	(86)	(74)	(52)
Total uses of funds	463	990	1,159	1,834	2,501	2,292	2,639	3,059	4,561	3,321	5,304	4,629	8,941	8,957	12,538

Source: S.A. Reserve Bank Quarterly Bulletin, various issues.

NOTES

1. I am grateful to Colin Stoneman and John Knight for helpful comments on this chapter, but they bear no responsibility for the views expressed or for any errors or omissions.
2. In South Africa, as in many other developing countries where poverty is widespread, the dividing line between consumption and investment may be difficult to draw. Some expenditures (e.g. on better food and clothing) which are normally regarded as consumption, but which could have profound effects on productivity, could be considered investment in capital.
3. This is *not* an argument against the employment of redistributive policies *per se*. On the contrary, a redistributive strategy will need to be an integral part of post-apartheid policies. But the point made in the text still stands.
4. Cf. Nattrass's claim that the country has achieved 'one of the fastest rates of economic growth' of any society in the world this century. J. Nattrass, *The South African Economy* (OUP, Oxford, 1981), p.xix.
5. B. L. de Jager and M. M. Smal, 'The potential gross domestic product of South Africa', *South African Reserve Bank Quarterly Bulletin*, December 1984.
6. The figure for 1984 — the last year for which data are available — was 3.1 (based on an estimated real fixed capital stock of R192 billion and real GDP of R61.6 billion, both expressed in 1980 prices). However, single year figures are potentially misleading, since the degree to which capacity is utilised can vary substantially over the business cycle. Thus, a period average is probably a more representative figure.
7. A constant aggregate capital : output ratio naturally implies, in turn, that the incremental ratio (ICOR) should also be constant. The net investment ratios in the paper have been calculated using the formula

$$g = \Delta y/y = 1/y \cdot \Delta y/\Delta K = 1/y \cdot 1/\text{ICOR}$$

where g = annual percentage rate of output growth
    y = output
    1 = net investment
    k = capital stock

8. After fluctuating between about 2.1 and 2.3 in the 1950s and 1960s, the capital-output ratio rose to around 2.5 in the mid-1970s, to 2.8 in the late 1970s and to about 3.1 from 1982.
9. Nattrass, *The South African Economy*, p.89.
10. It is worth noting that in the course of transition to a higher capital-output ratio, it might be necessary for the rate of growth of real investment to exceed 5.5% per annum. Certainly, in the absence of the various compositional effects discussed in the text, a higher aggregate ratio could be achieved only by virtue of an increase in the incremental ratio (ICOR) above the average level, which would (temporarily) require both a higher investment growth rate and a higher investment-income ratio. High investment growth rates have been achieved in the past — in 1960-82, for example, investment grew at an average rate of 6% per annum — but, under the assumptions made, even this would be inadequate for raising the investment-income ratio above one-third. It is also worth remembering that investment is the most volatile of all the major components of expenditure. Indeed, between 1977 and 1984, the level of real gross investment actually declined in no less than five years. In 1983, for example, it declined by no less than 9%. In contrast, three years earlier, it had registered an even more spectacular increase of 17%. No account has been taken of this volatility in the text, although it undoubtedly has important implications for achievement of the target growth rate.
11. There is no way of knowing *a priori* what effect a rise in the level of investment will have upon the level of depreciation. When new investment falls, there is likely to be a tendency to extend the useful life of existing capital equipment: conversely, a higher rate of investment may encourage the scrapping of existing capital. But many other factors (including the technological nature of the investments themselves) will affect the outcome. Partly for these reasons, and partly because of doubts about the quality of the data (which

are frequently obtained in the form of residuals), no attempt has been made here to allow for any refinements of the historical average rate of depreciation. In any event, it is unlikely that any reasonable adjustments would significantly alter the central point of the argument, which is that higher average living standards will necessitate devoting a significantly higher proportion of total income to gross investment.

12. After the war, the investment-income ratio fell from around 28% to about 23% in the 1950s. In 1959-62 it dropped to a mere 20%, before rising to around 26% under the impact of the post-Sharpeville major public sector investment programme. Subsequently, it has fluctuated widely around the 27% level, with lower levels being registered both after Soweto and during the upheavals of the past few years.

13. In fact, from an immediate post-war rate of only about 12% of income, the domestic savings ratio displayed a gradually rising trend, reaching an average level of 27% in the 1970s before declining sharply with the onset of recession in 1982.

14. Personal savings arise from the decision by households regarding the extent and timing of their consumption expenditures in relation to their incomes. Other things equal, both higher real interest rates and higher inflation are thought to raise savings levels, the former because the return to savings is higher, and the latter because the inflationary erosion of the real value of people's wealth induces them to save more to restore their wealth levels.

15. The fact that blacks have lower incomes on average obviously implies that their savings are likely to be smaller in *absolute* terms. The point being made here relates to the possibility that they may also save a smaller *proportion* of their income.

16. I am using the term 'capital market' in its most general sense, i.e. it incorporates all financial asset markets, including the money, equity and bond markets.

17. In the South African context, the exceptions — such as self-help housing and improvements to agricultural land — are not unimportant, especially in the context of black development.

18. See P. J. Drake, *Money, Finance and Development* (Martin Robertson, 1980), Chapter 2.

19. *Ibid.*

20. The *ceteris paribus* condition is particularly important where investment is concerned, since expectations are crucial. Witness, for example, the present situation in South Africa's capital markets, where, despite a reduction in the prime overdraft rate from a highly positive real interest rate in mid-1985 to a strongly negative rate in mid-1986, credit demand has collapsed.

21. See Susan Hickok and Clive Gray, 'Capital market controls and credit rationing in Mali and Senegal', *Journal of Modern African Studies*, Vol. 19, No. 1, 1981.

22. See Y. Lee and Y. C. Jao, *Financial Structures and Monetary Policies in Southeast Asia* (Macmillan, 1982). See also the classic works by R. I. McKinnon, *Money and Capital in Economic Development* (Brooking Institution, 1973), and by E. S. Shaw, *Financial Deepening in Economic Development* (OUP, Oxford, 1973).

23. There have been three occasions since 1970 — namely 1973, 1974 and 1980 — on which the government sector has had a financing surplus, but these are clearly only aberrations in an otherwise consistent picture.

24. The scope for terminological confusion here is considerable. However, the conventions of double-entry bookkeeping require that the transactions be viewed from the perspective of the relevant sectors. Thus, from the point of view of the rest of the world, a financing surplus corresponds to a South African deficit (and vice versa).

25. It would be nice to believe that some of the specific products of apartheid — such as the National Supplies Procurement Fund and the Community Development Fund — which fall within the ambit of this sector and which are undoubtedly a drain on its resources, will fall by the wayside. I confess to a degree of cynicism on this score.

26. Drake, *Money, Finance and Development*, Chapter 2, and D. J. Uys and S. J. van der Walt, 'National financial accounts for South Africa (1970-1979)', *S.A. Reserve Bank Quarterly Bulletin* (supplement), September 1981.

27. Although this equivalence is true in principle, in practice measurements of financial

flows are unlikely to yield precisely the same figures as those obtained from the income and product accounts. A balancing item is therefore normally incorporated in the financial accounts.

28. In the case of mortgages, the private sector is, in fact, a much larger demander of finance than a source of it.

29. See, for example, *Financial Mail*, Johannesburg, 13 June, 20 June, 11 July and 1 August, 1986.

30. Employer housing subsidies for black workers would also represent a means for securing wider access by blacks to housing finance.

A Rejoinder to Blumenfeld

COLIN STONEMAN

Jesmond Blumenfeld's argument assumes a politico-economic context of continuing capitalism and full integration into the world market, but the conclusions cannot be said to be optimistic, especially so far as raising employment levels are concerned. I want to argue here that the possibility of an orthodox capitalist solution to this problem is negligible, and then go on to explore the alternative assumption that liberated South Africa will be a democratic socialist state, with a degree of independence of the world markets. This assumption will relax one set of constraints, but introduce another.

ORTHODOX UNREALITY?

The set of constraints that Blumenfeld's chapter points to arises from the increasingly labour-saving nature of world technology. Often there is no longer the option to switch between capital intensity and labour intensity depending on relative factor prices. Because most modern technology has been developed in a capital-intensive, high labour-cost environment, there are often no viable labour-intensive alternatives. Even obsolescent technology may be no solution if, as well as requiring more labour for its operation, it also requires more material inputs, and sometimes even more capital. More suitable technologies for less-developed economies may in principle be developed, but only in India and China is much attention being paid to this.

So what it amounts to, is that to be competitive on the world market nearly always requires the use of capital-intensive technology, with the availability of cheap labour becoming increasingly irrelevant. This boils down under capitalism to the increasing cost of 'creating a job'. In South Africa estimates of this vary widely around R30-40,000; to be internationally competitive requires something more like the US figure, also varying widely in estimate around US $30,000. World Bank estimates[1] put the rise in the workforce in South Africa (people aged between 15 and 64) at 3.3% per annum, that is an increase of 670,000 per year. To 'create jobs' for this number of people every year would require investment of US $20bn or R40bn (that is about two-thirds of GDP) — plainly an impossibility. If we reduce the required investment to US $20,000 (at the cost of international competitiveness) we would still need R27bn or 44% of GDP; anything less and the numbers unemployed would continue to grow above the intolerably high present levels. Even if we assume that only half the work force are to be employed anyway, then 335,000 jobs still need to be created, still requiring R13.5 bn or 22% of GDP. This of course assumes that the people will be content with only 50% employment, that is with the absolute numbers of unemployed rising by 3.3% a year (even if the numbers employed are rising at the same rate).

But would it be possible even to invest at the rate required? Blumenfeld assumes that 55% of investment will be required to make good depreciation. To create 670,000 jobs annually would then require total investment of 98% of GDP annually, and even 335,000 would require 49%. I prefer to assume that depreciation will be relatively independent of new investment at around 12% of GDP, so my figures will be more optimisitic at 56% and 34% respectively. The latter is within the bounds of possibility,[2] but following the Harrod-Domar assumption would imply a steady GDP growth of over 7% per year[3] if the capital:output ratio is 3. Such a growth rate has been sustained in the past only for short periods by South Africa (or any other country); one reason for this is that because of the very high import content of investment consequent on the underdevelopment of the capital goods sector, the investment required for growth sucks in imports. Therefore either exports have to grow at a faster rate than GDP (with world trade typically growing at only 2-3% per year this implies a rapidly increasing share in world trade) or a balance of payments crisis will arise.

But the prospects for combining such an open 'export-led growth strategy' with full employment are even worse, for even if we accept the argument that competition on world markets requires high capital intensity and impossibly high levels of investment, labour costs remain a factor, as competition has to be with countries with very low *average* wage rates. Where, as in South Africa at present, half or more of the wage and salary bill is the cost of skilled labour and professionals at near international rates, the benefits of even the cheapest unskilled labour to capitalists is marginal. The outcome is that unless *all* employment costs can be kept down (as in South Korea and Taiwan in the 1960s), capital-intensity is forced even higher, and the mass of the population becomes excluded from the job market permanently. South Africa's racial domination would allow the ruling race to find this outcome acceptable, but after liberation, a capitalist South Africa would find itself in a similar dilemma to Zimbabwe's, in which maintenance of the living standards of the elite (white and black) and the interests of capital, demand international competitiveness at the cost of employment for the majority.

A SOCIALIST ALTERNATIVE?

The solution to this dilemma may only be through socialism (but one subject to the constraints caused by existing white skill domination and potential for sabotage as discussed below). Its components will have to include an at least temporary partial withdrawal from the world market to concentrate on the development of the internal market — that is, to provide employment to and raise the consumption levels of the vast majority of the population. This greater degree of self-reliance during a restructuring period (ultimately even socialist countries will not wish to remain isolated from world markets), would allow an approach which in effect treated every person on the job market as already in a job, albeit in many cases with extremely low productivity. With such a reorientation of thinking, the productivity of each person becomes central, suggesting the use of capital investment not to 'create' jobs, but to raise the productivity of existing jobs. That is labour, measured by the total number of jobs, has a demand for capital, rather than the number of jobs being determined by capital's demands. Initial overall growth rates measured in conventional terms would probably be lower on this approach than in the most optimistic projections for a conventional approach; but standards of living and productivity would rise faster for the majority, laying the basis for faster growth later.

In part the viability of such an approach is clarified by a change in accounting procedures: most countries cannot now simply expatriate 'guest' workers when labour is no longer required, imposing the cost of social security on the countries of origin; South Africa's attempt at this through the 'homelands' policy has clearly failed. Private firms everywhere, however, have a high incentive to 'repatriate' superfluous workers to the charge of the state, and yet the unemployed remain a charge on the country as a whole; this charge rises as education, health, housing and social services become institutionalised. So international competitiveness cannot simply be bought at the expense of greater unemployment through the high productivity of those remaining in work, because the country's productivity is not equal to the average of its firms' productivities. Of course in the end it may cost a welfare state only half as much to keep a person unemployed as it would to keep them on full pay where their marginal output was zero, so the benefit is not only to the private employer. But the converse is also true: the *social cost* of an employment-oriented policy is much less than the private cost to employers, even at the first-order direct level. Zimbabwe's experience in preventing retrenchment in recent years has shown that there are also numerous second-order benefits — through maintenance of demand, but also through the diversification forced on previously unenterprising companies featherbedded by secure monopolies, which have been obliged to find ways of creating productive employment for workers who would otherwise be a cost with no return. This may be seen as a paradigm for the future: when the South African state can no longer 'sack' workers and their dependants by sending them to the 'homelands', and when it is committed in any case to redistribution, it has an economic incentive to help them produce something rather than nothing.

If the resulting labour-intensive economy is not internationally competitive 'because of overmanning', the long-run remedy is clearly the provision of more capital per worker, to raise productivity. The short-run palliatives are either devaluation, which in principle for a country exporting manufactures in a competitive market, can always be continued until the price of the goods becomes competitive (at the expense of real wage rates). More appropriate in most developing country contexts might be export subsidies or wage subsidies. Again, planning to counter the inevitable external opposition (couched in ideologically loaded free-market rhetoric) would be important: it might be pointed out that the accounting could be recast with a proportion of the workers notionally transferred to direct state support (analogous to unemployment benefit) equal to the value of the subsidy, leaving the firm in question competitive by orthodox standards; or alternatively it might be pointed out that a disguised subsidy is received by firms in market economies that provide social security for the unemployed out of the common exchequer.

EXTERNAL CONSTRAINTS

For the purpose of considering likely constraints we will first assume a scenario in which a revolutionary process goes effectively to completion. This is still a real possibility because of the rising political consciousness faced by internal (and external) intransigence on the part of the supporters of white domination, from which capital is unable to distance itself sufficiently. Political will in this scenario would accept the initial economic costs and with a *de facto* alliance with the Soviet bloc and possible membership of the CMEA, the only effective constraints would be considerations of minimising economic disruption.

A more likely scenario, however, would involve a Lancaster House type agreement for South Africa which would guarantee some significant white property rights under majority rule. Trade, investment, and especially aid would then become conditional (as in Zimbabwe) on respecting the agreement. In effect aid would facilitate the implementation of those parts of the Freedom Charter approved by the West (such as expanded and improved education) on condition that no progress were made with the more radical elements.

These are not, however, the only two possibilities: constraints which have an implicit escalating battery of sanctions against their breaking, can cut both ways. In the case of Zimbabwe the country is too small, poor and vulnerable to have much freedom of manoeuvre. Realistic land reform or significant moves towards either nationalisation of industry or introduction of industrial democracy would provoke not merely a propaganda war, but also an uncontrolled outflow of skills and capital (and possibly sabotage), a suspension of aid, withdrawal of advisors, and maybe even invasion by South Africa. Every element of this scenario could be catastrophic for Zimbabwe. However in the case of a liberated South Africa, there would be negligible chance of military intervention, but the country would possess a real option of increased reliance on the Soviet Union. With the Cuban example in mind, more sophisticated Western policy makers would be reluctant to retaliate in response to marginal shifts by South Africa in a radical direction, because this might easily prove counterproductive. Thus if aid (which would almost certainly be designed to ease the costs to whites of redistribution) were to be withdrawn from primarily social projects, not only would leverage be surrendered, but popular anger (facilitating further radical shifts) would be aroused. Where the line would be drawn in terms of policy content is hard to judge, but a radicalising South Africa with sufficient political will could probably devise a strategy that progressively and irreversibly weakened both white economic ownership and control, and foreign influence, at a rate just slow enough to avoid serious sanctions. The existence of an implicit threat or option to move much faster — and if necessary into open alliance with the USSR — would be a key factor.

This is not to minimise the potential weight of the constraints that will exist. It is easy to envisage a West which had refused to stop buying white South African gold severely damaging a socialist South Africa by these means. Most other trade would be much less vulnerable. Sabotage and flight by capital and skilled whites could also be disastrous as Mozambique showed. But most whites will find it hard if not impossible to leave and would be highly susceptible to a strategy which in effect reduced their expectations but still left them with a lot more to lose if they failed to cooperate.

A RADICAL STRATEGY?

Here we may begin to pick out some key requirements for a successful radical strategy. Given the necessary condition of a high level of political will on a base of popular support, technical planning for land reform, socialisation of production under workers' self-management, central planning of trade and investment to meet popular needs, and so forth, could proceed, but only if coupled with equally careful planning to outflank the internal and external opposition or sabotage that would be inevitable. The essence of this planning would have to be to induce entrenched interests to cut their losses. As should be obvious, but is demonstrated well by the Zimbabwean case, a relatively poor country cannot sustain developed world per capita incomes and wealth ownership for a minority without extreme exploitation of the majority, so that even successful capitalist development requires redistribution. An approach which always threatens redistribution without actually doing much about it (as in Zimbabwe) seems to get the worst of both worlds: the bourgeoisie and their international supporters think that they are suffering but the poor feel no benefit and become demoralised. On the other hand a confiscatory policy would produce immediate non-cooperation and sabotage.

If on the contrary the policy were spelt out in such a way as to emphasise the benefits that would be left to the elite in a context of radical redistribution, those amongst the skilled whites with few prospects elsewhere (probably the majority) would choose not to lose everything. With the resulting freedom to manoeuvre, the state could then keep the option to marginally *relax* the impact of the policies on cooperating whites, psychologically a better way of reforming them than having undefined threats hanging over their heads, always feared, and sapping initiative. In more precise terms, white (and other high-paid) workers might be told that although (as in China after the revolution) the rate for the job was being greatly reduced to levels consistent with the country's wealth, this would not apply (or else only to a reduced degree) for present incumbents. It is not denied that this proposal would delay the introduction of nominal equality in the rate for the job, but two points should be made: first that whilst white economic power persists, actual equality will be circumvented anyway (via job redefinition etc.); and secondly that the apparent equality in Zimbabwe has been bought at the expense of confirming intractable and gross disparities in *average* rates between racial groups, because effectively all whites are in better paid jobs, and the effect on the average black earnings will be negligible even when as many blacks enter such jobs. Put another way, immediate racial equality in pay rates is in the interests of the black petit bourgeoisie, but *not* in the interests of black workers. Racial inequality in South Africa is integral to the economic structure, involving not only statutory restrictions and those derived from ownership, but also the whole process of skill acquisition. Inevitably, therefore, costs will be incurred in the process of dismantling this structure: the long-run costs of either the 'stroke-of-a-pen' approach, driving whites to flight and sabotage, or of immediate nominal equality, may be too high, preventing the attainment of even liberal, let alone socialist or egalitarian aspirations. It is suggested that in effect a start should be made immediately in paying the costs of dismantling the structural inequality, and part of this cost may be *temporary* continuation of nominal inequality.

Owners of capital would need different treatment: they could be formally expropriated, but then paid in government bonds redeemable according to a strict timetable, and under conditions related to how cooperative owners are during a transition period in aiding planning for a reorientation of investment; owners of small businesses, farms, etc., might become *de facto* managers (with exceptional salaries) of their former businesses.

NOTES

1. World Bank, *World Development Report 1984*, Table 21, p.259.
2. Although much higher than historical rates; see Blumenfeld, p.113.
3. Compare the historical record in Blumenfeld, p.111, or his target 5.5%.

9. Late Apartheid and the Urban Informal Sector

C. M. ROGERSON

INTRODUCTION

A post-apartheid government will face serious problems of urban unemployment and underemployment and will need to formulate a policy position towards the 'informal sector', defined here as urban small-scale enterprise.[1] The array of urban small-scale enterprises is remarkably heterogeneous with respect to type of activity, mode of organisation and overall social acceptability, and spans the entire spectrum from retail distribution, transport operations, personal services and petty production to begging, prostitution and crime. Organisationally, the diversity of small-scale activities extends from the capitalist backyard manufacturing 'sweat-shop', through the small family enterprise, workshop, market or street stall, to socialist forms of collectives or cooperatives. Small can be anti-social, inhuman or dangerous as well as 'beautiful'. If the pursuits of the hawker, backyard manufacturer or unlicensed taxi driver infringe certain existing conceptions of legality, rarely would such activities be viewed as socially threatening. By contrast, a listing of 'unacceptable' small-scale enterprises in most societies would encompass activities such as begging, prostitution and theft.[2]

This chapter aims to open a discourse on policies towards socially acceptable urban small-scale enterprises. Unlike unacceptable small-scale enterprises, such activities could anticipate a range of government policies from repression through tolerance to promotion. The parameters of this discussion are simply that, irrespective of the political complexion of a post-apartheid South Africa, small-scale enterprises *will* exist, *will* have problems and opportunities and that, in turn, these *will* be vitally influenced by changes in the economy, social organisation and role of the state.

The chapter has three sections. First, a conspectus is furnished on international academic and policy debates concerning the informal sector. Part Two investigates the current 'state of the art' of research in South Africa on urban small-scale enterprise. The concluding section argues that a post-apartheid government should, at the very least, plan for the existence of the urban small-scale sector.

THE URBAN INFORMAL SECTOR —
AN INTERNATIONAL PERSPECTIVE

Until the early 1970s most development scholars and policy analysts viewed urban small-scale enterprises as part of the 'traditional sector', an economic relic which itself was a by-product of the slow progress of modernisation.

The past decade has seen a re-evaluation of the role and developmental potential of small-scale enterprises. Far from being merely a transitory phenomenon or 'marginal' occupation for newly arrived migrants, it was acknowledged that urban small-scale enterprises not only were growing in increasing numbers but were a potentially dynamic force capable of attracting and sustaining in their own right.[3] Urban small-scale production assumed the status of a new panacea for the ills of urban unemployment and a favoured development tool of international development agencies. Controversies surrounding the urban informal sector centred on the debate between two broad schools of thought variously christened as 'dualists vs anti-dualists',[4] 'informal sector vs petty commodity production'[5] and 'the ILO vs radical groups'.[6]

Theoretical debates on the development potential of urban small-scale enterprise were launched by the assertions made by the International Labour Office (ILO) that such activities, albeit largely unrecorded, had a vital productive role to play in Third World cities and a potential to catalyse not only employment but also autonomous economic growth. At a time when many governments and international development agencies were concerned during the 1970s to foster 'employment-oriented strategies of development', the ILO argued that the promotion and upgrading of the informal sector was one means of realising the objectives of 'redistribution with growth'.[7] The urban informal sector could offer crucial contributions to employment and low-cost training. The ILO and the dualists maintained that notwithstanding their difficulties such as shortages of capital, inadequate tools, or the absence of a secure place of work, informal sector activities possessed opportunities for growth and autonomy. Government assistance with credit, public contracts and improved technical training would unleash the inherent economic dynamism of urban small-scale enterprise.

Through much of the 1970s the dualistic school's assertions became established as conventional wisdom in developmental studies. By the close of the decade, however, the orthodoxies of dualist analysis were coming under sharp attack. Perceptive observers were arguing that 'the concept of dualism has given a time honoured service to the analysis of underdevelopment but the time may well have arrived when it should be discarded'.[8] Dissatisfaction with the conventional wisdom mounted and a growing body of criticism was directed at the ILO and the dualist or informal sector approach. The first charge was that the informal sector concept merely offered a descriptive insight into the characteristics of certain occupational categories. Second, the dualistic classification was too simplistic, ignoring the subtle yet important differences between economic activities which might be styled intermediate or transitional. Third, the concept provided no criteria to identify a particular activity as formal or informal. Finally, dualists assumed the two sectors were autonomous whereas critics pointed to the nature of the interrelationship as one of domination/subordination.[9]

These criticisms of the dualist approach prompted the adoption of a perspective emphasising a continuum of productive activities and the need to investigate 'the structural linkages and relationships between different production and distribution systems'.[10] This second school, termed variously 'anti-dualist', 'radical' or 'petty commodity production', deploys an elaboration of Marx's theory of different modes of production and their articulation. As Caroline Moser avers, 'this is seen to contain a theoretical apparatus for explaining the internal dynamics of a particular form of production, the conditions necessary for its existence and the contradictions which lead to its eventual elimination'.[11] Those small-scale enterprises formerly identified as falling under the rubric of the informal sector are now conceptualised as 'petty commodity production', a form of production existing at the margins of the capitalist mode of production but nevertheless integrated and subordinate to it.

The petty commodity production school replaces the formal/informal sector dichotomy with a model reflecting the articulation of different forms and modes of production which are asymmetrically interwoven by relations of domination/ subordination. It is argued that these relationships may foster the restructuring and conservation rather than the dissolution of so-called urban informal sector enterprises. First, capitalists may allow the continuation of petty forms of production because of their preoccupation with the export economy and lack of interest in production and services for the domestic market. Second, the existence of an informal sector may be functional to the capitalist mode. The third reason advanced for the conservation of the informal sector relates to the advantages which accrue not to the capitalist mode of production but to the state in peripheral capitalist societies. The existence of an informal sector, characterised by labour intensity, alleviates the 'employment crisis' experienced in many areas of the Third World. Also, when household heads can offer welfare to their relatives the burden on the state to introduce adequate systems of social security and welfare is reduced. The state may further benefit through the ability of a thriving informal sector to blunt the 'revolutionary potential' of the lumpen classes. Finally, conservation stems from pressures emanating from within the informal sector itself. Against the common view of the passivity of members of the informal sector is set the ability of people to actively conserve their own activities under two internal pressures. First, it is evident that many components of the informal sector furnish vital goods and services targeted at the specific needs of low income populations, or which satisfy particular cultural requirements. Second, in situations where alternative income opportunities are bleak there are very real pressures for people to seek, in all possible ways, means to preserve their existing livelihoods. In certain circumstances the continued participation of people within informal income niches may even be interpreted as a form of 'hidden resistance' to capitalist exploitation.

The most fundamental contributions of the second school are those relating to identifying a continuum of forms of production from pure artisanal to capitalist, each representing a different degree of subordination to capital. What occurs is the growing differentiation among petty producers with two polar positions marked by a transition to petty capitalism (the minority trend) on the one hand and by progressive proletarianisation (identified as the dominant tendency) on the other. Policies which suggest that a few administrative reforms and a selective tinkering with the *status quo* could unleash the pent-up productive energies of urban small-scale producers were seen as naïve, short-sighted and downright cynical.

It is in the arena of linkages that the greatest strengths and weaknesses of the petty commodity production school lie. The petty commodity production analysts directed attention away from the characteristics of enterprises towards investigations of the linkages of different production systems. Nevertheless, Schmitz marshals empirical evidence to challenge many of the popular current myths propagated both by dualists and the petty commodity production school.[12] Small-scale productive enterprises face two growth constraints, *internal* (entrepreneurship and management) and *external* (access to resources and exploitation by large enterprises). Schmitz questions the internal constraint and stresses that 'factors internal to the small enterprise can be a source of strength rather than weakness'.[13] In addition, Schmitz examines two external constraints. The first emphasises the exploitation of small producers by large firms, the second points to their problems of access to product markets, technology and raw materials. His conclusions are worth citing at some length:

> While external constraints seem more important than internal ones, a word of caution is necessary. Fascination with the former can lead to deterministic and gloomy predictions, to the denial of all accumulative prospects and to a theory of marginalisation as the general paradigm of small-scale production in the periphery. ... The development of small-scale production is not just an outcome of pressures and constraints but also of opportunity and initiative. ... The pressures emphasized by those who warn about the dangers of marginalisation are real, but the conditions which determine their pervasiveness vary and must therefore be studied and specified.[14]

Finally, in one important respect both the schools of informal sector dualism and petty commodity production exhibit a common shortcoming, the gender-blind nature of their analyses. Thus ILO policies were slanted towards *male* informal sector workers and *male* heads of households. Notwithstanding writings demonstrating that much of the informal sector was primarily an arena of 'women's work', there was no attempt to design a set of policies specifically to advantage women. Equally problematic has been the treatment of women within the literature of petty commodity production.

The most important lesson to be drawn from this survey of literature on the urban informal sector is that many of the initial *a priori* assumptions concerning the 'sector' and its capacity to precipitate growth and employment have been seriously weakened by recent research contributions. Also, it would be wrong to conclude that urban small-scale enterprise has no potential. What it is crucial to grasp is that the diversity of small-scale enterprise makes a nonsense of sweeping statements on the role of the informal sector.

THE URBAN INFORMAL SECTOR — SOUTH AFRICAN PERSPECTIVES

Research into the informal sector in South Africa grew from three major influences. Interest was awakened by a growing recognition of the severity of structural unemployment, the surfacing of a stream of new historical research into the lives of the common people in South Africa's cities, and the apartheid state's belated encouragement of 'development' in the informal sector as an integral part of its so-called 'reformist' package.[15] The research frontier in South African studies has moved from dualism towards petty commodity production. At the same time, policy formulation and planning shifted from a position of outright repression of informal sector programmes towards increasing tolerance and, very recently, even tentative promotion of certain favoured segments of urban small-scale enterprise. In the main South African research on the urban informal sector has followed contemporary international literature. Early researchers sought to estimate the size of the informal sector, describe the characteristics of particular informal occupations, or catalogue and survey the range of informal sector enterprises or households at particular geographical locations. Typical of these forays are works conducted on the informal fabric of existence in urban townships such as Soweto,[16] Kwa Mashu[17] and Clermont,[18] or in so-called areas of squatter urbanisation, including Crossroads, Nyanga, and Winterveld.[19] This array of studies provided much valuable descriptive material and cross-sectional surveys gave the first approximations of the sheer significance of the urban informal economy in apartheid South Africa. Research in Soweto and Mdantsane suggested that a member from at least one in every three households was a participant in the informal sector;[20] from Kwa Mashu it was reported that the figure may be as high as one in every two.[21] A further finding revealed the relative underdevelopment of the production sphere.[22] By far the most common opportunities occurred in the areas of distribution or services, especially the pursuits of street vendor, shebeener, childminder, and unlicensed transport operator.

By the mid-1980s aspects of the informal sector had been investigated within the majority of urban townships appended to South Africa's leading metropolitan areas and, beyond these, in at least some of the 'first ring' of increasingly significant informal urban settlements.[23] Although they offered little concrete evidence for their assertions, the bulk of this group of students of South Africa's informal sector viewed its developmental potential in a highly positive light, mirroring the optimism that flowed from research inspired by the ILO.

The major shortcoming of these studies lay in their almost exclusive reliance upon the cross-sectional survey, which limited their capacity to deal with the complexity of internal and external constraints affecting the growth potential of urban small-scale enterprise. Further research has attempted to rectify this failing through both longitudinal research strategies and 'branch specific' studies to identify areas of constraint and opportunity affecting small-scale enterprise. Commonly, the petty commodity production approach replaced dualist analysis as the theoretical instrument utilised within this 'second wave' of investigations.

Impetus for the pursuit of longitudinal studies reconstructing the historical matrix of the urban informal economy in South Africa came from research associated with three History Workshops convened during 1978, 1981 and 1984 at the University of the Witwatersrand, Johannesburg[24] and the magisterial works by Charles van Onselen recovering the social history of the common people of the Witwatersrand in its formative years.[25] Several studies have documented the moving frontier of the region's informal producers, exploring the appearance, disappearance and restructuring of an array of activities.[26] Issues that have received detailed consideration include the rise and fall of coffee-cart trading in Johannesburg,[27] the survival of the township shebeen[28] and the changing historical spheres of women's participation in urban small-scale enterprise.[29]

Contributions to contemporary debates on 'developing' the urban informal sector have emerged from research into the dynamics of specific branches of small-scale production and distribution. Investigations of the hawker community in both central Johannesburg and Soweto revealed the widespread occurrence of relationships of 'dependent work' with many hawkers functioning as unpaid disguised sellers for formal sector retailing or wholesaling concerns.[30] Although returns in several areas of hawking, most notably the selling of live chickens and the vending of soft goods, were often quite substantial, the overall conclusion of these studies was that potential for substantially increasing incomes was limited. But, in later studies of the street trading scene in central Johannesburg, work conducted by Tomaselli[31] on the Indian flower sellers revealed accumulation of an order indicating mobility towards petty capitalism. Nevertheless, a clear concomitant of this was the marked trend towards the proletarianisation of other members of the flower-selling fraternity, notably their black assistants.[32]

Finally, a notable contribution to current critical analysis of reformist proposals for succouring the informal sector is furnished by Wellings and Sutcliffe, who utilise the petty commodity production framework.[33] Their findings reinforce certain earlier conclusions concerning the imperative for historical understanding and the heterogeneous nature of the informal economy as observed in the Clermont/Inanda region of metropolitan Durban. Most importantly, they penetrate and unravel the complex web of linkages and relations of domination/subordination that bond the informal sector to capitalist production, maintaining that 'this form of production and reproduction is undergoing a process of conservation and dissolution which is determined by the economic linkages that exist between it and the dominant capitalist mode of production'.[34] In their conclusions, Wellings and Sutcliffe aver that since the urban informal sector in present-day South Africa 'functions in spaces which are created and controlled by the formal capitalist mode of production, the opportunities for its autonomous development are severely limited'.[35] Indeed, their analysis strengthens the cumulative finding of empirical work from the Johannesburg area that the promotion of the informal sector would engender a growing differentiation among informal sector participants rather than a general amelioration of the exigencies of poverty and unemployment.

THE POLICY DOMAIN: FROM REPRESSION TO TOLERANCE

Policy formulation towards urban small-scale enterprise is in a state of flux. Until recently, the mass of participants in the informal economy of South Africa's cities were considered, by both national and municipal levels of government, as an unpleasant and ominous aberration, a blot on the urban landscape and an obstacle in the way of achieving the vision of a modern city. To a large extent, these perceptions of the urban informal sector and its actors were shared with governing elites in many parts of the developing world. The overwhelming policy thrust was towards repression of small-scale enterprises, seeking their excision from the urban landscape. In the aftermath of the Soweto uprisings, however, attitudes and policies towards urban small-scale enterprise in South Africa have been changing, albeit at a glacial pace in some spheres of government. At national and local scales of government, official recognition has been accorded to the imperative for creating a more favourable environment for the operation of urban small-scale activities.[36] It would be difficult, at the present juncture, to describe this shift as one from repression to promotion, for the state's enthusiasm for the informal sector is often more at the rhetorical level than at the grassroots of policy implementation. Nevertheless, a marked transition has taken place towards at least grudging tolerance of urban small-scale enterprise. Underlying this policy shift is the undoubted wish of the apartheid state to harness the urban informal sector as a base for establishing a petit-bourgeois class 'both complementary to the interests of white capital and dependent on the white state, which would act as a conservative influence on the poorer black classes'.[37]

In interpreting South Africa's history of anti-formal sector policies, it is possible to discern several sets of governmental concern which have prompted the innovation and continuation of repressive programmes. More especially, five underpinnings of repression may be identified. With one notable exception, each of these causes has parallels in the bases for anti-informal sector programmes found in other parts of Africa, Asia and Latin America.[38] First, the hostility of policy-makers towards urban small-scale enterprise reflects long-standing official endeavours to create and preserve the 'city beautiful'. In common with their counterparts in other parts of the developing world the urban managers of South Africa have sought to create an orderly, zoned, tranquil 'Garden City' with relatively low population densities, smooth traffic flows, an absence of congestion and a strict separation of housing functions from those of manufacturing and commerce. Efforts to forge such an urban environment have occasioned frequent prosecution of economic activities located in residential areas (such as backyard workshops, shops or even shebeens) and of all kinds of small enterprise which might precipitate congestion (most notably, street traders). In particular, the activities of hawkers in urban areas have been an affront to those visionaries of beautiful cities in South Africa.[39] Observing that 'informal' stalls, carts or tables attract crowds which, in turn, obstruct the city pavements and impede pedestrian flows, South African urban managers have consistently adopted a highly antagonistic stance towards the pursuit of street trading.

Further pressure for the enactment of anti-informal sector policies has been exerted by the powerful ideology of developmentalism. In essence, this consists of an almost obsessive belief in the desirability of 'modernisation ' or 'progress' coupled with a strong conviction that these goals can best be attained through imitating features of those societies and economies considered most 'modern' or 'progressive' (most commonly, North America and Western Europe). The all-pervasive belief in developmentalism has contributed to the neglect and subsequent persecution of activities which fail to accord with the prevailing desired image and direction of development. Typical examples of this would include the prosecution of petty service occupations, such as street vendors, the activities of paratransit operators and backyard mechanics or manufacturers. Moreover, a historical commitment to promoting all things 'modern' has resulted in the production and reproduction of urban environments in which the requirements of small-scale enterprise are largely eschewed.

The third common source of governmental repression is the creation of a host of lucrative work opportunities in the arena of regulatory employment. The imperative for 'control' of small-scale enterprise fosters a flourishing 'growth industry' in terms of the employment of licensing personnel, health inspectors, etc., and the formation of special repressive groups to oversee certain informal sector pursuits. The latter development is exemplified in South Africa by the spawning of special liquor squads with the objective of raiding shebeens, and of units whose task is to clear hawkers from their pitches on the pavements of the country's leading cities. An additional benefit of the making of a bureaucratic apparatus of control over small-scale enterprise is that it furnishes ample opportunities for government supporters and bureaucrats to profit from avenues of petty corruption. One final underpinning for negative, anti-informal sector policies in South Africa, which also has parallels in the developing world as a whole, is the process of containment (intended to give the impression of prohibition) which stops short of total elimination. Such a scenario, a classic example of double standards in policy implementation, occurs as readily in Colombia or Indonesia as in South Africa. It is, once again, best exemplified by street trading. Certain sanctions are introduced to restrict hawker numbers or to defend prestigious urban spaces, such as the central business district: however, given the mesh of linkages which tie street traders to powerful formal sector businesses, the goal is to contain the level of trading at some 'optimum' level rather than to eliminate it entirely from the urban scene. From the history of hawking in the Johannesburg area it would appear that such attitudes of containment have influenced the course of street vending in many urban township environs.[40]

Beyond these four root causes of repression are a set of additional factors specific to South Africa. As Wellings and Sutcliffe point out, the sphere of the informal sector was traditionally perceived (or more correctly, misconceived) by officialdom either as the recourse of the black unemployed or as a stimulus to rural-urban migration, situations which were antithetical to the designs of apartheid planners.[41] In addition, the designation of the informal sector variously as a 'social evil', 'health hazard' or as 'unfair competition' for formal sector businesses facilitated the initiation of measures to defend and succour the interests of white traders and manufacturers. The dysfunctionality of the informal sector with respect to the desired socio-economic order of the apartheid state is the final formative factor in accounting for South Africa's history of negative policies towards urban small-scale enterprise.

The closing years of apartheid have been marked by a transition in state policy away from the exclusive deployment of repressive measures towards urban small-scale enterprise. Indeed, since 1976 there has occurred a flurry of proposals for the activation of black-owned business and several 'concessions' in terms of the relaxation of former controls on the functioning of informal sector enterprises. Across a range of economic spaces, in manufacturing, services and distribution, some attempts have been made to move in the direction of greater 'tolerance' of the activities of small-scale operators. The most dramatic change is that with respect to manufacturing. Until as late as 1980 there were no industrial estates situated within the urban townships appended to South Africa's largest so-called 'white' metropolitan areas. Since 1980, however, a limited reversal of apartheid planning has been set in motion with a programme to stimulate the expansion of black manufacturing capital. Through the auspices of the Small Business Development Corporation, a joint state-private sector agency, and the private sector Urban Foundation, a series of industrial parks have been launched in fourteen different urban township areas.[42] The aim is to encourage both new black manufacturing enterprises and former backyard industrialists to locate in these areas. Assessments of the success of this programme must be necessarily tentative at this stage. It is clear, however, that the scheme has catalysed the expansion of certain black-owned manufacturing operations. Nevertheless, one ominous sign on the horizon of township industrialisation is the appearance and growth of 'sweat-shops' as white-owned enterprises take advantage of opportunities to sub-contract part of their manufacturing activities to township producers.

A further major area of small-scale enterprise in which the state has made strides towards 'formalisation' is the world of township liquor distribution and the shebeens. Currently, Soweto is being used as the proving ground for evolving a set of procedures to deal nationally with the issue of shebeens. The path towards shebeen legalisation opened in mid-1977 when the first steps were taken towards issuing licences to trade as legal taverns. Not surprisingly, the major liquor manufacturers, notably South African Breweries Ltd., have been prominent in the 'fight' for a more tolerant official policy towards shebeens in townships. It is striking, however, that the state has attached a series of very stringent conditions to the granting of tavern licences; indeed, conditions are so strict that few of the existing community of shebeeners can possibly meet them. Of Soweto's estimated 4,000 shebeens less than 40 had received all the necessary rezoning clearances and obtained licences that might allow them to function legally by 1985. The move towards a degree of greater tolerance of this component of small-scale enterprise is, of course, inseparable from the apartheid state's desperate endeavours to depoliticise the whole question of liquor and liquor selling in township areas.

Finally, the realm of street hawking is another area in which a shift away from policies of outright repression or containment is in evidence. For example, in Johannesburg this more tolerant attitude is mirrored in a decline in the persecution of hawkers for minor offences, most notably a relaxation in the archaic regulations which compelled traders to 'move on', relocating their stalls and goods set distances every twenty minutes. More importantly, however, there are the beginnings of several small schemes for the direct assistance of hawkers, the making of hawker malls and the preservation of a long-standing bazaar. These proposals notwithstanding, no attempt has been made or is even being mooted at present to throw open the central business area of South Africa's leading city to the street trading community. In Johannesburg, at least, the mood of tolerance goes only so far; the ideology of developmentalism and the beautiful city remain deeply embedded in the official mind.

THE URBAN INFORMAL SECTOR IN THE POST-APARTHEID ERA: REPRESSION, TOLERANCE OR PROMOTION?

It would be presumptuous to assert any concrete proposals regarding policy formulation and urban small-scale enterprise in the future, post-apartheid South Africa. Nonetheless, some broad guidelines for consideration undoubtedly do emerge from an examination of the international and local South African research experience of the urban informal sector. The context for this concluding discussion is set by acknowledging that urban small-scale enterprises have existed for a very long period of time in South Africa, that they exist in substantial numbers now, and that they will continue to exist, very probably in increasing numbers, into the post-apartheid years. In addition, because of the seriousness of the unemployment crisis that will be bequeathed to the makers of a post-apartheid South Africa, no future government could depend on large private capitalist enterprise, parastatal corporations, the bureaucracy and the armed forces to generate sufficient work opportunities in the urban areas. Moreover, it appears that lessons drawn from mistakes made in China or Mozambique in extending state control down to the level of the street corner, the market stall or the small factory workshop, are now widely appreciated. Accordingly, while they might not be accorded high priority in the shaping of a post-apartheid South Africa, small-scale enterprises should, at minimum, be recognised as a potentially vital element in reconstructing a future economy and in reducing levels of unemployment, destitution and poverty-induced crime.

As Ray Bromley points out, governments have only three broad sets of policy alternatives for dealing with small-scale enterprises which are deemed socially acceptable: 'repression' when constraints exceed supports; 'tolerance' when constraints and supports are of equal significance; and 'promotion' when supports exceed constraints.[43] The first option, repression, would have no credible justification in a post-apartheid South Africa. Persecution of small-scale enterprise would spawn an apparatus of repression directed at the urban poor in general and possibly at members of specific ethnic groups in particular. Inevitably, such an apparatus would be costly to operate; it would create avenues for petty corruption as well as causing considerable hardship and despair. We must concur with Bromley: 'Any concept of social justice, responsible government for the benefit of those governed, or humanitarianism, leads to the condemnation of repressive policies and of the governments which perpetuate them'.[44] Consequently, in a post-apartheid South Africa it will be essential to jettison the set of attitudes which are the root of repressive programmes towards urban small-scale operators. Not only must all vestiges of apartheid planning be dismantled but also there must be the abandonment of the pervasive ideology of developmentalism, the planning vision of 'beautiful cities' in the mould of Boston, Paris or Toronto, and the abolition of South Africa's army of health inspectors, licensing personnel and special policing squads whose exclusive *raison d'être* is to regulate the sphere of urban small-scale enterprise.

Total rejection of the option of repression narrows the debate to that part of the spectrum of policy options spanning tolerance and promotion. In suggesting this as the central arena for debate on small-scale enterprises in a post-apartheid South Africa, the dangers are acknowledged of fostering 'petit-bourgeois' mentalities or even perpetuating and reproducing work and remuneration conditions worse than those of workers directly employed in capitalist production. Nevertheless, it must be cautioned that in the contemporary world economy the future choice in South Africa may not be between 'small enterprise or accelerated industrialisation' (either of a capitalist or socialist genre), but between 'small enterprise or burgeoning urban unemployment'. If the point is conceded of the imperative need for future governments in South Africa to tolerate or actively promote urban small-scale enterprises, then the axis of discussion may be shifted to the several broad policy areas in which revision may advantage the small-scale operator.

Of an array of policy recommendations made in respect of assisting small-scale enterprise in Third World cities, four areas of policy have particular resonance in South African conditions. The most obvious area is how to channel direct governmental support to the urban informal sector. Emanating from the discussions set in motion by the ILO and other international development agencies are a host of proposals for providing small-scale enterprise with credit and finance, subsidised raw materials, privileged access to government marketing board products, technical training and support via direct state purchases. An imperative for decision makers in a post-apartheid South Africa will be to accord serious consideration to these proposals and a host of other suggested means of assisting the sphere of small-scale enterprise. It is significant, perhaps, that in Zimbabwe major debates are currently taking place over the most appropriate means to aid this sector.[45] A second area for policy reconsideration relates to deregulation, which represents the antithesis of constructing a repressive apparatus of control. An urgent priority for post-apartheid South Africa would be to achieve a drastic reduction in the morass of constraints which burden the daily existence of urban small-scale enterprises. Areas in need of massive revision are the abolition or simplification of licensing procedures; the regulatory by-laws which affect where, when and how enterprises may function; and the numerous trivial fees and taxes which almost certainly cost as much to collect as they yield in revenues. A third policy area for improvement concerns the design and construction of a range of favourable urban environments. Of crucial importance is to shape an urban form without the zoned segregation of small-scale manufacturing and commerce from housing: an environment with numerous sites for small informal enterprises, with high-density and pedestrian areas advantageous to markets and street traders, and with a transport mix that facilitates para-transit operations. Finally, considerable benefits may accrue from the promotion of organisations representing small-scale enterprises, their workers and petty entrepreneurs. The overall object of such organisations need not necessarily be to encourage expanded sub-contracting or patronage linkages, subordinating further the small to the large enterprises. Instead, trade unions of workers in small enterprises or associations of petty entrepreneurs could press for, *inter alia*, improvements in working conditions, better relations with larger enterprises (both private capitalist and parastatal) and expansion in levels of direct government support. As Bromley says,

> Such measures directly serving small enterprises may be reinforced by more sophisticated forms of economic organization, notably the formation of cooperatives to obtain raw materials, distribute products, handle banking and credit, and/or administer shared physical locations such as small-industry estates, markets and shopping centres.[46]

The innovative experiences of many Third World countries, not least the current experiments taking place in Zimbabwe, indicate that properly constituted organisations do have a capacity to uplift not only the growth potential of urban small-scale enterprise, but also the conditions of existence of their employees. These Zimbabwean experiences, debates and policy formulations, and the results achieved by current programmes, warrant close monitoring by the future makers of South Africa's post-apartheid economy and society.

NOTES

1. See the following: O.P. Mathur and C.O.N. Moser, 'The urban informal sector: an agenda for research', *Regional Development Dialogue*, No. 5, 1984, pp.ix-xxi; H.W. Richardson, 'The role of the urban informal sector: an overview', *ibid.*, pp.3-40; and T.G. McGee and R. Chandra, 'Comment', *ibid.*, pp.181-183.
2. R. Bromley, 'Introduction, Section V', in R. Bromley (ed.), *Planning for Small Enterprises in Third World Cities* (Pergamon, Oxford, 1985), p.249.
3. See ILO, *Employment, Incomes and Equality: A Strategy for Increasing Productive Employment in Kenya* (International Labour Office, Geneva, 1972); K. Hart, 'Informal income opportunities and urban employment in Ghana', *Journal of Modern African Studies*, No. 11, 1973, pp.61-89; T.G. McGee, 'The persistence of the proto-proletariat: occupational structures and planning of the future of Third World cities', *Progress in Geography*, No. 9, pp.1-38; T.G. McGee, 'An invitation to the "ball": dress formal or informal?' in P.J. Rimmer, D.W. Drakakis-Smith and T.G. McGee (eds.), *Food, Shelter and Transport in Southeast Asia and the Pacific* (Australian National University Press, Canberra, 1978), pp.3-27; T.G. McGee, *Doubts about Dualism: Implications for Development Planning* (United Nations Centre for Regional Development WP, Nagoya, 1978), pp.78-103; ILO, *Urbanisation, Informal Sector and Employment: A Progress Report on Research, Advisory Services and Technical Cooperation* (International Labour Office, Geneva, 1984).
4. C.O.N. Moser and J. Marsie-Hazen, *A Survey of Empirical Studies in Industrial and Manufacturing Activities in the Informal Sector in the Developing Countries*

(United Nations Industrial Development Organisation, UNIDO/IS, Vienna, 1984), p.470.

5. C.O.N. Moser, 'Informal sector or petty commodity production: dualism or dependence in urban development?', *World Development*, No. 6, pp.1041-1064.

6. P. Kennedy, 'The role and position of petty producers in a West African city', *Journal of Modern African Studies*, No. 19, pp.565-594.

7. See Moser, 'Informal sector', pp.1042-1051 for discussion.

8. McGee, *Doubts and Dualism*, p.25.

9. There is a large literature on critiques of the informal sector concept. For a review see C.M. Rogerson, 'The fist decade of informal sector studies: review and synthesis', *Environmental Studies*, Occasional Paper No.25, Department of Geography and Environmental Studies, University of the Witwatersrand, Johannesburg.

10. Moser, 'Informal sector', p.1061.

11. C.O.N. Moser, 'The informal sector reworked: viability and vulnerability in urban development', *Regional Development Dialogue*, No. 5, 1984, p.146.

12. H. Schmitz, *Manufacturing in the Backyard: Case Studies on Accumulation and Employment in Small-Scale Brazilian Industry* (Frances Pinter, London, 1982); and H. Schmitz, 'Growth constraints on small-scale manufacturing in developing countries: a critical review', *World Development*, No. 10, 1982, pp.429-450.

13. Schmitz, 'Growth constraints', p.432.

14. *Ibid.*, p.445.

15. C.M. Rogerson and K.S.O. Beavon, 'The awakening of "informal sector" studies in Southern Africa', *South African Geographical Journal*, No. 62, 1980, pp.175-190.

16. P. Morris, *Soweto: A Review of Existing Conditions and Some Guidelines for Change* (The Urban Foundation, Johannesburg, 1980).

17. G. Maasdorp and A.S.B. Humphreys, *From Shantytown to Township* (Juta, Cape Town, 1975).

18. G. Maasdorp and N. Pillay, *The Informal Sector in Clermont*, University of Natal (Durban), Department of Economics/School of Architecture and Allied Disciplines, Interim Report, No. 4, 1978.

19. See J. Maree and J. Cornell, *Sample Survey of Squatters in Crossroads, December 1977*, University of Cape Town, SALDRU Working Paper, No. 17, 1978; and T. Matsetela, 'The informal sector in the political economy of Winterveld', unpublished B.A. Honours dissertation, University of the Witwatersrand, Johannesburg, 1979.

20. T. Matsetela, M. Matshoba, D. Webster, P. Wilkinson, J. Yawitch and H. Zarenda, 'Unemployment and "informal" income-earning activity in Soweto', paper presented to the African Studies Seminar, African Studies Institute, University of the Witwatersrand, Johannesburg, 1980; and F.A. Jacobs, 'The urban informal sector in Ciskei', *Development Studies Southern Africa*, No. 4, 1982, pp.392-402.

21. P. Wellings and M. Sutcliffe, ' "Developing" the urban informal sector in South Africa: the reformist paradigm and its fallacies', *Development and Change*, No. 15, 1984, p.521.

22. See C.M. Rogerson and K.S.O. Beavon, 'Getting by in the "informal sector" of Soweto', *Tijdschrift voor Economische en Sociale Geografie*, No. 73, 1982, pp.250-265.

23. A. Mabin, 'Material and political factors in South African urbanisation, with some illustrations from the Transvaal', paper presented at a seminar, University of Natal (Durban), 30 May 1986.

24. See B. Bozzoli (ed.), *Labour, Townships and Protest* (Ravan Press, Johannesburg, 1979); B. Bozzoli (ed.), *Town and Countryside in the Transvaal* (Ravan Press, Johannesburg, 1983); and B. Bozzoli (ed.), *Class, Community and Conflict* (Ravan Press, Johannesburg, 1987).

25. C. van Onselen, *Studies in the Social and Economic History of the Witwatersrand 1886-1914*, 2 Vols. (Ravan Press, Johannesburg, 1982).

26. See K.S.O. Beavon and C.M. Rogerson, 'The persistence of the casual poor in Johannesburg', *Contree*, No. 7, 1980, pp.15-21; C.M. Rogerson, 'The casual poor of Johannesburg, South Africa: the rise and fall of coffee-cart trading', unpublished Ph.D.

thesis, Queens University, Kingston, Ontario, 1983; and C.M. Rogerson, 'Johannesburg's informal sector: historical continuity and change', *African Urban Quarterly*, No. 1, 1986.

27. See Rogerson, 'The casual poor of Johannesburg' and C.M. Rogerson, 'Feeding the common people of Johannesburg, 1930-1962', *Journal of Historical Geography*, No. 12, 1986, pp.56-73.

28. C.M. Rogerson and D.M. Hart, 'The survival of the "informal sector": the shebeens of Black Johannesburg', *GeoJournal*, No. 12, 1986, pp.153-166; and C.M. Rogerson, 'Consumerism, the state and the informal sector: the formalization of shebeens in South Africa's black townships', paper presented to the International Geographical Union, Working Group on Urbanisation in Developing Countries, Madrid, 28-30 August 1986.

29. K.S.O. Beavon and C.M. Rogerson, 'The changing role of women in the urban informal sector of Johannesburg', in D.W. Drakakis-Smith (ed.), *Urbanisation in the Developing World* (Croom Helm, Beckenham, 1986), pp.205-220.

30. On Johannesburg see S. Biesheuvel, 'Planning for the informal sector', unpublished M.Sc. (TRP) dissertation, University of the Witwatersrand, Johannesburg, 1979; K.S.O. Beavon and C.M. Rogerson, 'The "informal sector" of the apartheid city: the pavement people of Johannesburg', in D.M. Smith (ed.), *Living Under Apartheid: Aspects of Urbanisation and Social Change in South Africa* (Allen and Unwin, London, 1982), pp.106-123; and K.S.O. Beavon and C.M. Rogerson, 'Aspects of hawking in the Johannesburg Central Business District', *Proceedings, Geographical Association of Zimbabwe*, No. 15, 1984, pp.31-45. On Soweto see Rogerson and Beavon, 'Getting by'.

31. R.E. Tomaselli, 'The Indian flower sellers of Johannesburg', unpublished M.A. dissertation, University of the Witwatersrand, Johannesburg, 1983.

32. R.E. Tomaselli and K.S.O. Beavon, 'Johannesburg's Indian flower sellers: class and circumstance', *GeoJournal*, No. 12, 1986, pp.181-189.

33. Wellings and Sutcliffe, ' "Developing" the informal sector', pp.530-542.

34. *Ibid.*, p.537.

35. *Ibid.*, p.543.

36. The clearest expression of official attitudes in support of small-scale enterprise is found in Republic of South Africa, *White Paper on a Strategy for the Creation of Employment Opportunities in the Republic of South Africa* (Government Printer, Pretoria, 1984), especially pp.9-10.

37. Wellings and Sutcliffe, ' "Developing" the informal sector', p.524.

38. See the discussion provided in R. Bromley, 'Introduction, Section IV', in Bromley (ed.), *Planning for Small Enterprises*, pp.183-190.

39. C.M. Rogerson and K.S.O. Beavon, 'A tradition of repression: the street traders of Johannesburg' in Bromley (ed.), *Planning for Small Enterprises*, pp.233-245.

40. K.S.O. Beavon and C.M. Rogerson, 'Temporary trading for temporary people: the making of hawking in Soweto', paper presented to the International Geographical Union, Working Group on Urbanisation in Developing Countries, Madrid, 28-30 August 1986.

41. Wellings and Sutcliffe, ' "Developing" the informal sector', p.519.

42. Full details of the unfolding programme of industrialising the townships are provided by C.M. Rogerson and M. de Silva, 'From backyard manufacture to factory flat: the industrialisation of South Africa's black townships', paper presented to the International Geographical Union, Commission on Industrial Change Conference, Madrid, 24-30 August 1986. This section draws from material in that paper.

43. R. Bromley, 'Small may be beautiful but it takes more than beauty to ensure success', in Bromley (ed.), *Planning for Small Enterprises*, pp.321-341. Many of the ideas for this final section of the discussion are drawn from this thoughtful examination of the practicalities of dealing with small enterprises in Third World cities.

44. Bromley, 'Small may be beautiful', p.331.

45. The debates on the informal sector and small-scale enterprise in Zimbabwe were aired at an Informal Sector Study Seminar held in Harare, 27-30 September 1983. Of the many presentations at this seminar, the following are of particular interest: T. Chimombe, 'Financing small-scale industry in Zimbabwe: present policies and structures to assist

small-scale industries and their implications for the development of the informal sector'; R.B. Gadzanwa, 'The policy implications of women's involvement in the informal sector in Zimbabwe'; T. Mkandawire, 'The informal sector in the labour reserve economies of Southern Africa with special reference to Zimbabwe'; T. Sanangurai, 'Why Hawkers and Vendors Cooperative Society was formed'; and Zimbabwe Ministry of Community Development and Women's Affairs, 'The role of women in the informal sector'.
46. Bromley, 'Small may be beautiful', p.335.

10. Economic Policy Issues in the Education Sector

JAMES COBBE

What do we mean when we say we want people's education? We are agreed that we don't want Bantu Education but we must be clear about what we want in its place. We must also be clear as to how we are going to achieve this.

We are no longer demanding the same education as whites, since this is education for domination. People's education means education at the service of the people as a whole, education that liberates, education that puts people in command of their lives.

We are not prepared to accept any 'alternative' to Bantu Education which is imposed on the people from above. This includes American or other imperialist alternatives designed to safeguard their selfish interests in the country, by promoting elitist and divisive ideas and values which will ensure foreign monopoly exploitation continues.

Another type of 'alternative school' we reject is the one which gives students from a more wealthy background avenues to opt out of the struggle, such as commercially-run schools which are springing up.

To be acceptable, every initiative must come from the people themselves, must be accountable to the people and must advance the broad mass of students, not just a select few. In effect this means taking over the schools, transforming them from institutions of oppression into zones of progress and people's power.

(Zwelakhe Sisulu, 'People's Education for People's Power' (Keynote Address, National Education Crisis Committee, 29 March 1986), *Transformation*, No.1, 1986, p.110.)

INTRODUCTION

It is unnecessary to belabour the great inequality of educational access and achievement between the different races in South Africa (see Appendix A). What is less widely appreciated is the far-reaching and difficult nature of the economic policy decisions that will be required in the process of changing the nature of the education sector after the end of apartheid.

As is well known, the education system in South Africa is extremely complex, with many different authorities at different governmental levels having responsibility for the education of different groups of children according to their race classification, place of residence, and (in the case of Africans) 'nationality'. For many years, education has been administered separately for different races; more recently, not only has white education been administered through provincial governments, but much of African education has been placed, at least nominally, under the control of the various Bantustan authorities. This administrative complexity makes it very difficult to obtain comparable data for different groups, and also to make comparisons over time.

Despite much propaganda from official South African sources concerning the rapid growth of African education, the facts still confirm that an extremely unequal structure of education exists in South Africa. In 1983, well over half of all African pupils enrolled in school were in the four lower primary grades; recurrent expenditure per pupil for Africans in 1983/84 was only 11% of that for white pupils; whereas over two-thirds of the whites who were in Standard 1 in 1968 and 1969 were in Standard 10 in 1977 and 1978, fewer than 4% of Africans who were in Standard 1 in those years were still in school in Standard 10 nine years later; and in 1980 an African aged 15 to 19 years had only about one-ninth the chance of a white of the same age of passing matric (see below, Tables 10.1, 10.2, 10.6 and 10.8).

NUMBERS

In interpreting South African educational statistics, especially when they are broken down by race, it is important to remember that the demographic characteristics of different groups differ. The crude fertility rates of whites and Asians are very much lower than those of coloureds and Africans, and the absolute numbers of births per annum of groups other than African are falling quite rapidly (the crude birth rate of Africans is reputedly fairly static at about 40 per 1000, implying quite rapid growth in the number of births per year). These differences produce different age-structures of the population for different races, with implications for education. For example, Table 10.1 on the surface suggests a structure in which the majority of Africans can receive only a few years of education. The situation is not quite as bad as it seems; the age structure of the African population in 1980 has been estimated to be such that of the total 5-19 years old age group (representing about 53% of the African population), 37.7% were 5 to 9, 33% 10 to 14, and only 29.3% 15 to 19 (Simkins, 1981: 21).

In a rapidly growing population, younger age-cohorts always outnumber older age-cohorts, and thus even if nobody dropped out of school the numbers of pupils in lower standards would exceed those in higher standards. It is therefore much more revealing to look at progression rates over time through the school system than the enrolment distribution across grades or standards at a point in time. Tables 10.2 and 10.3 do this for South Africa, as estimated by Pillay (1984). Two points are extremely striking: the massive racial inequality in educational attainment implied by the figures, and at the same time the fairly rapid growth, at least until about 1979, of the progression rates for Asians, coloureds and Africans.

Attending school has costs, even if schooling itself is technically 'free'. These costs, primarily the costs of spending time in school that could have been used to earn income or engage in household production (but also often costs of clothing, travel, supplies, food away from home, etc.), have two important features in most countries. First, they rise with age (because the older the pupil, the more valuable the pupil's time in other activities). Second, the poorer the household, the higher such costs will be as a fraction of disposable income. Thus the probability of a child remaining in school tends to fall as the child's age rises and the family's relative position in the income distribution falls. We should expect inequality in educational attainment between races to persist as long as inequality of income distribution between races persists, except in so far as it is offset by other influences (such as cultural differences in attitudes to schooling, which may exist).

These rather banal observations are complicated by the circularity of the connections between schooling and income. Persons with more schooling tend, on average, to have higher incomes than those with less schooling. This seems to be true in societies with all forms of economic organisation in which formal schooling exists and data are available. It is summarised by economists in the notion of 'human capital', the process of schooling involving the acquisition of attributes that are valuable to society and are rewarded by higher income. It is therefore common to assert that part of the explanation of racial income inequalities in South Africa is the inequality of educational attainments by race. There is an immediate and disturbing implication: a society that removed racial discrimination would not automatically eliminate social and economic inequality between races for a very long time, if ever.

Equality of opportunity on its own will not achieve the outcome the deprived segments of the population expect, at least not for several generations. Measures will be needed, therefore, to compensate the disadvantaged groups, probably for a lengthy period. Such 'affirmative action' is inevitably costly; the obvious group to bear the costs, either through taxation or through 'reverse discrimination' is the group that has had the advantaged position (i.e whites in South Africa, or Chinese in Malaysia). However, a problem arises that is well illustrated by the behaviour of Malaysian Chinese. Excluded from Malaysian universities by preferential access for indigenes, Malaysian Chinese in large numbers go overseas for higher education, and a proportion do not return. Policies that seek to redress the racial imbalances in South Africa by imposing costs or limited access to education on whites will have the consequence of raising the rate of emigration of whites. It may well be true that post-apartheid South Africa will be able to afford to lose some of its white population, but those most potentially mobile are likely to be those with skills in shortest supply, and it is doubtful that it will be desirable to accelerate emigration of this group very much. Zimbabwean experience in this regard may be instructive, as we shall see below.

The fundamental problem that we have been skirting here is one of time scales. Popular expectations in post-apartheid South Africa will demand rapid movement toward racial equality of outcomes with respect to educational attainments and income distribution. This demand will conflict with short-term economic objectives, requiring the retention of a large part of the skilled, highly educated white population. Retaining these people may require that educational opportunities for their children are not drastically curtailed, and that they are not taxed too heavily in other ways. The danger is that this may lead to severe economic difficulties (the extreme analogy is Mozambique's problems arising from withdrawal of Portuguese settler skills), or to popular disillusion with consequent political problems. As background for the discussion that follows, I assume that in post-apartheid South Africa the education sector will involve no discrimination by race or ethnic group. Further, I assume that a substantial part of the white population will remain, and that it is an objective of government to encourage skilled whites to do so. Lastly, I assume that government has as an objective the elimination of racial differences in educational attainment and income distribution as rapidly as is consistent with other economic policy objectives such as maintaining employment and the growth of the economy.

FINANCE

In recent years, the expansion of school enrolments by Africans has been very rapid. The bulk of African enrolment is still, however, at primary levels. One of the consequences of the end of apartheid will be an explosive growth of enrolment by Africans at secondary levels, expanding the trends of the late 1970s. Even quite conservative assumptions suggest that by the end of the century the bulk of matriculation passes will go to Africans (see Table 10.7). The potential magnitude of the problem of financing this expansion can be illustrated by a simple (non-realistic) arithmetic exercise. If per pupil education expenditures in 1983/84 had been the same for other groups as for whites, total education expenditures would have been over R14 billion, rather than the actual figure of under R4 billion. This would have represented well over 10% of GDP, a level of spending on education unprecedented anywhere in the world. In practice, given the differences in distribution of pupils over grades between groups, and the increase of per pupil expenditures as grade level increases, equalisation of spending per pupil across races by grade would not require such a large increase. Even so, there are several policy issues that will affect per pupil expenditure levels that will need to be faced. The most important concern teacher salaries and the extent and nature of direct parental contributions to the costs of education.

Teacher salaries in most countries make up between 85% and 95% of total recurrent expenditures on education. In most countries, and South Africa is no exception, teacher salaries are on scales that relate pay to qualifications and experience. Reportedly, all white teachers in South Africa have matric and 97% are also professionally qualified; about one third of the professionally qualified also have university degrees (Pillay, 1984: 17). In contrast (see Table 10.9) over 20% of African teachers are not professionally qualified. Over 60% have Junior Certificate or less as their highest educational attainment, only about a quarter have completed high school, and only 2.5% hold a university degree. There is already a severe shortage of qualified African teachers in South Africa. Although there will be good political and educational reasons for emergency action to upgrade the qualifications of the African teaching force after apartheid, this will have severe implications for the education budget unless changes are made to the relative salaries of teachers with different qualifications. I have not been able to find precise data on South African salary scales for teachers, but the data in Table 10.13 showing 1985 Zimbabwean salary scales gives a notion of what is involved. An initial rapid expansion of the school system after apartheid would almost certainly require hiring large numbers of unqualified teachers. It will be desirable to upgrade the best of these, and to replace the rest with newly-trained teachers. But this process is likely to impose continuing heavy strain on the educational budget, unless the differentials between more and less qualified teachers are reduced. The difficulty is that it is likely to be thought desirable to retain some university graduates in the teaching force, and their salaries will have to be competitive with those of graduates entering other occupations.

However, there is in a sense a prior problem, concerning the kind of school system that will emerge after apartheid. Schools are currently segregated (except for some private and church schools) and facilities are unequal. After apartheid it can be assumed that most people will want the best education they can obtain for their children. Whites will resist what they perceive as decline in the quality of the schools their children attend, and will emigrate more rapidly if they think the decline is too great. At the same time, both they and the richer members of other races will also be willing to pay to maintain higher quality in schools than the state feels able to afford. One pragmatic approach would be to follow current policy in Zimbabwe, where some aspects of school control and finance have been passed to parents who, via elected bodies, have the power to set fees for individual schools, supplementing the resources provided by the state. However, there are obvious problems with this approach. It will produce schools that are stratified by income class and therefore to some extent also by race, with lower income pupils excluded by the level of supplementary fees voted by parents. Given the level of residential segregation in South Africa, such a system would slow the rate at which equality of opportunity and outcome could be achieved. In an educational system with a unified examination structure (assuming exams are not abolished), the inequalities would quickly become apparent — indeed, exaggerated in the public mind.

The pragmatic solution is thus easy to describe but of dubious political feasibility. It would amount to determining a level of per pupil subsidy to be paid by the state to each recognised school, and then giving parents control of the individual schools, permitting them to set supplementary fees and hire whatever teachers they wanted at whatever salaries they wanted to pay. In one sense this would equalise matters by giving each pupil the same level of state resources (possibly rising with grade, but perhaps not); it would also keep the whites fairly happy and be welcomed by the more affluent members of other races. But in fact the system described would perpetuate inequality of educational opportunity by income, while still fostering substantial *de facto* segregation of schools by race.

THE ZIMBABWEAN EXPERIENCE

There are ways in which Zimbabwe's experience since independence is not a good guide to what may happen in South Africa after apartheid, given the differences between the two countries in racial composition and the strong influence of the protracted war on the education system in Zimbabwe. Nevertheless, the experience in Zimbabwe is suggestive of some of the problems that are likely to occur in South Africa. Tables 10.10 and 10.11 summarise some data on total pupil enrolments and teachers for selected years. Before independence, African pupil enrolments were constrained by both the effects of the war (which closed many schools) and official government policy on places for Africans. Since independence, selection has in effect been abolished at the former choke points in the system (Grade 7 to Form 1, Form 4 to above), with all those passing the relevant exam permitted to continue. The growth in enrolment has been explosive. Primary enrolment more than doubled between 1979 and 1982; since then, growth has been slow and is unlikely to be much faster than population growth for the foreseeable future. At the secondary level, however, enrolment went up more than five and a half times between 1980 and 1984 and, if selection is not reintroduced, is likely to continue to grow very rapidly until 1990 (by which time there might be as many as one million pupils in secondary schools).

This expansion has required more teachers. Pupil : teacher ratios in primary schools have remained close to unchanged, on average, but the proportion of untrained teachers in the primary schools has had to grow rapidly, so that by 1983 over half the primary school teachers were untrained. The total number of teachers in secondary schools over this period went up about two and one half times. Untrained teachers were held to only 22% of the total in 1983 by the introduction of sandwich-type teacher training systems by which student teachers were placed in schools almost immediately on starting training (and regarded in the statistics as trained) and then received their training by distance and in-service methods. In addition, the authorised staffing ratios (given the number of teachers government would pay for) were changed from 1:20 in government schools and 1:22.5 in private schools, to 1:30 for Forms 1-3, 1:28 for Form 4, and 1:20 for Form 6 in all schools in 1983. Three types of school were inherited by Zimbabwe at independence: government Group A, government Group B, and 'private'. Table 10.15 gives the numbers of each of these types of school for each year from 1978 to 1983. The Group A schools were basically white, the Group B schools largely for urban Africans, and the private schools rural and mission-run. Since independence, the growth in number of schools has been largely in the private category, which now includes schools started by district councils and other bodies. The central government has provided very little for school construction, although it does pay teachers according to its staffing ratios and salary scales in all recognised schools. However, the historical legacy still exists in terms of the qualification of teachers, physical facilities, the socio-economic origins of students, and examination results — with the exception of a few elite private schools, Group A schools do better than Group B, and Group B better than private. Furthermore, the system whereby the parents of children in a particular school can vote to impose fees on themselves to pay for hiring more teachers and providing more materials, together with residential patterns that segregate the population by income, if less by race than in the past, tends to strengthen these inequalities.

Finance

Despite the fact that the government of Zimbabwe has made moves to shift part of the cost of education onto parents and communities, the budget has grown very rapidly. By the mid-1980s, the government's total spending on education and training was probably over 8% of GDP, and around 7% of GNP. This is a high figure: for 1981, the World Bank has reported estimates for sub-Saharan African countries ranging from 0.3% to 8.1%, with a weighted mean of 3.4% of GNP. However, it is probably significant that the other countries with ratios at the high end — 7 to 8% — are concentrated in Southern Africa (Botswana, Lesotho, Swaziland). There is, I believe, a regional effect here stemming from proximity to South Africa, and a historical legacy of neglect under colonial rule of African education plus generous provision for white education.

This is reflected to some extent in such things as pupil:teacher ratios and teacher salary scales. The official staffing ratios in Zimbabwe are generous for anglophone Africa, although comparable to South African pupil:teacher ratios. Trained teachers in Zimbabwe receive salaries that, although not high in comparison with salaries for teachers in South Africa or other professionals in Zimbabwe, are nevertheless a large multiple of GNP per capita or of average earnings in communal farming — perhaps as much as fifteen times the latter. Given that about 60% of the labour force is engaged in communal farming, the implications of paying teachers such a large multiple of average earnings in that sector are disturbing.

The implications are that Zimbabwe will have to make changes in education sector policy. These changes will be made more difficult by a decline in quality (reflected in examination pass rates), and continuation if not exacerbation of inequalities of opportunity between children in different types of school. The most obvious things government could do are to permit the real incomes of teachers to decline (not hard to do in theory when inflation is occurring), to increase pupil:teacher ratios, and to slow the rate at which untrained teachers are replaced by trained ones (the latter influenced by provision of training spaces for teachers). One might go further, and restrict the growth of enrolment at the secondary, sixth form, and (most expensive of all) university level by reintroducing selection rather than open access at the various choke points in the system.

However, this last step would run into several important difficulties. The progression rates through the system in 1983-84, when there were no constraints on enrolment at higher levels if exams had been passed, would imply, if maintained, that out of 1,000 children entering Grade 1, 776 would reach Grade 7, 567 would reach Form 4, and 113 would reach upper Form 6 (at the end of which A levels are taken, the university entrance requirement). Although these numbers are high for sub-Saharan Africa, they do not represent universal primary education. They illustrate that there are still very substantial costs, and perhaps only small rewards, of attending school in Zimbabwe. But would it be politically feasible for government to constrict opportunity by rationing places? As many Zimbabweans have remarked, one of the things the war was fought over was access to education. If places are rationed, whose son (and whose daughter) will not continue?

There is also the problem of how such measures would affect the equity issues in the education sector. Would it be possible to prevent the wealthy from buying more education for their children, as they can by subsidising school fees? If not, measures such as those suggested would make the inequality of outcome by income group, and perceived inequality of opportunity by income group, more severe than it already is.

Lurking in the background is an even more serious problem, politically explosive in Zimbabwe and potentially in South Africa as well. Historically, educational access for Africans was constrained. As a result, the distribution of educational qualifications in the labour force was distorted, with fewer persons with any given level of education above zero, and in particular fewer Africans, than would otherwise have been the case. This situation helped to support a wage and salary structure that gave very high rewards to formal education, and also discriminated against Africans, thereby skewing the income distribution in favour of whites. Rapid growth of education, and particularly secondary and higher education, has the effect of changing the relative qualifications of the labour force. Persons with more education are likely to become more plentiful in the labour force quite rapidly. The consequence has to be, first, a steady decline in job opportunities for holders of particular educational qualifications and, over time, a slow erosion of the relative real incomes of those with more education and an escalation of the qualifications demanded of new entrants into various occupations. The typical initial symptom is unemployment of recent graduates — the school leaver unemployment problem was already apparent at all education levels in Zimbabwe in 1985. The process is made more disruptive and costly to society if it is resisted by attempts to maintain 'traditional' real income differentials between those with different levels of education. This tends to exacerbate the unemployment problem, because recent school leavers spend longer attempting to get first jobs before being willing to settle for less well paid occupations, and also because it increases the supply of graduates. The latter occurs because current pupils and their families tend to base the economic part of decisions on whether to stay in school on their observations of current relative incomes of holders of various educational qualifications, which of course tend in these circumstances to reflect past supply and demand and not the larger supplies of educated persons likely to be available in the future.

STRUCTURE, CURRICULUM AND ECONOMICS

So far I have avoided discussion of the issues raised by the quotation with which this chapter opens, the issue of whether in post-apartheid South Africa there should be continuity in terms of the curriculum and the structure of formal education, as has happened in Zimbabwe; or whether there should be a radical break with the past in keeping with the ideological aspirations of those who have overturned apartheid. A radical break would be difficult and perhaps dangerous, but it may be the only way in which a continuing crisis of conscience and policy choice over issues of equity, finance, and access in the education system in post-apartheid South Africa can be avoided.

Educational systems tend to be inherently conservative with strong elements of continuity even across marked changes of government, political and economic systems. Educational systems in francophone Africa are invariably recognisable as 'French', just as in anglophone Africa they are clearly 'English'; allegedly there are many features of Soviet education that are direct inheritances of pre-1917 Russian education rather than results of conscious policy decision. Similarly, many African countries have encountered considerable resistance from parents and pupils to attempts to make curriculum or system changes that appear eminently sound, such as localising examination systems, but which represent breaks with the familiar. In South Africa, with its history of Bantu Education, this popular conservatism is likely to be extremely pronounced. If the educational system were to be changed radically, to one that attempted to give equal opportunity to all but which was structured to reflect probable demands for labour and the economic realities of the post-apartheid state, it would have to be a system from which the rich and powerful could not opt out. This in turn implies that the introduction of such a radically reformed system would very probably drive out of the country a large proportion of the more skilled sections of the population, not fully committed to the ideology of radical reform and disturbed by the perceived damage it might do to their children's life chances.

Thus radical reform involves not just an educational decision but an economic and political one. It would exacerbate problems of 'white flight' and skill shortages, causing economic disruption, at least temporary unemployment, and so on. This suggests a minor paradox: the more disrupted the economy becomes during the shift to the post-apartheid state, the more radical reform is likely to be. The opposite case might also be made, however, arguing that if there has already been much disruption and much loss of skills, the economy cannot afford to drive out any of those remaining that it can hold on to. It may be that an argument along these latter lines has had some influence on educational policy in Zimbabwe. The crucial point may be the extent to which the 'modern' economy can still be said to be functioning when the decision has to be made. If it is still operating at some reasonable level, then there will be many who will argue against doing things to the educational system that will drive out the skills that keep it running. But on the other hand, if the modern economy is already in a shambles, there may be little left to lose. This suggests a rather pessimistic conclusion: a truly radical reform may be likely only if the economy is first reduced to something close to absolute chaos — in which circumstances it is doubtful whether the resources, skills, determination and initiative to carry through a radical reform will be available.

What might a radically reformed system look like? It should have the following features: it should give each child an equal chance of 'success', however defined; it should produce graduates with skills and attitudes appropriate to the realities of the economy, polity, and society; it should be affordable from the point of view of society, families, and pupils, and it should not permit the advantaged to buy or extort advantages for their children; and it should be responsive to the wishes of the people. The details would obviously depend on the actual nature of the economy and society that emerges in the post-apartheid situation, but one can speculate about some aspects now.

My own guesses would run along the following lines. The system would be unified and compulsory. The first cycle would last eight years. It would emphasise language (with probably much emphasis on English), mathematics, civics/social studies/political studies, and practical skills. Primary teachers in this first cycle would have training (and retraining) specifically for the first cycle, and would have relatively low salaries and status. The curriculum and syllabi would be set by the state, but schools would be subject to considerable control and influence in day to day matters by elected bodies of parents. On completion of the primary cycle, at about age 14 to 15, all pupils would be expected to enter the labour force for a period of at least three years. Secondary schools would be academic, and entry would be on the basis of primary school record, aptitude exams, interview, and recommendations from employers and other authorities (such as perhaps political parties). The secondary course would be rigorous, but places would only be provided for numbers consistent with fairly conservative projections of demands for labour with the educational background represented by complete secondary education. The secondary academic cycle would be, say, four years long, culminating in an examination. It would be followed by two years of compulsory 'National Service' at relatively low pay, and selection for further academic study or technical training would be based on both the results of the leaving examination and reports on performance during the service period. The service could be in the military or civil branches of government, or in labour battalions, farming, industry, rural services, or whatever. Secondary and higher education and training would be free to the pupils, as would primary, and in addition pupils would receive small living allowances based on family need, intended to reduce the probability of pupils dropping out because of family economic difficulties. However, each pupil entering secondary or higher education would have charged against a notional individual education account the full costs to the state of their secondary or further education. After graduation, each such student would be subject to a surcharge on their individual income taxes, at a rate such as 20 per cent, that would be credited to their individual education account, until such time as they had repaid to the state the resources expended on their education.

Such a system would be a radical departure, and I believe it could overcome many of the equity problems that are likely to be such a thorny aspect of the education system in post-apartheid South Africa.

South African Data

Table 10.1: African Pupil Enrolment by Standard, 1983

Standard	Enrolment	% of Column Total
Sub A	1,024,944	18.5
Sub B	795,087	14.3
1	735,112	13.3
2	591,520	10.7
Subtotal, lower primary	3,146,663	56.8
3	553,992	10.0
4	449,595	8.1
5	395,968	7.1
Subtotal, higher primary	1,399,555	25.2
Subtotal, all primary	4,546,218	82.0
6	317,902	5.7
7	256,635	4.6
8	227,205	4.1
9	112,634	2.0
10	86,873	1.6
Subtotal, all secondary	1,001,249	18.0
TOTAL	5,547,467	100.0

Source: SAIRR, *Race Relations Survey, 1984*, p.660.
Note: These data cover all Africans in South Africa, including Bantustans.

Table 10.2: Pupil Progression Rates by Race, Std 1 to Std 10

Years in Std 1	Std 10	Std 10 Enrolment as % of Std 1 Enrolment			
		Whites	Indians	Coloureds	Africans
1967	1976	59.9	21.5	5.9	3.2
1968	1977	66.8	25.5	9.1	3.7
1969	1978	69.0	34.4	10.5	3.9
1970	1979	68.4	48.5	11.4	n.a.
1971	1980	68.9	42.1	12.0	n.a.

Source: Pillay (1984), p.9.

Table 10.3: Pupil Progression Rates by Race, Std 6 to Std 10

Years in Std 6	Std 10	Std 10 Enrolment as % of Std 6 Enrolment			
		Whites	Indians	Coloureds	Africans
1969	1973	55.9	29.1	11.8	4.8
1970	1974	58.5	32.4	12.5	5.0
1971	1975	56.7	28.4	13.5	6.1
1972	1976	60.1	25.3	13.0	6.9
1973	1977	65.3	30.8	18.3	7.7
1974	1978	68.3	40.6	22.3	7.8
1975	1979	68.0	60.3	24.1	n.a.
1976	1980	69.5	53.1	24.8	n.a.

Source: Pillay (1984), p.9.

Table 10.4: Pupil:Teacher Ratios

Africans (1982)	45.0:1
Coloureds (1984)	26.0:1
Indians (1984)	23.0:1
Whites (1984)	18.9:1
Africans (excluding TBVC, 1984)	40.7:1

Sources: SAIRR, *Race Relations Survey, 1984*, p.650; and Vermaak and Verwey (1984), p.8.

Table 10.5: Total Education Expenditures, 1984/85

	Million Rand	% of Column Total
African education	1,460	30.7
Coloured education	571	12.0
Indian education	259	5.5
White education	2,465	51.8
Total	4,755	100.0
Total as % of total central government expenditure		19.1%
Total as approximate % of GDP		4.8%

Source: SAIRR, *Race Relations Survey, 1984*, pp.201, 647.

Table 10.6: Per Pupil Recurrent Expenditure, 1983/84

	Rand	As % of Recurrent Expenditure Per Pupil for Whites
Africans (excluding TBVC)	166.63	11.0
Coloureds	501.11	33.2
Indians	905,00	59.9
Whites	1,511.00	100.0

Budgeted total per pupil expenditure in 1983/84 in TBVC was

Transkei	171.97	11.4
Bophuthatswana	245.64	16.3
Venda	174.00	11.5
Ciskei	161.24	10.7

Source: SAIRR, Race Relations Survey, 1984, pp.648, 649.

Table 10.7: Projections of Matriculation Results

Year	Total		Percentages			Growth Rate, % Per Annum, Between Years	% of All Passes Univ. Exemption Passes
		Wh	Col	As	Af		
University Exemption passes:							
1972	22,200	84.6	4.1	2.7	8.6		42.8
1980	35,100	72.6	4.6	5.7	17.1	5.89	39.3
1990	49,500	55.7	6.1	7.7	30.5	3.50	32.1
2000	67,300	37.9	6.8	6.4	48.9	3.12	30.7
Senior Leaving Certificate passes:							
1972	29,700	80.5	3.0	8.1	8.4		
1980	54,300	41.8	9.9	5.2	43.1	7.61	
1990	104,900	23.9	7.9	4.1	64.1	6.81	
2000	151,600	14.6	6.8	3.0	75.6	3.75	

Notes: Wh - white, Col - coloured, As - Asian, Af - African.
  University Exemption pass permits entry to university; without University Exemption the Senior Leaving Certificate pass permits entry to technicons (polytechnics or training colleges) and teacher training institutions. These projections are of course dependent on their assumptions, for which see the source.

Source: C.E.W. Simkins, 'South African matriculation passes: analysis and projections from 1972 to 2000', SALDRU Fact Sheet No. 6 (Saldru, Cape Town, January 1985).

Table 10.8: Projections of Relative Probabilities of Persons Aged 15 to 19 Years Old of Passing Matriculation

Year	Whites	Coloureds	Asians	Africans
1972	100.0	6.3	32.6	2.2
1980	100.0	18.4	46.8	11.3
1990	100.0	28.0	62.1	20.7
2000	100.0	36.9	72.0	25.7

Notes: This table implies that compared to whites, in 1972 Africans had only a 2.2% as good a probability of passing matric, i.e. the fraction of the age group among Africans passing matric was only 2.2% of the fraction of the white age group passing matric. The projections are of course dependent on their assumptions, for which see the source.

Source: C.E.W. Simkins, 'South African matriculation passes'.

Table 10.9: Qualifications of African Teachers, 1983 (excluding TBVC)

Professionally qualified, with:	Number	Percent
Standard 6	6,754	7.6
Junior certificate	39,951	44.9
Technical certificate	694	0.8
Standard 10	19,810	22.3
Some university	1,554	1.7
University degree	1,651	1.9
Special teacher certificate	423	0.5
Subtotal	70,837	79.6*
Unqualified, with:		
Junior certificate	14,857	16.7
Technical certificate	566	0.6
Matric or Senior certificate	1,507	1.7
Some university	709	0.8
University degree	501	0.6
Subtotal	18,140	20.4
Total	88,977	100.1*

* rounding error

Source: SAIRR, *Race Relations Survey, 1984*, pp.665-666.

Zimbabwe Data

Table 10.10: Enrolments, 1977-84

	1977	*1980*	*1984*	*1984 as % of Column Total*
Grade 1	174,551	376,392	359,559	14.0
Grade 2	155,080	207,889	341,503	13.3
Grade 3	141,626	170,420	360,829	14.0
Grade 4	124,544	144,746	372,641	14.5
Subtotal	456,229	899,447	1,434,532	55.8
Grade 5	111,850	125,977	313,987	12.2
Grade 6	97,636	112,890	214,922	8.4
Grade 7	85,853	97,099	182,742	7.1
Subtotal	295,339	335,966	711,651	27.7
Subtotal, all primary	892,651	1,235,994	2,147,898	83.6
Form 1	19,632	22,201	140,045	5.4
Form 2	17,656	17,125	107,052	4.2
Form 3	14,558	15,891	93,232	3.6
Form 4	12,927	12,926	71,632	2.8
Form 5	3,687	1,815	3,164	0.1
Form 6 lower	1,566	2,641	4,218	0.2
Form 6 upper	1,367	1,413	2,962	0.1
Subtotal, all secondary	73,335	74,966	422,584	16.4
Total	965,986	1,310,960	2,570,482	100.0

Note: Components do not add to subtotals and totals because of omission of 'special' classes (never more than 2,500 pupils).
Source: Central Statistical Office, Government of Zimbabwe, *Quarterly Digest of Statistics*, December 1984, Table 5.1, p.5.

Table 10.11: Teachers, 1979-83

	1979	1981	1983	% Increase, 1979-1983
Primary, trained	16,825	22,654	25,954	54.3
Primary, untrained	1,658	15,119	26,548	1,501.2
Primary, total	18,483	37,773	52,502	184.1
Untrained as % of total	9.0	40.0	50.6	
Secondary, trained	3,258	4,608	6,874	111.0
Secondary, untrained	276	266	1,934	600.7
Secondary, total	3,534	4,874	8,808	149.2
Untrained as % of total	7.8	5.5	22.0	

Note: 'Trained' includes ZINTEC trainees; some teachers working in so-called 'upper tops' (secondary schools physically located in primary school facilities) are misclassified as primary.
Source: Government of Zimbabwe, *Annual Report of the Secretary for Education* (Government Printer, Harare) for years ended 31 December 1979, 1981, 1983.

Table 10.12: Apparent Pupil Progression Rates

Years in Grade 3	Years in Form 4	Form 4 Enrolment as % of Grade 3 Enrolment
1970	1978	11.3
1971	1979	11.1
1972	1980	10.7
1973	1981	12.3
1974	1982	11.6
1975	1983	17.8

Years in Form 1	Years in Form 4	Form 4 Enrolment as % of Form 1 Enrolment
1970	1973	57.4
1971	1974	59.1
1972	1975	59.2
1973	1976	67.0
1974	1977	68.1
1975	1978	71.0
1976	1979	65.5
1977	1980	66.7
1978	1981	81.7
1979	1982	85.9
1980	1983	110.4

Note: The Form 1 to Form 4 rates are obviously distorted by the effects of the war (both white emigration and African pupils unable to attend secondary school and then returning to school after the end of the war).

Source: Calculated from enrolment data in the *Annual Reports* of the Secretary for Education, Government of Zimbabwe.

Table 10.13: Portions of 1985 Zimbabwe Education Salary Scales

April 1985 salary scales in Zimbabwe dollars, per annum:

Untrained	1,764 by 5 steps to 2,832
ZINTEC trainees	2,376 by 10 steps to 5,040
A1/2 scale	3,288 by 13 steps to 7,152
B-D scales	6,072 by 15 steps to 12,096
E-H scales	6,072 by 20 steps to 13,824
Head 3 (primary)	9,936 by 6 steps to 12,528
Head 2 (primary)	11,664 by 6 steps to 14,256
Head 1 (primary)	12,528 by 8 steps to 16,068
Head (secondary)	12,960 by 8 steps to 16,548

Note: Newly trained teachers start at at least Z$6,072 per annum, more than twice the maximum theoretical salary of an untrained teacher.
Source: Government of Zimbabwe.

Table 10.14: Education Expenditures

	1981/82	1982/83	1983/84	1984/85
Total central government education expenditure Z$ million (approximate)	297	380	442	n.a.
% of total central government expenditure	18.9	18.9	18.2	17.7
As % of GDP	7.0	8.3	8.0	8.7

Source: Author's estimates from published government sources and *Standard Chartered Business Trends* (Harare), February 1985.

Table 10.15: Number of Schools of Different Types

Year	Primary Govt. A	Govt. B	Private	Secondary Govt. A	Govt. B	Private
1978	135	111	2,715	37	29	124
1979	134	123	2,144	36	34	107
1980	85	130	2,905	28	35	126
1981	83	145	3,418	26	103	557
1982	117	155	3,586	34	115	589
1983	115	156	3,691	34	110	646

Note: In 1980 and 1981, there was a fourth category, 'community schools', of which in 1980 there were 8 secondary and 41 primary schools, and in 1981 8 secondary and 40 primary schools. Unaided schools are omitted up to 1980; therafter the full title of the private category is 'registered private'.
Source: Government of Zimbabwe, *Annual Report of the Secretary for Education*, for the years 1979, 1981, 1983.

REFERENCES

PILLAY, P. N., 1984. 'The development and underdevelopment of education in South Africa', Second Carnegie Inquiry into Poverty and Development in Southern Africa Conference Paper, No. 95, Cape Town, April.

SIMKINS, C.E.W., 1981. 'The distribution of the African population of South Africa by age, sex, and region-type 1960, 1970 and 1980', Saldru Working Paper No. 32, Cape Town, January.

VERMAAK, D. and VERWEY, C.T., 1984. 'Current statistical profile of education in the developing states in the South African context', Second Carnegie Inquiry into Poverty and Development in Southern Africa Conference Paper, No. 100, Cape Town, April.

11. The South African Mining Industry After Apartheid

PETER ROBBINS

SOUTH AFRICAN MINING INDUSTRY —
OWNERSHIP, STRUCTURE AND PRODUCTS

Ownership

To the lay observer, the South African mining sector would appear to be dominated by five major groups: Anglo American, General Mining Union Corporation (Gencor), Anglovaal, Gold Fields of South Africa and Barlow Rand Ltd. Other groups with comparatively minor mining interests are RTZ, African Exploration and Lonrho. These eight groups collectively control over 95% of all mining in the country.

This variety of ownership is often cited as a sign of healthy competition and an indication that South Africa's most important industrial sector is a shining example of the capitalist system. However, an examination of the shareholdings and the boards of directors of these companies reveals a different picture. Each group consists of a variety of holding companies, investment companies, subsidiaries and joint subsidiaries as well as an incestuous complex of minority holdings in each others' companies at all levels of the structure.

Of the 450 or so directors of the 128 top mining companies, 72 have more than four directorships. One man has twenty-seven directorships, including several chairmanships and several managing directorships. This apparent thirst for directorships would signify less if companies only encouraged directors to sit on boards of subsidiary or sister companies, as indeed they seem to do. But there are, in fact, 135 cases of cross-directorships. All the major mining groups are integrally connected. There are many examples of commercial cooperation between the groups and of apparent coordination in sales policy. The gold mining companies also present a joint front in negotiations with unions through the South African Chamber of Mines.

When one examines the true picture of ownership and control of these mining groups, one can immediately see its monolithic nature and by implication its high degree of central control. If a new regime in South Africa decided to take the mining industry into public ownership, or exercise some other form of government control, it would not be faced with the complications to be expected if the mining groups were less integrally connected by virtue of ownership and the huge pool of common directors.

The general policy and coordination of all mining in South Africa is almost certainly in the hands of less than a hundred men. Most of the major South African groups own or partly own mining companies outside South Africa. Mining in Namibia, Botswana and Zimbabwe is dominated by South African companies who also have interests in Canada, the USA, Australia, Portugal, Spain and several other countries.

Products

South Africa produces a great many mineral products and metals, though the volume recorded is not always significant as a percentage of world production. The production of copper, silver, nickel, titanium ore and aluminium is low by world standards although all of these materials are exported. The following metals are produced in large enough quantities to be especially significant: 48% of the world's gold; 30% of its chromium; 22% of its manganese, 36% of its vanadium; 40% of its metals in the platinum group, and 25% of Western production of uranium.

The export revenue obtained by the sale of metals represents the bulk of all foreign earnings: gold exports account for almost half of foreign earnings, while base metals and other minerals bring in about 16% of the total. The export of gold and all other minerals represents about 17% of gross domestic product. The total asset value of South African mining companies amounts to some 30 billion rands, most of which is retained in South Africa.

The prices of all mineral commodities were hit hard by the last six years of recession, but the mining companies have increased profits due to the falling value of the rand: costs being in rands and revenue in US dollars. Disruption of production by strikes has the effect of increasing the value of the metal produced at the mine where the strike has occurred. The price of platinum, for instance, rose by 20% after the lock-out at Impala mines in early 1986. This price increase does not necessarily benefit the producing company, however, as the loss of production means they have less to sell at the higher price.

ANC POLICY AND OTHER OPTIONS

The ANC has always maintained that it would bring the 'commanding heights' of South Africa's mining sector under public ownership once it has assumed power. For the purposes of this chapter I shall assume that this means the nationalisation of the 'big five" mentioned above, together with all their subsidiaries and jointly owned companies.

Without exception these companies are not only vertically integrated but have diversified into other commercial areas: farming, building materials, plastics, light and heavy engineering, chemicals, financial services and many more. Vertical integration within the mining sector goes all the way through geological survey and prospecting, venture financing, concentration, refining and production of semi-fabricated and fabricated products. It may be that the ANC has in its mind to treat the diversified industries in a different way, but for the purposes of this chapter I shall mainly concern myself with the finding, mining and processing of minerals in South Africa. The nationalisation of these commercial groups means the taking over of several hundred mines, concentration plants, smelters and refineries as well as fabricating factories. In my discussion of the problems likely to be faced in this huge task I shall refer to the experiences of Zambia and Zimbabwe. Both countries are very different from each other and both are very different from South Africa, but many lessons can, I think, be learned.

Zambia nationalised its mining industry and at first did well as the price of copper, its main product, increased through the late 1960s and 1970s. The Zambian economy has now become a slave of this one product which has absorbed most of the country's available investment and has concentrated political power around the mining industry. Zimbabwe has taken over almost none of the mining industry and has instead tried to regulate the activities of the multinational mining companies by setting up parastatal bodies to control mining development and marketing. These efforts have not, however, prevented the closure of mines and transfer pricing on a large scale, nor has it benefitted Zimbabwean miners. Both countries have encountered the problem of corruption which is endemic in the mining business; and neither country has been capable of training enough indigenous personnel, particularly in administrative and marketing skills.

All other Third World countries who have attempted to take control of their own mining industries have faced difficulties using approaches which recall the experience of Zambia and Zimbabwe. The policy followed in Australia, where the government insists that Australians should have a majority shareholding in all mining companies, suggests a third approach. It seems certain that any country which is determined to bring its mining industry under the control of its government will face three main problems: subversive activity from the multinationals; finding the necessary quantity and quality of skilled engineers and managers loyal to the cause of independence; and corruption. Even if all these problems are solved, the mining industry is still the slave of world market conditions and market manipulation by Western governments and multinational companies. It should perhaps be remembered that metals have been mined in huge quantities in Southern Africa for over one hundred years and that, taking into account a considerable depletion of mineable stocks by these activities, the net benefit to Africans after all this activity has been zero.

ESSENTIAL ELEMENTS OF A MINING INDUSTRY

1. Policy

What place should mining hold in the economy? The overwhelming importance of the mining industry to South Africa is as a source of foreign exchange. The mining sector has, therefore, as much to do with the government's fiscal and banking policy as it has to do with its industrial policy. The importance of foreign exchange to a majority ruled South Africa falls outside the scope of this chapter. The importance of the mining sector as a provider of employment also falls outside the present topic, except to say that the number of people employed has probably reached a peak. The major mining companies in South Africa have been contemplating massive programs of mechanisation for some years.

Inspired by political considerations more than economic ones, the industry would like to make its mines less dependent on, especially, unskilled labour. Threats of mechanisation have been used as a weapon against the trade unions but the shortage of investment funds has forced many of these plans to be shelved and it is unlikely that a majority government would want to implement them without full consultation with unions. Mechanisation would only be used to improve the working conditions in mines. It is not the imminent threat of mechanisation, thus, that is likely to set a limit on the mining workforce. A stronger factor is the expectation of mining output which, for the next few years at least, indicates a sluggish growth in demand for metals, especially for those in the steel industry. Increasing production would lower prices and not increase overall revenue.

The other major importance of the mining industry lies in its potential for vertical integration, more advanced in South Africa than any other African country. The domestic steel industry, for instance, can completely satisfy the domestic market and provide a surplus for export. Production of semi-manufactured metal items such as window frames, pipes, rolled products, wire, solder, etc. can completely satisfy local demand. Massive further scope for vertical integration could be found in many areas of the metals and minerals sector — in, for instance, the manufacture of electronic components, quality jewellery, fully finished engineered products, special steels and super alloys, and inorganic chemical products. In addition there is considerable scope for increasing capacity to export more mining products with greater added value.

We do not know the extent of the influence on centralised mining policy of the present South African regime, but it should be noted that quasi competition between the major mining groups has almost certainly acted to reduce total revenue for the country; also, many policy mistakes have been made in recent history, such as the failure to predict the boom in demand for South African metals in the second half of the 1970s and the expansion of production before the global recession. South Africa's isolation from other producers of the same minerals has also contributed to its failure to maximise revenue. Centralised policy making for the South African mining industry would almost certainly enhance efficiency and revenue for the country as well as improving the conditions of miners.

2. Technical

Exploration, prospecting and geological surveillance are at present largely controlled by major mining companies, as are the decisions to close, develop or open new mines. In my experience South African mining companies are not especially good at the timing of these decisions. Nevertheless, the tasks of research, costing, directing investment and raising capital are highly sophisticated, and if the experience of Zimbabwe is anything to go by personnel with the relevant experience are hard to come by outside the existing mining companies. The work is of such crucial importance that the government should have absolute trust in the findings of the experts involved. It may be that those who are attempting to formulate policies for a future majority government should attach some priority to the need to train personnel in all technical aspects of the mining industry.

Most west and east European countries offer training facilities for these skills. Canada and Australia are heavily committed to the mining industry and more recently the Chinese have become especially skilled at solving difficult mining and logistic problems. It is certainly not too early to start a programme designed to meet the need of a new South African mining industry for skilled technical staff.

Running existing mines may present fewer difficulties, especially as the unions have had at least some success in forcing the mining companies to employ black workers in some skilled and highly skilled areas of production; help in this area will nevertheless be required, especially in the financial control of mining enterprises. The marketing of minerals and metals will constitute the greatest challenge. We shall come back to this point later.

3. Control

Political control of a nationalised mining industry would rest with the Ministry of Mines, which should make policy and carry it out through bodies completely under its control. The essential functions to be coordinated are: financial control at national and individual plant level; training; recruitment of and negotiations with personnel; exploration and development; market research; transportation and shipping; stores and mining supplies; and marketing.

We can assume from the integrated ownership structure of the giant mining companies that there is already a degree of centralised control through the Chamber of Mines of such matters as labour relations, production development, and port facilities. Marketing policy is also centralised to a greater or lesser extent depending on the product. The marketing of uranium, diamonds and gold is, for instance, completely centralised. Market research, too, is pooled either directly among the mining houses or at conferences or by published papers. Many functions remain, however, in the hands of individual companies, even mines. Safety control and working conditions vary considerably from mine to mine. Transport and financial control are mainly the problem of individual companies.

In my opinion the control mechanisms set up by a new government should retain a certain amount of administrative power at the mine and plant level within the guidelines of government policy, but all marketing should be centralised and training programmes should be centrally directed, as should overall development, exploration and market research. Stores/mining supplies and recruitment should not be considered as areas suitable for centralised control.

Inevitably there will be a great deal of hostility both from within the South African mining industry and from the capitalist world to government control of the mining sector, especially as a new government may not feel that it would be just to compensate the present owners with the full value of the facilities taken into public ownership. Evidence should now be gathered and prepared which can be used to demonstrate the just basis of nationalisation.

Reading recent annual reports of the major South African mining companies, one could be led into thinking that these companies were the epitome of liberal thought. Each competes with the other to prove that its only goal is the advancement of black people, a fiction for the consumption of shareholders outside South Africa. In fact, of the hundred or more mines owned by the major groups, each with a separate board, not one director is black. Even the very recent history of the industry has been a tale of vicious exploitation, playing off indigenous workers against migrants and seeding many other forms of factional disputes leading to wholesale dismissals. A new government should be ready with a complete dossier of mismanagement by mining companies and the anti-worker record of the industry, together with its failure to take advantage of market movements.

Consumers of metals, in my experience, are unlikely to reduce their interest when faced with the prospect of buying from a newly nationalised mine. They are only interested in price, quality and reliability of supply. They were as happy, for instance, to buy copper from Chile under Allende as under Pinochet, and continued to buy metals from Peru when mines were nationalised in that country. The governments of consuming countries are a different matter however, and some may increase tariff barriers against metal from a country whose policies they disagree with. South Africa's leading position as a producer of several metals gives it a strong hand in such international dealings. Other major metal producers, of course, will be ready to exploit any difficulties that South Africa may experience during a period of transition.

A menacing prospect is the possibility of the major mining companies raping the mines before the transition can occur. Evidence is now emerging that De Beers have exploited diamond deposits in Namibia almost to extinction. This can be done in almost any mining operation. All mines have a variation in the richness of the ore body. To give the mine its longest possible commercial life, the good ore is taken out with the poorer ores and overload. If the owners expect to lose control of the mine in a period which is shorter than the natural life of the mine, they can exploit only the good ore, allowing the overload to fall in over other exploitable material. This operation has the effect of boosting the short-term revenue of the mine, but shortening its life. Arrangements should be made *now* with the unions to monitor any changes in mining practice during the period up to transition. It is in the interest of the miners, after all, to keep their jobs for as long as possible.

4. Marketing

The first and obvious point to be made about the price of metals is that although the price of a given metal may be very volatile and change in value by hundreds of percent over the period of a year, the price of that metal at any given time will be the same all over the world. Communication between consumers, producers and metal merchants is highly developed these days and variations of prices paid for a metal in any part of the world on a given day will differ by a maximum of no more than 1% or so.

Formal and informal markets

About a dozen metals are traded formally. That is to say they are traded on one or other of the world's commodity markets such as the London Metal Exchange (LME) or the New York Commodity Exchange (COMEX). Metals produced in South Africa which are traded in this way are gold, silver, platinum, palladium, copper and nickel. Other metals not traded on any formal exchange include chromium, manganese, vanadium and antimony. A market for these metals is made by international merchants and the prices of the transactions are reported by Reuters and trade journals such as the *London Metal Bulletin* and *Metals Week* published in the USA. The diamond and uranium markets are complicated by international cartel arrangements and marketing restrictions. The prices of metals which are formally traded are much influenced by speculators from outside the trade, but these markets are far more liquid than those of the non-formally traded metals and the markets can be used for hedging forward production. The non-formally traded markets are heavily influenced by the large international trading companies who often manipulate prices up and down for their own gain.

Most of the world's metals and minerals are, however, traded directly between producers and consumers. In the case of formally traded metals the contract price is usually made on a formula based on the moving price of the commodity exchange. Non-formally traded metals are sold to consumers either on a formula based on the price quoted by one of the trade journals or at fixed prices for 'spot lots' of the metal.

Marketing arrangements

Metal and mineral producers usually use the services of a sales agent in the consuming country to do the marketing work; only the largest producers can afford to have branch sales offices in the main consuming centres. In the present arrangement, gold is marketed centrally under government regulation although Swiss banks play a large part in market advice and research and in distribution. Diamonds are sold through the ubiquitous De Beers marketing system that even the Russians abide by. Uranium is sold by a cartel of producing companies but with heavy South African government participation and under the regulation of international uranium marketing systems. All other metals are marketed by the producing companies making heavy use of sales agents who are normally international merchants.

Marketing arrangements vary from producer to producer, from metal to metal, and from consuming territory to consuming territory. It is almost impossible, for instance, to sell directly to Japanese consumers without appointing a major Japanese trading house as sales agent, and although the major South African mining houses boast offices in many parts of the world, these companies often prefer to use merchants with local knowledge to sell products to the consumers.

There has been an interesting trend in the marketing structure for South African metals recently. For many years South African companies have used some of the largest merchant houses as sales agents, but recently some of these companies have ended these arrangements because of anti-South African pressure and new agents have had to be appointed. Several of these have emerged in Switzerland; often run by rather shady individuals, these are companies whose ownership is hidden by the secretive Swiss commercial law. South Africa is a long way from all its major metal markets. Historically, the mining companies have depended on branch offices, subsidiary companies and agents to market their metals; there are very few people with the necessary marketing skills to be found in the whole of South Africa.

Marketing control

When the Zimbabwe government decided to take control of the marketing of its metals it found that the job of replacing the network of marketing structures that had been set up by the mining companies was just too complicated. To this day 99% of all metals and minerals produced in Zimbabwe is sold through agents who are under the direct control of the producers, not the government.

This has led to a continuation of transfer pricing that is probably costing Zimbabwe about 20% of its entire mining revenue. Transfer pricing is a technique used by the mining companies to get money out of the country in which the metals are produced. This is done in several different ways, but the most common method is to sell metals from the country of origin to an agent, say in Switzerland, at a price which is substantially below the market price. The agent then sells the metal on to a consumer at the correct price and deposits most of the difference in the producer's foreign bank account.

If a future South African government wishes to avoid this problem a new marketing system will have to be set up. One positive result of centralising the marketing of South African products will be that the cost of running foreign branches of a South African metals marketing board will be justified by the huge volume of trade that the combined output of all South African mines would represent. Branches would need to be set up in all the main consuming areas of the world. This would not, however, solve the problem as branch sales offices would be useless if they could not be staffed with skilled salesmen who were above corruption. New agents who were not under the influence of the mining companies would have to be appointed, not only to sell the products, but to conduct market research and to train personnel employed by the metals marketing board.

Unfortunately, there are not many metal sales agency companies who have the skill to market metals and who are trustworthy. As I have said earlier, corruption is endemic in the mining world. Many buyers for even the most prestigious consuming companies in the world actively encourage suppliers to bribe them. A good few bargains are struck in bars and nightclubs. The temptation to gamble on these very volatile markets is very great. Metal dealers are some of the most highly paid individuals in the world. Great care will need to be taken by the metals marketing board when appointing agents and brokers, especially as the deposed mining companies and erstwhile agents will do their best to sabotage these efforts. A team of completely trustworthy inspectors will have to be appointed at an early stage to oversee this process.

International cooperation
Another important aspect of marketing, and one which could work to the advantage of a new government, would be cooperation with other producers and producing countries. The present South African system is extremely isolated from other Third World countries, preferring to believe the fiction that it is part of the industrialised white world. There is a great deal of scope for metal producers (of chromium and manganese particularly) to act together to improve the terms of trade for Third World countries. The Pretoria government has rightly believed that its backing from Western countries can be attributed partly to the fact that it has been a supplier of very cheap metals to the industrialised nations. It has so far been able to do this by keeping workers' wages and conditions at a low standard. Even in areas where South Africa dominates the world market such as platinum and gold, export prices have been kept low. A new administration would find many countries, especially in Africa, eager to discuss cooperation in the management of output to maximise mineral and metal export prices.

Platinum
In the case of platinum group metals, there are specific problems to be faced. Almost all of these metals are used either for jewellery or industrially in a semi-manufactured form. Much of this manufacturing work is done in industrialised countries by companies who have a long and close relationship with the South African producing companies. The work is so specialised that it would be very difficult to find alternative partners immediately. Ultimately it would be wise to consider transferring as much of this work as possible to South Africa, but this could take many years as the necessary skills do not exist there at the moment. Some type of deal will have to be struck with these manufacturing companies but, again, close inspection of their profit margins will have to be made as they will be in a powerful position to demand low prices for raw materials until alternative manufacturing facilities can be found.

Metals and Minerals Marketing Board of South Africa
The necessary elements in a marketing board are, firstly, the functional tasks such as transport and shipping control, maintenance of adequate stock where needed, liaison with mines and plants, financial control, technical service to customers, etc. The second category of necessary elements are of a more entrepreneurial nature, such as bargaining with customers, predicting markets and the tactics of competitors, appointing and liaising with sales agents, market research, making pricing policy and cooperation with other producers.

A new marketing board will probably find the functional elements relatively easy to create, but the entrepreneurial resources will be much harder to find. The people involved in these areas need skill, experience and the utmost probity. Such people do not exist in South Africa today, nor has any other African country managed to fill this gap. They have instead decided to rely heavily on agents and metal dealers to do this work. In my opinion it will become absolutely essential to have a trained nucleus of people familiar with international metal trading before a transition of ownership is executed. In the period leading up to independence in Zimbabwe the present political leaders of that country were far too occupied with the war to settle on a policy to control the mining industry: in consequence, they have had to put up with a state of affairs where the chief foreign currency earning industry is still almost completely controlled by self-interested and often hostile shareholders. The South African mining industry is an order of magnitude larger than that of Zimbabwe and is at the core of South Africa's economic future. A detailed policy on mines and a training programme for future managers of the industry should, in my opinion, be instigated at the earliest possible opportunity.

Investment

As I have said previously, a great deal of investment has been made in the mining industry, particularly in the five years prior to 1984 after which a combination of the recession, low metal prices and international disinvestment in South Africa reduced both the need and the ability to invest.

All mines have a finite life and the cost of developing new ones is very high. In addition, a certain amount of technology in existing mines and refineries has to be updated to compete in the world market and to make maximum use of low grade feedstock. Existing companies can raise capital by virtue of their stock in international markets.

If a state-owned mining industry has to be capitalised entirely through the government it should be possible to raise investment through consumers. For instance, a major consumer may be prepared to finance a new furnace or rolling mill in return for a long-term supply contract where the cost of the equipment was paid for in the product it produced. This method of finance is now extremely popular in China and South America. One negative aspect of these so called buy-back deals is the loss of control of the product as the buyer can sell it onto the market in competition with other material sold from the plant.

Vertical Integration and the Domestic Market

Separate attention should be paid to policy concerning vertical integration and supplies of mined products to the domestic market. We do not know as yet whether a new government would take the manufacturing end of the giant mining companies into public ownership. Assuming that it would not, the South African consumers of metals and minerals mined in the country nevertheless constitute an important outlet — not only as a proportion of sales, but also because they represent a major part of South African industrial activity. If they were provided with metals at below the international price, it would have the effect of boosting industrial activity; but it would also represent a transfer of revenue from the public to the private sector. If, on the other hand, they were asked to pay the international price for metal raw materials they might fail to compete with foreign imports.

On the assumption that a new government would wish to stimulate production of such items as pipes, steels, wire, alloys, inorganic chemicals, etc., one would assume that its metal supply policy towards these industries, whether or not they would remain in the private sector, would be dovetailed into its general industrial policy including such matters as import restrictions and tax.

Rob Davies would like to thank Sipho Dlamini, Jacques Depelchin, Judith Head, Bridget O'Laughlin, Albie Sachs and Gottfried Welmer for their comments on an earlier draft of the present chapter, and Stephen Gelb for helping correct a few errors in the Appendix. Final responsibility is, of course, mine.

12. Nationalisation, Socialisation and the Freedom Charter

ROB DAVIES

The Freedom Charter adopted by the Congress of the People on 26 June 1955 includes the following well-known and much discussed clause:

> The national wealth of our country, the heritage of all South Africans, shall be restored to the people: the mineral wealth beneath the soil, the banks and monopoly industry shall be transferred to the ownership of the people as a whole. ...

This extract from the Charter represents one of the most direct and controversial statements of economic policy by the national liberation movement. Formulated at a moment in the struggle when liberation was a distant goal, it represented a general statement of aspiration. It showed the movement's awareness that the achievement of national liberation would depend on the radical transformation of the capitalist economic system in a way which would undermine the stranglehold of the monopolies.

However, the Charter itself, understandably, did not attempt to identify the extent of monopolisation of the economy, nor to discuss the implications of transferring monopolies to public ownership. An analysis of the Charter made by the ANC National Executive Committee at the 1969 Morogoro conference identified certain of the monopolies which should be transferred to public ownership, stating:

> It is necessary for monopolies which vitally affect the social well being of our people such as the mines, the sugar and wine industry to be transferred to public ownership so that they can be used to uplift the life of the people.[1]

These, however, are clearly meant as examples and in no way constitute a final strategy for achieving the objectives defined in the Freedom Charter.

The aim of this chapter is to contribute certain tentative reflections to a debate on the contemporary significance of this section of the Freedom Charter in a post-apartheid society. As such it does no more than raise pertinent questions about a process of transferring the monopolies to the ownership of the people under current conditions. No attempt is made to discuss two related sections of the Charter: the clause stating, 'All other [non-monopoly] industries and trade shall be controlled to assist the well being of the people' and the section headed, 'The land shall be shared among those who work it'. Policies in both these areas will, of course, be of critical importance in a liberated South Africa. The non-monopoly sector, although small relative to the monopoly sector of the economy, is quite substantial in comparison with that in other African countries. As in other African countries, it can be expected to be an important site of potential class formation and struggle after apartheid restrictions are lifted. The question of how non-monopoly capital is to be controlled to make sure that it serves the interests of the people is thus of central importance. Likewise, the land question opens up a number of critical and thorny issues — how should the land be redivided; what will be the new forms of production to be created; what will the relative balance be at different phases between state farms, cooperatives, small and large-scale capitalist agriculture, and family production; how will a transfer of agricultural monopolies be effected? Important though these questions are, they cannot be discussed adequately in the present chapter, which will instead confine itself to the issue of transferring the monopolies to the people.

The chapter begins with a discussion of the extent of monopolisation of present day South African capitalism, highlighting developments in the period since the adoption of the Freedom Charter in 1955. It will deal with the various forms which nationalisation can take, emphasising the distinction between nationalisation as a change in the legal form of property and socialisation. It will argue that if nationalisation is to be part of a broader process of socialisation it needs to be accompanied by concrete changes in the organisation of labour processes and decision making at enterprise level, which permit the working masses themselves to gain control progressively over their means of production. Indeed, it will suggest that in some cases prior advances at this level may lay a firmer basis for later socialist transformation than premature defensive nationalisations. In this respect we will offer some brief reflection on the Mozambique experience. The chapter will conclude by pointing to the importance of developing policies which allow for a prioritising and sequencing of tactical objectives within an overall strategy aiming at achieving the objectives defined in the Freedom Charter.

1. THE DEVELOPMENT OF MONOPOLY CAPITALISM

As is generally known, South African capitalism has long been dominated by monopoly capital. The onset of deep-level gold mining in 1896 led to a very rapid process of centralisation and concentration of capital in the mining industry. Within twenty years, the industry was controlled by a small number of mining 'houses' or 'groups', with strong links to financial institutions. These were organised in the Chamber of Mines, which ran its own monopoly labour recruitment organisations as well as presenting a common 'industry point of view' in state structures. However, although the mining industry was characterised by monopoly capitalist relations of production from a very early period, other sectors were not. It was only in the post-Second World War period that monopoly capitalism began to penetrate the other sectors of the economy. A number of phases in the development of contemporary South African monopoly capitalism can be identified.[2]

The first phase, from 1945 until the post-Sharpeville crisis of 1960-63, saw the emergence of monopoly capitalism in secondary industry. This was part of a general global trend, which saw the 'multinationalisation' of certain capitals based in the metropoles of capitalist production. In South Africa, as in a number of other peripheral social formations, foreign industrial capital began establishing subsidiaries based on the transfer, in a certain form, of the technologies and the corresponding organisation of labour processes from the centres of advanced capitalist production. Subsidiaries or associates of foreign concerns became the dynamic force within the South African manufacturing sector, stimulating a process of concentration and centralisation of capital in the industrial sector. The Nationalist regime, although rhetorically committed to an anti-monopoly stance, eventually opted for a pragmatic approach, confining its interventions in practice to seeking favourable terms for 'Afrikaner capital' in the emerging dominant relations of monopoly capital. Throughout this phase, however, capitalist agriculture remained characterised by competitive capitalist relations of production.

The second phase corresponded to the post-Sharpeville 'boom' of 1963-73. This saw the consolidation of monopoly capitalist relations of production in manufacturing and the beginning of a continuing process of concentration and centralisation of capital in the agricultural sector. Between 1960 and 1980 the number of 'white farmers' fell from 106,000 to 70,000. By the 1980s it was estimated that 40% of white-owned farming land was held by just 5% of farmers.[3] The other feature of this phase was that it saw the start of a process of interpenetration between monopoly capitals. Mining monopolies, such as Anglo American, began investing in industry, finance, property and agriculture, establishing subsidiary holding companies to control interests in these sectors. Monopolies which developed initially in the industrial sector, such as Barlow Rand, acquired mining subsidiaries. Financial groups, including the Afrikaner banks and insurer groups — Volkskas and Sanlam — as well as established non-Afrikaner institutions such as SA Mutual, acquired substantial industrial, commercial, agricultural and other subsidiaries. Sanlam too acquired a mining subsidiary — Gencor — virtually handed over to it in 1963 by Anglo American in an attempt to 'encourage moderation' among important forces within the Afrikaner nationalist alliance. As a result of these developments, sectoral differences between capitals became less and less important. Moreover, non-Afrikaner monopolies, Afrikaner monopolies and foreign multinationals all began buying into one another, thus reducing the importance of the different 'national origins' of monopoly capitals. The monopoly conglomerate, with subsidiaries in many sectors and substantial investments in other conglomerates, emerged as the dominant force in South African capitalism.

The period from 1973 to the present constitutes the third phase, corresponding to the multiple organic crises of the apartheid system and state. With the exception of the 1979-81 temporary 'upswing' resulting from the sharp rise in the gold price, this phase has in general been one of low or negative growth. As is generally the case in periods of capitalist crisis, the current recession in South Africa has seen the elimination of a large number of small capitals and a corresponding further centralisation of control over capitalist production in the hands of the monopoly conglomerates. It has also seen a process of further centralisation within the conglomerates themselves. For example, in *The Struggle for South Africa*, written in early 1983 on the basis of data for 1981, eight private conglomerates — Anglo American, Sanlam, Barlow Rand, Volkskas, Rembrandt, SA Mutual, Anglovaal and SA Breweries — were identified as the controlling forces within South African capitalism, together with state corporations and a small number of foreign multinationals.[4] A number of medium sized conglomerates pursuing policies of aggressive acquisition were also mentioned, two of which — Liberty Life and the Kirsch group — were described as the most important. Since then one of the major conglomerates, SA Breweries, has ceased being an independent corporation and now falls under the control of Anglo American; SA Mutual has assumed effective control of Barlow Rand; the Kirsch Group has been swallowed up by Sanlam; and there has been a high level of interpenetration between the conglomerates and banks (in particular, SA Mutual/Nedbank, Rembrandt/Volkskas and, after the November 1986 sale by Barclays (UK) of its South African subsidiary, Anglo American/Barclays).[5] Liberty Life, on the other hand, has entered the 'big league', controlling assets valued at R13,535 million in 1985.[6]

This process of further centralisation of power in the hands of the monopoly conglomerates has been accelerated by withdrawals by foreign multinationals from direct investments — a reflection of the general loss of confidence by foreign capital. Within a few months of the removal of exchange controls in February 1983, three major foreign owned companies — Premier Milling, Rennies and Metal Box — were sold to Anglo American, SA Mutual and Barlow Rand respectively at a total cost of R604 million.[7] The first deal strengthened Anglo's stake in the food industry and also gave it effective control over SA Breweries. The second gave rise to the merger of Safmarine and Rennies, giving SA Mutual effective control over the vast bulk of all shipping and forwarding operations in southern Africa. The third reinforced Barlow's already substantial stake in the packaging business. By the beginning of October 1986 an estimated 73 companies from the United States alone had quit South Africa, many of them selling out to South African monopolies. Since then, partly in response to the passage of the 'Comprehensive Anti-Apartheid Act' by the US Congress despite President Reagan's veto, the pace of withdrawals from direct investments has increased. While some of the most recent disinvestments — for example, those by General Motors and IBM in October — have involved sales to consortia formed by local management, others have involved yet more sales to local monopolies. The latter include the deal leading to the incorporation of Ford's South African operation into the Anglo-controlled Sigma Corporation, and the purchase in November 1986 by Anglo American of the South African subsidiary of Barclays Bank — the largest banking operation in the country.[8] Such deals have of course not only expanded the asset base of the domestic monopoly conglomerates, but also altered the relative weight of local monopoly and foreign capital in favour of the former.

2. CURRENT INDICES OF THE MONOPOLISATION OF SOUTH AFRICAN CAPITALISM

Several calculations of the extent of monopoly control have been made. Nearly ten years ago, the *Report of the Commission of Enquiry into the Regulation of Monopolistic Conditions Act of 1955* concluded that there was 'an exceptionally high degree of concentration of economic power in the major divisions of the South African economy'.[9] A study undertaken by the Commission calculated that in 1972 10% of firms in the manufacturing, construction, wholesale, retail and transport sectors controlled 75% or more of the market, whilst 25% of the firms controlled approximately 90%.[10]

Another way of examining the extent of the economic power of the major monopolies is to consider the assets they control. The Appendix represents an attempt to update the analysis made in *The Struggle for South Africa*. It shows the assets in 1985 of the mining, industrial, construction, trade, transport and finance companies listed in the *Financial Mail*'s 'Top 100' and 'Giants' League', controlled by the major conglomerates. Comparing the 1985 table with that for 1981, a number of important changes are evident.

Firstly, the total value of the assets of the top 130 or so companies has more than doubled from R157 billion to R371 billion. This represents an annual average rate of increase of 23.98%. This is in excess of both the annual average rate of inflation, which varied between 10.97% and 18.45% in the period since 1981, and the annual average rate of depreciation of the value of currency against the US on the foreign exchanges, which works out at 20.15% in the period until just before Botha's August 1985 'Rubicon speech'.[11] It is thus a reflection of the fact that the recession has been a period of further centralisation of capital in the hands of the big corporations.

Secondly, the proportion of the total assets held by state corporations has declined slightly from 26.61% in 1981 to 24.59% in 1985. This is largely due to the selling off of Safmarine to SA Mutual in 1983. Nevertheless, it is extremely relevant in any discussion of nationalisation and socialisation to remember that nearly one quarter of the total assets of the top companies are in the hands of the state corporations. These not only control central banking, communications, and the bulk of the transport sector, but also key strategic production sectors, notably iron and steel, energy (electricity and synthetic fuel from coal) and armaments production. In addition, through the Land Bank and the Industrial Development Corporation (IDC), the state has a substantial effective stake in capitalist agriculture and the non-monopoly industrial and service sectors. Moreover, the rate of accumulation of some of these corporations has been extremely rapid. The assets of Sasol, for example, have increased from R1,232.5 million in 1981 to R5,120.8 million in 1985 as a result of the substantial investments (partly privately financed) in the Sasol II and III projects.

A third important change since 1981 has been in the composition of the 'top non-state group'. This has changed as the result of the swallowing up of two formerly independent groups (SA Breweries and Barlow Rand), the inter-penetration of two groups with banks (SA Mutual/Nedbank and Rembrandt/Volkskas), and the entry of one newcomer (Liberty Life). Instead of consisting of eight corporations, it now consists of six.

Finally, there has been a significant increase in the percentage of the total assets of the top 137 companies controlled by the leading conglomerates. Thus, in 1981 the top 8 controlled 61.66% of the total assets of non-state corporations. In 1985 the top 6 controlled 71.26%. If we compare the position of the top three (Anglo, Sanlam and SA Mutual/Barlow Rand) with that of the same companies in 1981, we find that their share has gone up from 50.68% to 57.78%. Most dramatic has been the increase in the Sanlam group's share from 16.82% to 18.62% and the SA Mutual/Barlow Rand/Nedbank group's from 10.29% to 18.06%. These figures reflect a process of extremely rapid centralisation of capital which has occurred over a short (four-year) period.

A similar conclusion about the extent of monopoly control has been reached by Robin McGregor through a study of the percentage of the total Johannesburg Stock Exchange (JSE) shares controlled by the different groups. McGregor estimated that 80.2% of JSE shares are controlled by four groups, while 90.5%

are controlled by ten identifiable groups. The top four are Anglo American, Sanlam, SA Mutual and Rembrandt, of whom Anglo alone controls 54.1%.[12]

The above figures are all of course indices of the centralisation of capital in South Africa. There is no equivalent aggregate data to show the precise extent to which the process of rapid centralisation has been accompanied by a concentration of capital. However, recent studies of particular industrial sectors have documented how the transition to monopoly capitalism in the late 1960s and 1970s led to profound reorganisations of production into larger production units based on more mechanised labour processes.[13] A similar trend has also been evident in the mining industry since the mid-1970s, and current plans envisage both the combination of existing mines into 'mega-mines' and the further mechanisation of a number of production processes.[14]

However one looks at it, it is clear that South African capitalism is today characterised by the domination of a few conglomerates over all sectors of production, distribution and exchange. At the time of the Congress of the People, monopoly capital controlled the mining industry and banking and was beginning to penetrate manufacturing. Today the monopolies dominate all significant sectors of the economy — mining, manufacturing, agriculture, banking, wholesale and retail trade and even service sectors like hotels, entertainment and tourism. The conglomerates control vast empires with hundreds of subsidiary and associated companies penetrating into all spheres of the economy. There is no significant production, distribution, exchange or service sector in which these do not control the vast bulk of 'economic activity'. This has important implications for any discussion of the contemporary significance of the Freedom Charter. It means that under today's conditions the objective of transferring the monopolies to the ownership of the people can mean nothing less than establishing popular control over the major part of every sector of the entire economy.

3. NATIONALISATION AND SOCIALISATION

Transferring ownership of the monopolies to the people is sometimes regarded as equivalent to a call for some form of nationalisation. However, nationalisation is of itself only a change in the legal form of property. More precisely it is a transfer of legal property rights to a state. As such it may take a variety of forms, occur under different forms of state, and in the context of several possible patterns of social relations of production.

In common parlance, the term 'nationalisation' has been used to describe such diverse situations as that where a state:

(1) takes a minority shareholding in an enterprise (usually termed partial nationalisation);

(2) takes a majority shareholding, but leaves managerial control in the hands of the private minority shareholder(s);

(3) takes over, with or without compensation, 100% ownership of an enterprise but enters into a management contract handing over management to private capital;

(4) takes over the management of an enterprise which continues to have a minority or majority private shareholding;

(5) takes over, with or without compensation, both 100% ownership and management of an enterprise.

Any of the above may or may not represent an attempt to subordinate the actions of enterprises to some form of state plan.

Nationalisation, in any of the above forms, may take place under very different state forms. In advanced capitalist social formations, nationalisations of ailing and unprofitable industries and sectors, which are nonetheless socially necessary (from the standpoint of national capital accumulation), have been undertaken by openly bourgeois as well as social democratic regimes. In peripheral social formations, regimes dominated even by comprador bourgeois elements have nationalised certain enterprises and created parastatals to provide an opening for capital accumulation by domestic class forces. In apartheid South Afica, we have already noted that a substantial state sector, embracing strategic areas of production as well as central banking, transport and communications, already exists — created by successive racist minority regimes.

There has been some debate about whether the Freedom Charter 'really' represents the interests of the working class. Taking up this point, Raymond Suttner and Jeremy Cronin have written:

> This doubt sometimes arises from a confusion between working class demands that are also in the interests of other classes, and demands which are primarily beneficial to workers ... while the Charter is not a programme of the working class alone, it nevertheless primarily reflects its interests. Some of the clauses in the Charter are socialist in orientation and are addressed much more profoundly to working class interests than would be the case with any bourgeois document.[15]

Billy Nair makes a similar point, saying:

> Right the way through [the Charter] you will see workers' interests represented, but not in isolation from other popular classes. Take for instance: 'The people shall share in the country's wealth'. That is fundamentally a working class demand but the emphasis on the *people* is still relevant in that it shows the broad unity of all classes.[16]

In short, the Charter is a document formulated in the process of struggle, articulating the demands and aspirations of an alliance of class forces, in which the working class has a leading role. As such, although it is true that 'the economic clauses in the Freedom Charter are not specifically socialist',[17] the demand to transfer the ownership of the monopolies to the people clearly envisages more than a transfer of legal property rights to a state seeking no more than the creation of opportunities for capital accumulation by some new exploiting class. Put another way, the Congress of the People was not calling merely for the creation of new Iscors, Escoms and Sasols. The Freedom Charter is quite specific on this. It calls for much more than an extension of state ownership. It calls for a transfer of ownership of the monopolies *to the people*.

For a transfer of the monopolies to popular control to be complete it is necessary for the people to assume both the *powers of economic ownership* and the *powers of possession* in sectors currently under monopoly control. The former refers to the powers to assign the means of production to this or that use, to dispose of the objects of labour and to control the social process of accumulation. The powers of possession refer to the ability to put the means of production into operation — the powers related to the organisation and direction of labour processes.[18] A *necessary* condition for achieving a transfer of the ownership and control of the monopolies to the people is clearly the establishment of a form of state in which 'the people shall govern' and the working class assumes 'the leading role' within a broad alliance of oppressed class forces. However, nationalisation —

as a legal transfer of property — is not, even under such a state form, a *sufficient* condition for a transfer to the people of the powers of either economic ownership or possession.

Writers from Lenin onwards[19] have made a clear distinction between national-isation and socialisation. In particular, socialisation can in no sense be reduced to nationalisation. While nationalisation is a change in legal property relations, socialisation is a much broader process of collective reappropriation by producers of control over the means of production. Nationalisation by a people's state is a necessary element in a process of socialisation, but only in conjunction with other transformations. More specifically, if nationalisation is to contribute to a process of socialisation it needs to be accompanied, first, by the introduction of a process of planning in which social need rather than profit increasingly becomes the criterion in decisions about the allocation of resources; and, second, by transformations in the organisation of management and labour processes which permit direct producers to assume increasing control over decisions at enterprise level, currently the preserve of capital. The dialectical relationship between the centralising tendency of the macro-economic planning process and the decentralising tendency of greater workers' control at enterprise level is one of the most important issues in any experience of attempted socialist transition.

The *sine qua non* for any process of socialist transition in South Africa is clearly the creation of a people's state, in which the working class assumes the hegemonic role. Although there are many battles still to be fought — and the national liberation movement is quite correct in giving priority to organising and mobilising for these — it is becoming increasingly apparent, and indeed this is the *raison d'être* of the present study, that the end of racist minority rule is in sight. As ANC president O. R. Tambo put it in his 1986 New Year message, the developing mass struggles have reached the point where 'the Botha regime has lost the strategic initiative'.[20] This is reflected in its inability — either through restructuring ('reform') or repression — to produce any long-term solution to the deepening crisis.

The creation of some form of popular state in South Africa in the foreseeable future is thus becoming a real possibility. However, the limits and possibilities, as well as appropriate strategy, for a struggle for socialism will depend to a large extent on the precise balance of class forces under which such a state was established as well as on the outcome of class struggles taking place after liberation. Both the balance between formerly oppressed/exploited and former oppressors/exploiters and that between the different class forces among the formerly oppressed/exploited will obviously be relevant. These by definition are currently unknown elements — to be determined in future struggles — and no attempt will be made here to speculate about their possible or likely outcome.

Nevertheless, it is clear that monopoly capital is preparing to do battle on the terrain of a post-apartheid — or at least post-National Party ruled — South Africa. Ideally, it would like to force through some kind of federalist or consociational system, which would permit the emergence of a 'black government', but severely constrain its capacity to transform the basic structures of capitalist power or mechanisms of capitalist exploitation. As a fall back, it would probably be prepared to settle eventually for a deal which offered guarantees protecting certain legal property rights for big capital but probably not precluding nationalisation altogether. In this respect it is notable that leading figures associated with the monopolies have 'accept[ed] ... a measure of state planning and intervention ... to compensate for the errors of omission of the apartheid era'.[21]

The rest of this chapter will argue that whatever concessions may or may not have to be made to monopoly capital in the course of struggle — and even if in the end no concessions at all have to be made — the struggle to achieve the objectives of the Freedom Charter in so far as the transfer of control of the monopolies is concerned can only be seriously conceived of as a protracted *process*. It is one which necessarily will pass through various phases and stages. Moreover, while nationalisation by a people's state will in South Africa as elsewhere be an essential element of a process of socialisation, it is necessary, in my view, to break from the kind of mechanistic conception which sees nationalisation as a process which has to be completed before the struggle for other transformations can begin. Significant advances towards socialist planning and workers' control at enterprise level may be made before the achievement of full nationalisation and, indeed, may lay a firmer basis for nationalisation as part of a process of socialisation than premature offensive or defensive nationalisations by a state lacking sufficient cadres to take over the running of enterprises.

Under the concrete conditions of South Africa, the struggle to place the monopolies under popular control will, in my view, have to be seen from the outset as a war of position involving action on a number of fronts. It will have to base itself in the first instance on consolidation in the two areas where the forces of the people are likely to be relatively strong — in the apparatuses of the central state, and in shop floor organisation at enterprise level. Coordinated and mutually reinforcing action at both levels will be necessary if an advance towards socialism is to be achieved under the likely concrete conditions of a post-apartheid society. A one-sided reliance on action at the level of apparatuses of the central state may result in the predominance of statist, bureaucratic and ultimately undemocratic practices. A one-sided reliance on shop floor power will tend to spawn workerist practices, unable to distinguish between the short-term interests of particular groups of workers and the longer-term interests of the working class as a whole.

4. SOME REFLECTIONS ON THE MOZAMBICAN EXPERIENCE

Some aspects of Mozambique's experience of attempted socialist transition would seem to be relevant to a discussion of the relationship between nationalisation and socialisation, as well as the possible role of shop floor organisation. However, this is decidedly not to hold up the Mozambican case as either a positive or negative 'model'. The Mozambican experience has its own specificities — its own concrete conditions determining the limits and possibilities of a process of transformation, and its own history and traditions of struggle — all of which are very different from those in South Africa. Nevertheless, it offers some points for reflection in a discussion of a possible process of transition in South Africa.

Mozambique's attempted socialist transition took place in a society which had been characterised, under colonialism, by extreme coercive and backward forms of labour exploitation. At independence Frelimo inherited an economy displaying all the classic features of chronic underdevelopment. Agriculture was the most important activity, and the overwhelming majority of agricultural producers were peasants who relied on hand tools. Industrial development was mainly centred on import substitution of luxury goods for the urban settler markets, and production for export was principally of agricultural produce, cotton, sugar, tea and cashew. Urban development was restricted to the nine provincial capitals, of which Maputo (Lourenco Marques) was far and away the largest. Transport networks served neighbouring states, and Mozambique possessed no direct road/rail link between the north and south of the country.

Labour exploitation after 1930, when colonial rule was consolidated under the facist regime of Antonio Salazar, took three main forms. The south of the country was essentially a labour reserve for South African mining capital. From the beginnings of gold mining on the Rand, Mozambican workers have been an important component of the labour force with upwards of 100,000 men a year working on the mines in the peak years of labour recruitment. Settler capitalist agriculture in this area was characterised by its technical backwardness and its dependence on a labour force paid even lower wages than those on the mines. Unable to compete with the mines, settler agriculture relied on forced labour.

The central part of Mozambique, barred since 1913 to labour recruiters for the mines, was dominated by a number of capitalist plantations — producing sugar along the Zambezi river, copra along the coast around Quelimane, and sisal and tea inland and on the Malawi border. These plantations also relied on migrant labour, but labour drawn from the colony itself on six-month contracts. This too was 'mobilised' by a number of coercive mechanisms.

In the northern parts of the colony, peasant cultivation of cotton emerged as the dominant economic activity. Large concessions of land were granted to individual settlers and companies who were permitted to organise peasant producers within them to grow cotton. Investment was limited to the provision of seed, the establishment of a few rudimentary shelters which served as markets, wages of overseers and a ginning factory. Prices were set by the colonial state's cotton board in consultation with the concessionaires. Profits depended on the production of as much cotton by as many producers as possible, and hence on the exploitation of the labour of the peasant family.

The system of exploitation was maintained and reproduced by the colonial state through a series of repressive labour and tax laws. These limited physical and social mobility, and denied the colonised any civil or political rights. Workers could be punished for a whole series of infringements of the law which included their behaviour in the workplace. It was illegal to break the contract, to refuse to obey orders, to work slowly, etc. Punishment ranged from extension of the contract period to unpaid labour services for the colonial state. Physical punishment was also common, and workers who were in any way vocal went in fear of their lives.

All these factors militated against labour organisation. Although there is evidence that workers — particularly those in the ports and railways — participated in various forms of industrial action, this did not reach the state of union organisation. The only unions which existed before independence were the tame *sindicatos* promoted by the fascist state. Until the 1960s, these were open only to whites, and after the 1960s only to whites and 'assimilated' blacks.

After it came to power in 1975, as a deliberate policy measure Frelimo nationalised only the health service, legal practices, education, funeral services and rented property. Later, during the war with the Rhodesian Smith regime, the oil refinery and fuel distribution were taken over. Apart from these areas no deliberate decision was taken to nationalise productive enterprises. Nevertheless, by 1982 only 27% of 'industry' (including construction and service activities) remained in private ownership — the rest being either state owned, 'intervened' (state managed) or mixed state/private.[22] No equivalent figures for agriculture are available, but it is clear that the major part of the former settler owned farms as well as plantations had become state farms. The process under which the state in Mozambique came to control the vast bulk of productive enterprises as well as the banking sector, retail outlets and the service sector was essentially one of *defensive* nationalisation. The abandonment of property by former settler capitalist owners, frequently after prolonged processes of asset stripping and even physical sabotage, forced the state to intervene and take over the management of enterprises. Later these were in a number of cases restructured and incorporated into state companies. Likewise, the banking system was taken over and restructured following the virtual collapse of the sector in the wake of the nationalisation of rented property. While the process was at one point seen as positive in the sense of creating a base for socialism, it was in fact extremely disruptive to production, overstretched the existing cadre, and made it difficult to introduce a planning process prioritising and hierarchising specific tactical measures within an overall strategy. State intervention became a reactive response to emergencies created by the actions of fleeing settler capitalists. State appointed managers, frequently with no previous experience of the sector to which they were assigned, could often do little more than engage themselves in a day to day *ad hoc* struggle to restore production under existing conditions.

Perhaps understandably in this context, the rapid creation of a state sector gave rise to an initial triumphalism. A number of costly and voluntaristic attempts were made to 'leap forward' into mechanised large-scale production based on the notion that the priority for an advance to socialism was a quantitative expansion of the state sector rather than a qualitative transformation of relations of production within it. The particular example here was the case of the Limpopo Agro-Industrial Complex (CAIL). Vast sums of money — 50% of the agricultural sector's capital budget and 30% of the capital budget of the entire country in 1977 — was poured into this project with little attention to the cost effectiveness of the investments being made.[23] The CAIL experiment was eventually abandoned in 1983 with huge losses and vast quantities of useless idle equipment. The complex was divided into a number of smaller more manageable units, some of which have been handed over to cooperatives, family agriculture and even to small private capitalist farmers and foreign multinationals.

Under these circumstances, which were probably largely unavoidable in view of the specific conditions of labour coercion on which capital accumulation in colonial Mozambique had depended, the fact that the production decline was arrested in 1977 and that production increased by 12% in real terms between 1977 and 1981 were remarkable achievements. Nonetheless, the fact remained that the state was technically unable to effectively manage and control all the nationalised enterprises, while the working class was far from having assumed collective control over the means of production. In short, from the perspective of socialist transition, the process of nationalisation — the change in the legal form of property — had in the case of Mozambique far outstripped that of socialisation and indeed had reached the point where it was impeding the processes of establishing an effective planning process and transforming production relations in enterprises.

However, while the above represents a sketch of the general situation, there were within the broad Mozambican experience a number of cases where a different pattern of transformation was evident. An example here is the case of the TEXLOM textile factory in Maputo, studied by the Centre of African Studies in 1980[24] — before the onset of the current crisis. What was notable about TEXLOM was that it became a nationalised enterprise (technically intervened) not through the usual process of abandonment by previous owners and an intervention from the top, but as a direct result of workers' struggles on the shop floor — struggles which directly challenged management's prerogative on key issues affecting the control of the enterprise. Moreover, this was done on the basis of a relatively high degree, by prevailing Mozambican standards, of shop floor mobilisation.

The TEXLOM company was established in 1966 by a consortium of Portuguese and settler capitalist interests. The factory was completed and began producing in 1973. It was the second largest textile plant in Mozambique and one of the most modern factories in the country. When independence came, the initial investment had not been paid off and the capitalist owners stood therefore to make a significant loss if they abandoned it.

Prior to the Portuguese coup of 25 April 1974, there was little by way of labour organisation or workers' action. With the coup, however, workers began to organise and put demands to the firm's management. A workers' committee was formed in June 1974, which demanded an end to racial discrimination in the factory; a revision in the wage scale; and the desegregation of facilities — the canteen and company buses — restricted to Portuguese workers and *assimilados*. When this was refused a strike broke out in July 1974. Management's response was to call in the police, who in the new conditions refused to break the strike and instead persuaded management to make concessions. The workers returned home that night in the previously segregated buses, having won a clear victory. Thereafter management was compelled to recognise the workers' committee as a force. It was consulted on a number of key issues and negotiated several wage increases and other benefits. This situation continued for some time after independence, until in 1976 another conflict erupted. Management, responding to the exodus of Portuguese foremen and technicians, attempted to reinforce its position by promoting to supervisory positions a number of its lackeys. This move was opposed by the workers who considered the new appointees unqualified and the promotions themselves a manoeuvre to consolidate management control. The workers refused to accept the new appointees or to take orders from them. Deadlock ensued and when the state structures refused to back the position of management, the senior managers resigned and TEXLOM became a state intervened (effectively nationalised) enterprise.

The point about the TEXLOM example is that the firm became nationalised as a result of workers' struggles which challenged the prerogative of bourgeois management on key questions, and not through action from above. When the Centre of African Studies visited TEXLOM in 1980, it was evident that the experience of workers' shop floor organisation and struggle in the factory had created a much more secure base for state management than in many other intervened enterprises. Workers had already begun to participate in the administrative decision-making process, previously the exclusive preserve of bourgeois management. The production council, elected by the workers, was represented on the management council and made a significant input to management decisions. Regular shop floor meetings were held to discuss a variety of problems and by 1980 there was also some rudimentary but real involvement of the workers in preparing plans for the enterprise — a practice which has unfortunately not continued. Since 1980, there have been changes and TEXLOM has been affected by the crisis brought on by destabilisation and the bandit war. Nevertheless, at a particular moment and in the context of specific concrete historical situations, it represents in my view a relevant experience with potential lessons.

5. CONCLUSIONS

Returning to the South African case, it is clear that the level of shop floor power of the working class is much greater than it was in Mozambique. Over a million workers are organised in unions, which have a history of militant struggle and an established presence in the industrial, mining, distribution and service sectors. Already questions of workers' control have been raised in the course of concrete struggles. For example, the current struggle against redundancies has seen unions demanding information about company plans and challenging management projections and plans. Moreover, the South African working class has developed a tradition of democratic collective organisation not only in unions, but also in community and political organisations as well as, more recently, in the embryonic structures of popular power that are being created in residential areas.[25] These are obviously points of strength in the broad liberation movement which will have to be built on and developed in a struggle for socialism in a liberated South Africa.

On taking power a people's government in South Africa will, of course, inherit the existing, already substantial, state sector. At the same time, it will undoubtedly be obliged to make a number of immediate interventions in the existing 'private sector'. For example, it will be necessary, even as a defensive measure, to establish effective state control over the banking system at an early stage. There is already a substantial and increasing outflow of capital from the country. For some years all the major monopolies have been making large investments abroad.[26] If and when a process of socialist transition begins, we can expect a rapid acceleration in the rate of capital outflow if adequate controls are not imposed immediately. In addition, state intervention will, of course, be necessary from the outset in the struggle to realise the objectives in relation to employment, housing and social services defined in the Freedom Charter. To take another example, we can expect a rapid increase in the rate of urbanisation after liberation. Yet the trend in capitalist production is towards increasingly mechanised production with a corresponding expulsion of labour from production. In such circumstances, 'market forces' are not going to provide employment for the growing urban population. The establishment of new productive state enterprises producing goods to satisfy the needs of the people as well as providing employment will have to be an urgent priority.

It will also be necessary at an early stage both to submit the existing 'private sector' to a measure of supervision and control, and to create conditions for a transfer of the monopolies to popular control. In this respect, the current structure of monopoly control might ironically in the end be turned to advantage. It has created a small number of control centres over the vast bulk of capitalist production. In principle, gaining control (through partial or full nationalisation, or even through the introduction of regulations) of the parent boards of Anglo American, Sanlam, SA Mutual, Rembrandt/Volkskas, Liberty Life and Anglovaal should provide the basis for a substantial measure of real control over the major 'macro' decisions affecting the vast bulk of capitalist production without it being immediately necessary to take over the management of each of the hundreds of component enterprises.

None of these or any other of the likely immediate priorities of a transformation process would, however, necessarily be enhanced if the available cadre were absorbed in taking over the day to day management of the large number of existing enterprises as a result of a process of premature nationalisation — either forced or willed by a conception that socialism depends on an immediate far reaching change in the property relations. It is precisely here that the question of shop floor workers' organisation will be of crucial importance. Workers organised at the point of production will be an indispensable element of a process of controlling the actions of the existing bourgeois managements, elements of which will have to remain at their posts for some time if severe disruptions of production are to be avoided. At a certain point, as the TEXLOM example suggests, the defensive struggle of workers to control or resist manoeuvres by bourgeois managements is likely to pass over into a struggle in which their continued control over the enterprise is called into question. This is one possible route through which part of the *process* of transferring the ownership of the monopolies to the people might be accomplished.

At all events, what will be necessary will be the sequencing of tactical measures within an overall strategy. All will not be possible on 'one glorious day'. Priorities will have to be selected within the range of possible actions. Above all state action and the actions of workers organised at the point of production will have to be mutually complementary and reinforcing. Only in this way will it be possible to realise the objective of transferring control of the monopolies to the people.

APPENDIX

Centralisation of Capital as Reflected in
Financial Mail's 'Top 100' and 'Giants' League' 1985

Group	Group's Assets	% Total Assets Top 137 Cos	% Total Assets No. State Cos
1. State Corporations			
Escom	31,252		
SATS	17,262		
SA Res Bank	13,500		
Landbank	7,939		
Post Office	6,825		
Sasol	5,120.8		
Iscor	4,486		
I.D.C.	2,882		
Armscor	1,635		
Uscor	253.2		
Subtotal	91,155	24.59	
2. Anglo American			
Anglo	14,546		
De Beers	9,823		
Amgold	5,325		
AMIC	4,516.8		
Southern Life	4,437		
SA Breweries	3,594.6		
Vaal Reefs	2,855		
JOI	2,783		
Premier	1,902.7		
AEOI	1,800		
Tongaat	1,634.7		
Dries	1,589		
Hiveld	884.6		
OK Bazaars	670.1		
LTA	390.3		
Edgars	371.5		
Argus	370.5		
Suthsun	304.5		
Amrel	272.8		
Afcol	233.2		
McCarthy	216		
ONA Gallo	149.8		
Ovenstone	145.1		
Cullinan	136.7		
Subtotal	58,951.9	15.91	21.1

3. Sanlam

Bankorp	13,612		
Gencor	10,473		
Sanlam	7,785		
Trustbank	7,277		
Sappi	1,981.7		
Saambou	1,723		
Sentrachem	1,393.8		
Fedvolks	1,380.8		
Kirsch	1,029.1		
M & R	870.3		
Messina	486.5		
Haggie	481.5		
Tedelex	479.2		
Protea	442.3		
Malbak	441.3		
D & H	438.9		
Fedfood	400.4		
Kanhym	371.5		
Kohler	251.7		
Ellerine	213		
Trek	192.4		
Group 5	171.3		
Abercom	169.5		
Subtotal	52,065.2	14.05	18.63

4. SA Mutual/Barlow Rand/Nedbank

Nedbank	14,561		
Old Mutual	13,501		
Barlows	9,607.7		
OGS Food	2,494.6		
Safren	1,987.4		
Rand Mines	1,450		
Tiger Oats	1,438.2		
Nampak	1,128.2		
Plate Glass	782		
PPO	649.3		
Reunert	573		
Metal Box	548.9		
ICS	514.9		
Wooltru	329.8		
Romatex	316.4		
Rob	233.5		
Frasers	188.6		
Plevans	163.4		
Subtotal	50,467.9	13.62	18.06

5. Rembrandt/Volskas			
Volkskas	11,402		
Remgro	3,114.3		
Lifegro	1,857		
Metkor	1,409.6		
Dorbyl	1,041		
Bonuskor	165		
Subtotal	18,988.9	5.12	6.79
6. Liberty Life			
Liberty Holdings	6,867		
Liberty	6,668		
Subtotal	13,535	3.65	4.84
7. Anglovaal			
Anglovaal	2,170		
AVI	1,195.5		
Anglo Alpha	1,093.9		
Consol	272.7		
Grinaker	235.9		
I & J	190.3		
Subtotal	5,158.3	1.39	1.85
Subtotal Top 6			
Private Conglomerates	199,167.2	53.73	71.26
8. British Multinationals (listed companies only)			
Barclays*	22,944		
Stanbic	19,310		
Goldfields	4,098		
Afrox	423.7		
Dunlop	177.6		
Lonsugar	162.7		
Subtotal	47,116	12.71	16.86
9. Building Societies			
(5 companies)	19,306	5.21	6.91
10. Others			
(37 companies)	13,906	3.75	4.98
GRAND TOTAL	370,650.2		

Source: Financial Mail Survey of Top Companies, 23 May 1986.
Note: The caveats in Notes A and B on p.64 of Davies, O'Meara and Dlamini, *The Struggle for South Africa* apply equally here.
* The table refers to ownership pattern in mid-1985. There have been a number of changes since then, the most important being the acquisition of Barclays by Anglo in November 1986. If this had been included, Anglo's share of the total assets of non-state companies would have risen to 29.30% and that of the top six to 79.47%.

NOTES

1. 'An analysis of the Freedom Charter adopted at the Consultative Conference of the ANC, Morogoro, Tanzania, April 25–May 1, 1969', reprinted in *ANC Speaks: Documents and Statements of the African National Congress, 1955-1976* (1977).

2. This section is based on the analysis developed in R. Davies, D. O'Meara and S. Dlamini, *The Struggle for South Africa: A Reference Guide to Movements, Organisations and Institutions* (Zed Books, London, 1984), Chapter 2.

3. *Ibid.*, p.118.

4. *Ibid.*, pp.58-61.

5. Robin McGregor, *McGregor's Who Owns Whom* (McGregor, Purdey Publishing, 1985) has been used as the basis for determining ownership patterns.

6. See *Financial Mail Special Survey: Top Companies*, 23 May 1986, p.150.

7. This was analysed in a Centre of African Studies dossier (23.40), 'Background on recent disinvestments by foreign capital from South Africa', Maputo, 25 July 1983.

8. See 'An analysis of recent disinvestments from South Africa by multinational corporations', Centre of African Studies dossier (33.80), Maputo, December 1986. There the point is made that despite these disinvestments, transfer of technology from the former foreign parent company in many cases continues.

9. Quoted in Davies, O'Meara and Dlamini, *The Struggle*, p.57.

10. *Ibid.*, p.58.

11. On the average annual rates of inflation see *The Citizen*, 21 Jan. 1984 and 22 Jan. 1986. The calculation of the rate of depreciation in the value of the rand was based on the rate for 25 December 1981 given in the *Financial Mail* (R1–$1.033) and that just before the 'Rubicon speech' given in *Business Day*, 16 Feb. 1986 (R1–$0.48). The rate before the speech was used as many of the asset figures in the *Financial Mail* Survey refer to mid year.

12. Quoted in *Weekly Mail*, 13 March 1986.

13. See, for example, Eddie Webster, *Cast in a Racial Mould: Labour Process and Trade Unionism in the Foundries* (Ravan Press, Johannesburg, 1985).

14. See *Financial Mail*, 17 Jan. 1986, 31 Jan. 1986; and Centro de Estudos Africanos, 'Changing labour demand trends in the South African mines with particular reference to Mozambique', mimeo, 1986.

15. Raymond Suttner and Jeremy Cronin, *30 Years of the Freedom Charter* (Ravan Press, Johannesburg, 1986), p.143.

16. *Ibid.*, pp.145-146.

17. *Ibid.*, p.129.

18. On this see Charles Bettlehelm, *Economic Calculation and Forms of Property* (Routledge and Kegan Paul, London, 1976), p.69.

19. See V.I. Lenin, ' "Left-wing" childishness and the petty-bourgeois mentality', May 1918, Part III.

20. 'Message of the National Executive Committee of the ANC on January 8th 1986, delivered by President Tambo', mimeo.

21. See article by Gavin Relly in the *Sunday Times*, 1 June 1986.

22. See *Economist* Intelligence Unit, *Country Profile: Mozambique 1986-7*, p.8.

23. See Kenneth Hermele, 'Contemporary land struggles on the Limpopo: a case study of Chokwe, Mozambique 1950-1985', Uppsala, Akut paper No. 34, 1986.

24. Centro de Estudos Africanos, *Capacidade Produtiva e Planific-acao na TEXLOM* (Maputo, 1980).

25. On this see Tony Karon and Max Ozinsky, 'The working class in the national democratic struggle', *Work in Progress*, No. 42, May 1986.

26. See David Kaplan, 'The internationalisation of South African capital: South African direct foreign investment in the contemporary period', *African Affairs*, Vol. 82, No. 329, October 1983.

13. The Politics of International Economic Relations: South Africa and the International Monetary Fund, 1975 and Beyond

VISHNU PADAYACHEE

Revolutionary movements caught up in the struggle for state power have invariably attached low priority to issues of economic transformation. Even when economic transformation is discussed, both in the pre- and post-revolutionary phases, such discussion is usually dominated by questions of material production, of raising output and the distribution/redistribution of that output. The sphere of production overshadows the sphere of finance — i.e. the money, banking, capital flow and price system — at both the national and international levels.

This chapter examines the limits and constraints on a post-revolutionary government's economic and political transformation process that arise out of its international economic relations — in particular its relationship with the International Monetary Fund (IMF). The post-apartheid South African state will act as the 'model' for this analysis.

In order to consider this question we need to: (1) say why, in South Africa's case, it is important to be aware of the implications for transformation of our international economic linkages; (2) locate the role and ideological predilection of the IMF within this international system; (3) examine the nature of the relationship between the apartheid state and the IMF in the last decade or so; (4) assess the basis of South Africa's role in the world capitalist economy and hence its special relationship with the IMF and (5) speculate on the nature of this relationship and examine the consequences thereof for the post-apartheid state. This will involve, amongst other things, an analysis of the class-representative basis of alternative forms of such a state.

THE IMF, THE WORLD ECONOMY AND ECONOMIC TRANSFORMATION IN SOUTH AFRICA

Especially after the Second World War and with the emergence and consolidation of the hegemony of American capitalism, new conditions and rules were established to ensure the international expansion of capitalism. The international monetary system that was planned at Bretton Woods in 1944, which established the IMF and the IBRD (World Bank), established and laid the monetary foundations for facilitating this expansion. South Africa was one of the 29 countries that signed the Fund's Articles of Agreement on 27 December 1945. This all-pervasive system has left virtually no part of the globe outside its sphere of influence and control. As a country whose industrialisation had its origins largely in the flow of international capital, technology and goods, the South African economy has been closely connected with international developments. The discovery of diamonds and gold in the second half of the nineteenth century precipitated large inflows of foreign capital for the purpose of exploiting the country's mineral resources. The subsequent export of gold and other mainly primary products and the import of machinery, equipment and technology for the growing mining and industrial sectors led to an increase in trading relations with the rest of the world. In short, South Africa has, in the last hundred years, become in this way an integral part of the world capitalist economy. Since the Second World War in particular the economy has become a markedly open one — its international sector (exports and imports) has been and is an important stimulus to economic growth. Foreign investment has played a significant role in economic growth especially in the late 1950s and 1960s. As part of the international economy South Africa has not, however, remained unaffected by cyclical and structural shifts and changes in the balance of power relations within the world economy.

As might be expected, therefore, numerous studies[1] have shown that if South Africa is to expand its productive capacity and grow sufficiently to enable it to meet the demands of a post-apartheid state, it will be hard pressed to do so without some role for international trade, capital flows and technology transfers.

In short, a post-apartheid government will inherit an economy which has for long depended upon and which, in all likelihood, will continue to depend upon its links with the international economy. What implications does this hold for the politics of accumulation in the period of economic and political transformation? Are these international links costless? If not, how do they bear upon the tasks and objectives of economic and political transformation? For as Payer (1974) stresses 'the internal political evolution of a nation is intimately and structurally connected to its external economic situation.' The literature on development abounds with case studies that illustrate the pervasive and perverse influence of certain types of international economic linkages for development. These are the issues which we need to examine and understand clearly. Not all of this, however, can be dealt with in this chapter. Within this larger task the chapter will attempt to examine the influence of South Africa's relations with the IMF on its past and possible future development and independence. It has been established (Payer, 1974; Torrie, 1983; Girvan and Bernal, 1982, among others) that the IMF is more than just an international agency that lends to countries experiencing short-term balance of payments (BOP) difficulties — that in fact it has for long held centre stage as the control and surveillance arm of international economic relations; it has reflected, imposed and maintained, behind a cloak of neutrality, the dominance of Western industrialist capitalist interests, most notably those of the USA. In this role it has, except for a few short uncertain years after 1971, continued to cast a shadow over the world economy. Numerous countries in the developing world have failed to understand, let alone come to terms with, the nature of this international economic agency. A post-apartheid South African state that is at all serious about transforming the political, economic and social distortions of a century of capitalist development — based on the centrality of a racial form — will ignore or underestimate these problems at its peril.

THE IMF AND THE APARTHEID STATE, *c.*1975—*c.*1985

South Africa's membership of the IMF coincides, except for the first three years, with National Party apartheid rule. Smuts, in what was to be his last term as United Party premier, had displayed his 'renowned international statesmanship' in the creation of the United Nations system which included the IMF and the World Bank. Behind its facade of political neutrality, the IMF, despite the increasingly strident and forceful condemnation of South Africa's apartheid policy from the UN, for long felt itself under no obligation to question either the economic or political system of the only country in its membership practising legislated racial discrimination. That only changed in 1983, and only after popular and workers' struggles had brought into question the profitability of continued foreign investment and the stability of the apartheid state in this region — both crucial factors for Western interests in Southern Africa. It is now evident that these Western interest groups — despite some evidence of tension among them — are seeking to influence the direction of political development in South Africa so as to ensure the continuation of the country's present place within that sphere. The international economic system, and the IMF in particular, with all its power to open and close aid and loan 'doors', will be a significant though unseen part of any Western package deal working towards a 'post-apartheid South Africa of a special kind'.

Let us now look briefly at the relationship between the apartheid state and the IMF in the period 1975-1985. South Africa received its first stand-by credit arrangement from the IMF in 1957/58. These loans were agreed to without conditionality or phased disbursals, which even in those early years of IMF lending were being imposed on other borrowers, most notably the Latin Americans. This rather cosy relationship was to characterise South Africa-IMF dealings throughout the history of the IMF and in many respects continues to this day.

The Seidmans (1978, p.75) note that by 1972 the IMF was still providing almost 60% of all short-term non-direct investment funds available to South Africa from the central government and banking sector. This, and later, BOP support, provided by way of loan arrangements in the mid 1970s and again in 1982, best illustrates the special nature of the relationship between South Africa and the IMF. It should be noted at the outset that the loans will be judged against the IMF's own lending policies rather than against any other norm. This will enable us to determine the extent of any preferential treatment received by Pretoria in its dealing with the IMF.

The IMF provided credits in 1975, 1976 and 1977. These mid-1970s borrowings were, according to South African and IMF sources, in support of the government programme to strengthen the country's BOP position. The 1976 credit, for example, was made under the Fund's Compensatory Financing Facility (CFF) with respect to an export shortfall experienced by South Africa during the twelve-month period ended August 1976. The success of the US policy to depress the price of gold in the mid-1970s (directed mainly at the USSR and Europe and carried out partly through IMF gold sales) badly affected South Africa's gold exports and hence its balance of payments. Despite efforts to cut gold production as a counter to the failing gold price the country slid rapidly into a deep recession. South Africa's current account BOP weakened from 1974 as a result of the decline in the price of gold, the prolonged recession experienced by the country's trading partners, increases in the cost of imports because of inflation in the West, the increase in oil prices and what the IMF called expansionary demand management policies.

The case that South Africa put to the IMF thus emphasised mainly externally induced factors: lagging exports, declining reserves and a deterioration in the BOP. But there were other factors affecting the BOP as well, such as the rapid increases in defence expenditure which led to the budget deficits and, in turn, to increases in money supply, to inflation, to a weakening rand and, finally, to BOP problems.

Though defence and law and order expenditure had been increasing from the early 1970s, following internal resistance and external concerns (Namibia), the sudden *urgency* for funds around January 1976 — the month of the first application to the Fund in that year — must be placed within a wider context. As Johnson so dramatically notes (1977: 111):

> By January 1976 all eyes in South Africa were fixed upon a single object — the advance of Cuban troops towards the Namibian border ... beside this all the crises of the 1970s paled. The thing which Pretoria had so long predicted, but so little really believed, had come to pass. A communist army was marching through Angola towards her.

And Soweto — the single word that has come to symbolise the uprising of 1976/77 whose roots were in themselves not unrelated to the recession — was to prove a major influence in the further downward drift of the economy. In the 'politically sterilised' offices of the IMF Executive Board these matters must have loomed large, but were never raised directly.

In November 1976, five months after the Soweto uprising began, South Africa returned to the IMF with another aid request — this time under the CFF. Whereas to gain approval for its earlier standby it had merely to show a need and a programme to correct its BOP, for the CFF (a temporary export shortfall facility) South Africa had to argue that its BOP was caused by factors outside its control. An IMF staff analysis of export performance supported the request for aid. However the staff analysis was severely criticised by some of the Executive Board directors at the IMF meeting.

Over the forty-year history of the IMF it is extremely rare that applications for loans that reach the executive board of the IMF are debated at all. In fact any request that reaches the executive board is assured of approval. Thus the objection to South Africa's application was unusual and yet despite this the dominance of the US and UK vote on the IMF was sufficient to steamroller these requests through.

The IMF loans in 1976/77 helped to steady foreign bank creditors in the face of the Soweto riots, which may also have been the intention behind the loans of 1960/61 following Sharpeville. Thus the IMF and especially the US and UK vote within it played an important support role by overriding economic and the obvious but unvoiced political and moral objections to support — in times of political uncertainty — a member country which was closely integrated into its international network of trade, investment and strategic interest. In fact the IMF BOP assistance to South Africa for the two years 1976/77 was greater than the combined IMF assistance to all other African countries for the same period. In those two years only two other countries, Britain and Mexico, were bigger beneficiaries of IMF aid.

1977-81 witnessed an increasing deterioration in the world economy — affecting most developed and developing countries. Problems of unemployment, inflation and mounting debt dominated international financial discussions. By the early 1980s 'fears' that the IMF was going 'soft' on developing countries were being dispelled following the Thatcher (1979) and Reagan (1980) electoral successes. A much tougher line as regards financial assistance to developing countries was beginning to emerge. South Africa's finance minister, Horwood, was nevertheless able to report at the annual IMF-WB meetings in these years that the country was doing rather well, having turned around the 1974-76 BOP deficit. He attributed the success to monetary and fiscal restraint. However, in 1981 with the gold price declining sharply from over $800 an ounce and imports surging, South Africa again ran up a deficit on the current account of the BOP in the order of a massive $4,380 million. By mid-1982 when it appeared that there was little likelihood of an improvement on the current account, South Africa — despite numerous denials by top financial officials[2] — approached the IMF for a stand-by loan of $1.1 billion. South Africa had already drawn $122 million from its reserve position in the Fund and declared its intention to borrow an additional $132 million through the SDR account. These are automatic and non-conditional borrowing rights that a member may choose to exercise.

South Africa's approach to the Fund was made in mid-1982 but on USA advice was not announced until October 1982 — a few weeks before the IMF executive board meeting. The expectation that the application would be controversial was to prove correct. Opinion ranged from those who urged that the loan not be approved under any circumstances to those who stated that the loan should be approved on condition that South Africa abolished 'apartheid imposed' rigidities, etc. Five IMF executive directors lodged strong technical and economic arguments against the loan at the Board's meeting of 3 November 1982. They argued that the South African loan did not meet the standard of conditionality imposed on other borrowers, in addition to questioning the need for the loan based on IMF predictions of a $1.6 billion trade surplus for 1983.

Altogether seven executive directors representing 68 countries refused to support the loan and called for a postponement. However, executive directors representing the USA, Canada and Western Europe backed the loan. This latter group vote added up to 51.9% of the IMF total and the loan was approved.

SOUTH AFRICA'S PLACE IN THE WORLD CAPITALIST ECONOMY

In 1978 President Carter's national security adviser, Zbigniew Brezinski, identified Iran (still under the Shah), Brazil and South Africa as 'regionally influential nations' noting that changes within these countries will have profound consequences throughout the areas in which they are situated and in the major centres of world capitalism. South Africa's particular role within the global structure of capitalism is, like that of Iran (at the time) and Brazil, that of serving to limit the scope and possibilities for political and economic changes within smaller and weaker states in these regions. Factors such as its constellation of South African states initiative, its vital transport and communications network in Southern Africa, its active market penetration of neighbouring states, its employment of thousands of workers from Lesotho, Mozambique, etc., its regional investment, its numerous military adventures and support for UNITA and the MNR — all are indicative of its involvement in this region and of its destabilising capacity. That South Africa is very aware of the role it plays in this region, and within this sphere of Western interests, is evident from the reaction of top government ministers and officials to the threat of Western disinvestment and sanctions. These officials are quick to point to the damage, both economic and political, that would befall its vulnerable neighbours in the event of such action. And the West too, is well aware of the economic collapse and consequent political destabilisation that will follow any punitive measures South Africa might take against countries as far north as Zambia and Zaire. But these strategic concerns arising out of East-West struggles are not the only tune that South African spokesmen can play. There are, in addition, financial and economic factors that make the fate of South Africa of no small signficance to advanced capitalist countries. These are familiar and well-worn arguments and will be noted here only in the briefest terms. Large-scale Western (US, UK, West German) investments and loans mainly by multinational corporations and international banking institutions generate a substantial proportion of earnings for specific firms and countries in the core areas of the capitalist world economy. Especially during the 1960s and early 1970s South Africa experienced rapid industrial growth and the inflow of large amounts of foreign capital.

It is these profitable outlets and strategic concerns that worker and popular struggles are now threatening, a development which the West is having to come to terms with. For there is now an increasing recognition that the apartheid form of the South African state is becoming an economic and political liability to these Western capitalist interests.

If South Africa in the apartheid years had established its preferential and favoured relationship with Western capitalist interests in general and with its 'specialised agencies' such as the IMF in particular because of its place and functions within the global power structure after the Second World War, then it would be reasonable to conclude that the future form of this relationship will depend crucially on the extent to which a post-apartheid South Africa will continue to play this role — whether this arises willingly, by compromise or by virtual blackmail. This in turn will depend, among other things, upon the class-representative basis of the post-apartheid state which will determine its path of development and its international economic relations and policy.

The form, nature and class character of the post-apartheid state will depend upon a set of objective and subjective factors arising out of the dynamics of working class and popular struggles and there is, in the context of this chapter, little to be gained by any speculative academic forays into this minefield and indeed into how such a non-racial society emerges. However, it is possible and useful to sketch out two or three very broad and admittedly theoretically unrefined scenarios for a post-apartheid South Africa so as to provide a rudimentary basis for evaluating the limits and constraints on its transformation. Within these scenarios development goals and strategies that may arise out of any interaction with the international economic system, and with the IMF in particular, can be assessed. Given the 'openness' of the economy, an already heavy foreign presence, its recent foreign debt problems and the understandable temptation and perceived necessity to encourage continued capital flows these are issues that have to be addressed now.

THE IMF, DEPENDENCY AND THE POST-APARTHEID STATE

There is little in the theory and practice of non-capitalist transformation and development that can be drawn upon by post-revolutionary governments seeking autonomy and independence from the politics and institutions of the world economy. Invariably what this has led to is a development *within* the framework of the world capitalist economy, even when (as in India's experience of the 1960s) this was undertaken in the name of socialism or within a pro-Soviet bloc foreign policy. Two major paths of this type of development may be distinguished. We shall touch upon the first of these and then move on to the second — the mixed economy model — that is more relevant to (and fits the political language that dominates) the current debate on the nature of the post-apartheid South African economy.

The first path would entail — for want of a better word — a classic capitalist path of development with (substantial) reliance on foreign capital and investment as growth generators. Such a development strategy — whether monetarist or Keynesian in character — would arise out of and reflect the dominance and exploitative structures of capitalist relations of production. In other words, the elimination and dismantling of apartheid would, in terms of this model, leave intact the structures of capitalist exploitation. A post-apartheid South Africa under this type of development will find great favour in Western capitals and in the institutions of international finance: the existing rather cosy relationship between the apartheid state and the IMF, for example, will continue. In the absence of the hassle factor of South Africa's racial policies, the relationship may even 'blossom'. And while Western interests in this region will be guaranteed there will be other (local) beneficiaries as well. However, while such an arrangement of the post-apartheid economy will secure the interests of the Reagans and Thatchers of this world, of foreign multinational interests and local economic and political interest groups such as Inkatha, NAFCOC, the FCI, ASSOCOM, etc., the losers will always be the working class and the rural poor whose subjugation or cooption will be crucial to securing continued foreign loans and borrowings from the IMF and the private banks who wait upon the IMF's stamp of approval.

The second path is that of a 'national/popular, mixed economy' or social democratic development option — an admittedly broad range of economic and political policy options bounded on the right by the classic capitalist strategy above and on the left by a socialist model based on workers' control, although obviously excluding the latter. Although clearly the content and form of this particular version of a possible post-apartheid state cannot be specified, in general it would emphasise a strong role for the state, especially in the sphere of the distribution of income/wealth, land reform, nationalisation of 'strategic' industries, some control over national and foreign monopolies, infrastructural development, rural upliftment programmes, and protectionist trade and foreign exchange regulations. The commitment to the social and economic welfare of workers and the rural poor may be and usually is high. In East/West terms the foreign policy of such a government is more than likely to be non-aligned. Two other policies however, invariably characterise such a mixed economy option. First, there is rarely — as evidenced by post-colonial history — an immediate or even gradual attack on the class structure of the society, i.e. the capitalist relations under which accumulation occurs. The result is that control and ownership of a substantial part of the means of production is retained by the bourgeoisie.

Second, given the urgent tasks which have to be faced and met in any post-revolutionary society there may emerge (as in the Nicaraguan experience) a growth strategy that relies heavily on foreign financing. There is the danger that the problem of debt and dependency and its implications for the stability of the state may be overlooked or ignored at this stage. To secure foreign investment and to guarantee an inflow of loans, together with the support of the IMF and (hence) private international banks, offering a place to the bourgeoisie in the 'revolutionary government' may be seen as both necessary and attractive — even if this means acceding to the demands of the bourgeoisie. For example, in post-1979 Nicaragua the 'international community' was regarded as one of the four agents of national reconstruction (Vilas, 1986: 107), in the first development programme of the revolutionary government, 'along with the working people, the *patriotic business sector* and the revolutionary state' (p.107, emphasis added).

This path of development is attractive, and in South Africa it is held by some to be a possible developmental option in the immediate post-apartheid period. It promises a reform of the repressive apartheid state, economic adjustment aimed at alleviating poverty and redistributing income, internal legitimacy and international respectability in the world community of nations. Most of the current anti-apartheid leadership appear to favour this kind of option. Some see it as an interim phase on the road to socialism, while there may even be some support for an option between this one and the first.

Yet there are problems and contradictions in this mixed economy approach which we in South Africa must recognise and come to terms with. In short, the issue is this: what are the implications for economic transformation and development based on such a model that arise from and inform our relationship with the international financial network? The question must be raised now. For it has happened too often that, when revolutionary governments finally understand and pay attention to these questions, what were initially disequilibria have turned into enormous problems: in the final analysis, both the stability and structure of the state can be jeopardised, paving the way for IMF type solutions. While it is unlikely that the West's and the IMF's immediate response to this type of post-apartheid state will be hostile, this does not mean that such a non-aligned national/popular, social democratic government may not be subjected to pressure to adopt a more openly pro-IMF type of development if and when it finds itself having to borrow from the IMF and/or private international banks.

In surveying the mixed economy, post-independence/revolutionary experience of Jamaica, Peru and Portugal — countries which had a sufficient variety of economic, political and historical circumstances to offer conclusions of general applicability, Girvan (1980) comments that:

> Despite these variations, the common bond of their experiences was the overriding impact of the external sector on the behaviour of their economies. It was this factor that provoked economic and political crises when the model of economic growth broke down, paving the way for the intervention of the IMF in the national political economy.

Such a breakdown may be fuelled by the fragility and contradictions of a 'national popular' policy, being an attempt at maintaining mass welfare programmes within a fundamentally capitalist framework incorporating a national and international bourgeoisie. Thus for example, Omvedt (1980) notes in relation to India's national development path that:

> Populism within the framework of imperialism is internally contradictory and it is perhaps natural that now India's ruling class — who after all have no desire to break this framework — are casting envious eyes abroad at countries like Brazil, South Korea, the Philippines which have been following a path of open dependence.

This model of economic growth breaks down because of an inherent crisis of accumulation within its fundamentally capitalist framework. Such crises provide the point of entry to agencies such as the IMF, especially when the country's economy is closely integrated into the world capitalist system. When the crises occur, and especially when BOP problems have surfaced, international financial pressure increases for a 'reform' of this national/popular development strategy as a precondition for investment and loans that will be more acceptable to the West, the IMF and consequently the private international banks. Under this pressure such a government — however strong its commitment to the well-being of the masses — may have little option but to grant even greater powers to the bourgeoisie. It may have to free markets, to freeze wages, to reduce subsidies on food, etc. — in general, to make the turn to the right that spells the end of national sovereignty, involves the capitulation to Western capitalist interests and ensures defeat for the goals and strategies of this development model. There are no glib solutions for overcoming these enormous difficulties in dealing with an inherently antagonistic Western controlled international economic system. Let us look briefly at the experience of other mixed economy countries in this regard.

Given the pressures arising from the Reagan administration's hostility to the Sandinista revolution and the implications this would have for Nicaragua's national reconstruction, in which as we have noted already there was a significant role for the international economy, the Sandinistas attempted to draw the bourgeoisie even closer to its goals — to try to make it 'understand this revolution and its own role in it'. However, as Vilas (1968) notes:

> The basic unity is not so much class but political-ideological support of the aims of the revolution. But given the clearly antagonistic forces involved, the reproduction of this antagonism as an alliance facing another antagonism which appears more urgent at [that] stage requires complex and delicate political leadership. ...
>
> The basic needs of the working classes are not those of the bourgeoisie or the middle sectors. Therefore keeping fractions of the national bourgeoisie within the scheme of national unity and the mixed economy implies having to satisfy some of the needs of this class.

Whereas initially the strategy of national popular unity, a mixed economy and the foreign support that accompanied the strategy was designed to promote economic development, Vilas notes (1986) that — despite the profound commitment of the popular classes, particularly the workers and the youth, to revolutionary transformation — the first six years of the revolution have shown up the 'reluctance of most fractions of capital to undertake commitments that guaranteed their integration in the reconstruction stage at considerable cost to economic growth and the well-being of the masses'. The mixed economy approach to Nicaragua's transformation is no longer a means to economic development but a strategy of survival: breaking with the bourgeoisie 'in response to its negative behaviour — that is to its place in the class struggle' may lead to the severance of Nicaragua's remaining international links. The Sandinistas, moreover, are suspicious of worker autonomy and have severely braked workers' movements.

In Jamaica, Prime Minister Manley was caught in a political contradiction arising out of the class representative basis of his democratic socialist experiment. Faced with falling living standards among the urban and rural poor, the sectors that voted for him, and increasing pressure to abandon his reforms before international investment and loans were resumed, Manley

> attempted to appease his popular base through radical rhetoric while on the other [hand] he tried to appeal to Jamaica's private sector to collaborate with him. Jamaica's businessmen were alarmed

by the rhetoric and they refused to cooperate with the government. Instead they sabotaged its efforts through a virtual investment strike and capital flight. Manley was left with two alternatives, to radicalise his programme toward structural changes in the economy which would involve a confrontation with Jamaica's business and landowning class or to capitulate to IMF policies which essentially favoured that class and fell most heavily on his own political base. Manley opted for the latter and in the process paved the way for his own massive election defeat in 1980 (Latin American Bureau, 1983).

And despite India's particular development path — supposedly a national populist and 'socialist' one — neither the government nor the Indian national bourgeoisie were at odds, in accepting a 1982 IMF loan, with the obviously pro-Western stance of the IMF or with the repression inevitably in store for the dominated classes. Opposition bourgeois political parties, and even the socialist forces in the Janata Party were, according to Omvedt (1982) consistently sabotaging all efforts proposed by left forces to unite in opposition to anti-working class measures. The most significant point that emerges from the Indian experience here is that:

India's IMF loan reveals a situation where IMF conditions, specifically the maintenance of a capitalist path are (in diluted form) not simply forced on Third World nations *but acceded to without much disagreement as a result of the crisis coming from the nature of their own capitalist development*(Omvedt, 1982: 137, emphasis added).

To summarise: it would appear that the seeds for IMF intervention in the management of development in national/popular or mixed economy countries lies in the crisis and contradictions that are intrinsic to their fundamentally capitalist development — crises that may well be exacerbated by welfare and redistribution programmes that initially the government may support. Conflicts of interest may arise between the different classes 'represented' in such a revolutionary government and this may lead to economic and political compromise at both domestic and international levels. Girvan and Bernal (1982) note that for countries dealing with the IMF

Domestic contradictions within the government and the ruling party as well as a lack of a coherent economic strategy which integrates political philosophy with economic management and popular mobilisation can prove fatal to the political survival of the government.

Now it may be argued that South Africa is not Jamaica, or Nicaragua, or India or just 'any other developing or Third World country' for that matter: that the inherent production strengths of the economy, its natural and human resource capacities, existing infrastructure etc. make it qualitatively different from such countries and therefore more resilient to the pressures that might, in a post-apartheid era, emanate from its international economic relations. Thus it may be held that the legitimate concern expressed here on the dangers for a mixed economy model, arising say from entanglement with the IMF, may be overstated. It is true that in comparison with many other developing countries South Africa is much better endowed and developed. Its gold and platinum reserves, especially, may improve its bargaining power in international economic relationships. However, as even Britain discovered in the late 1970s and Australia may soon learn, this is no guarantee against BOP disequilibrium and IMF intervention and discipline. There is no way by which we might even hazard a guess as to the probabilities of disequilibrium in the BOP of a post-apartheid South Africa, as who is to say what will happen to the price of gold, to capital movements, etc. However, the country's present heavy involvement in the world economy; its present integration into and place in the world capitalist system; the uncertain effects of national/popular, post-apartheid internal and external policies on its international links; the economic and political response by the West to such policies — all this, at one level, suggests that the sophistication of the South African economy (its infrastructure, resources, etc.) is in itself no guarantee against possible IMF intervention in its internal economic affairs and autonomy.

At a more fundamental level, however, our point is this: that the substance and logic of the post-1970 revisionist literature and recent analysis of the current crisis have demonstrated that this crisis is not only one of legitimacy — stemming from the apartheid form of state — but is fundamentally one of capitalist accumulation. It has been shown that the apartheid form is itself an historically evolved expression of the way in which capitalist production has developed in South Africa, and that the symptoms of the present crisis — unemployment, inflation, foreign debt, investment slack, etc. — are more than just 'apartheid related'.[3] The present crisis is at base one of capitalist accumulation. The 'mere' dismantling of apartheid will not resolve this crisis. Thus a post-apartheid mixed economy that retains the essence of this capitalist framework predisposes a seemingly more resilient South Africa to crises and hence to vulnerability from external sources. It has yet to be shown that a post-apartheid South Africa incorporating both a national and international bourgeoisie in its transformation can or will be more immune to such intrinsic crises than any other fundamentally capitalist economy.

Given the ideological bias and role of the IMF in the world economy any such intervention will have immense negative implications for the demands of popular and working classes in such a post-apartheid state and for its capacity to pursue an independent path of development, whatever its commitment to these goals may be. One final point is worth making. Those who subscribe to some version of a two-stage view of the transformation from apartheid to socialism, and who therefore support a mixed economy/social democratic interim phase, have yet to reveal or spell out those processes and dynamics inherent in this stage that would begin the irreversible movement to socialism. To leave all this simply to the first stage post-apartheid state's commitment to the well-being of the masses would be to rely on an extremely unusual and mechanistic view of the 'state'. For the power and capacity of agencies such as the IMF both to subvert the goals of a mixed economy form of development, and to brake the transition from a mixed economy to socialism, must not be underestimated.

If the contradictions and tensions of a mixed economy development path, and the costs involved, are so problematic then what are the chances for a socialist option, a 'politics of accumulation' representing the hegemony of working class interests? The problems and pitfalls of a socialist path to reconstruction and development — based on the hegemony of working class interests — are enormous, especially for a country like South Africa which has for long been incorporated in the capitalist world economy.

Any socialist option would be interpreted as a threat to Western economic and strategic interests here and the real danger is that the West will immediately use its financial leverage through organisations such as the IMF to choke off loans, investment and technology flows. The effect will be to slow down economic growth and the ability to extend and improve health, education, social services and rural development among other objectives. There is the danger that a post-apartheid South Africa based on a socialist model characterised by the hegemony of working class interest would be isolated in an attempt to destroy its economy and destabilise it politically, creating conditions for a return to a pro-Western, pro-IMF model of economic and political development. But there is no reason to base a socialist model on the assumption that such a state would inevitably have to go it alone. Cutting all international economic relations is not in itself a prerequisite for a successful socialist transformation. However, if as the outcome of the struggles against the apartheid/capitalist state such a model for development emerges, its class cohesion will help it to negotiate and control the terms on which international economic relations will be conducted, and to withstand and survive the consequences of any international economic backlash. In the socialist model a state founded and functioning as a unitary actor in class terms would not face the contradictions which predispose capitalist or mixed economy models to crises with the conflicts and tensions that facilitate IMF intervention on behalf of Western capitalist interests. This is not, however, to imply that all problems emanating from its international links will be resolved magically. The effect of possible investment, trade and technology boycotts on economic growth and development, and the consequences this will have for political stability, will pose extremely thorny problems and prove a great test of the viability and very survival of a socialist post-apartheid state.

ASSESSMENT AND CONCLUSION

Revolutionary governments, especially in the developing world, have found that it has often been as hard to live with the IMF as it has been to live without its support. A country like South Africa, whose particular form of development has been tied intrinsically to its extensive international economic relations, will find the task of 'living' with this historical legacy in the post-revolutionary era particularly challenging. Its relationship with the Fund is likely to be characterised by increasing tensions, conflicts, pressures and struggles as the scenario moves from the pole of a democratic capitalist state to one of socialism under workers' control. Thus for the working and popular classes, increasing control over their lives may be accompanied by an increasing threat to the very existence of such a state from Western capitalist states seeking to maintain or reassert their economic and strategic interests in this region — which they have identified as being crucial to 'mediating' crises that arise from their own capitalist form of accumulation. In short, the IMF, a supposedly apolitical international agency, can very well form an integral part of the formidable weaponary available to the West in shaping the emergence, nature and development of a post-apartheid South Africa.

We have thus far in this chapter noted (1) the ideological basis and economic philosophy of the IMF; (2) South Africa's integration into the world capitalist system; (3) its place and function in that system; (4) the preferential treatment that the apartheid state has received thus far in return for its role in this region; (5) the experiences of some 'mixed economy' developing countries in their relationship with the IMF; and (6) the potential for and possible effects of IMF intervention in a post-apartheid South Africa.

We have in the end not been able to proffer any easy solutions for managing international economic relations in post-apartheid South Africa. There are in fact no such solutions, short of a fundamental change in the nature of power relations in the world economy. But understanding the difficulties now, and working through the options however limited they may be, is preferable to the inevitability of failure which arises from total neglect or shortsighted dismissal of this aspect of economic transformation and development.

In this spirit we need finally to inquire into some of the areas of planning and policy formulation that might reduce our vulnerability to these pressures — especially those arising from the availability, cost and terms of capital flows and our trading relations with the world economy. As we have noted, virtually all the major sources of credit in the developed capitalist world will refuse to lend to a country which persists in defying IMF 'advice'. Non-capitalist sources of credit/loans would appear to be severely limited, if we are to go by the experiences of even some Warsaw-Pact countries. The following broad issue thus has to be addressed: 'in the area of international economic relations what particular mix of policies, external and internal, will minimise the impact on the living conditions of the masses, maintain room to manoeuvre in the choice [sic] of direction of development strategy' (Girvan and Bernal, 1982), and facilitate the process of transformation to and the development of a stable post-apartheid South Africa.

The first and most fundamental point to be made in this regard is this: that these policies and the development strategies followed are not, except in a technical sense, 'chosen' — they flow naturally from the politics of accumulation, i.e. the class interests that are represented in the pre- and post-revolutionary movement/ state and in the process and manner through which decisions are taken and plans for transformation and development are formulated. This class representation will determine whether or not there will arise a system of production which makes a firm break with those predicated upon capitalist accumulation and the power relations that flow from that system. Outside of this, however, the following policy issues must be considered. We need firstly to understand the need for financial discipline and 'the often painful adjustments in the structure of production [that] are necessary for the health of the balance of payments' (Payer, 1974). In urging developing countries to adopt financial discipline the IMF is perfectly correct, but as Payer notes the problem is that 'by conniving in the rich countries' use of foreign aid as a bribe, the IMF is deliberately frustrating the very type of financial discipline and production adjustments which are most badly needed.' Thus we must have the determination to rationalise and restructure our production, our range of products, our techniques of production, our sectoral priorities, and to discipline our consumption — especially of imported goods — in short, to refashion production to the new demands of a post-apartheid state. Secondly, South Africa is, unlike many other developing countries, well endowed with natural resources and the development of our industrial, agricultural and energy sectors must make maximum use of local resources and develop national technological capabilities. Thirdly, we would need to give greater attention to expanding export markets into Africa, Asia, the East Bloc countries and Latin America, and to give serious attention to a regional development strategy such as SADCC — now including South Africa, of course, as an equal rather than hegemonic partner. For there is sound economic and marketing sense in a regional development strategy, especially a socialist one. The coordination of development within a regional bloc in southern Africa can go some way towards increasing the entire region's 'power coefficient', as it were, in international economic negotiations. Finally, physical controls and planning — in foreign exchange allocation, foreign trade policy, import budgeting and credit and investment budgeting — are direct instruments for coping with our BOP and international economic relations policy. Their use, extent and timing must be debated.

NOTES

1. This has been shown or suggested in numerous studies that have recently been reviewed in the South African press and also by others such as Aubrey Dickman, Gavin Relly, etc.
2. See, e.g., *Financial Mail*, 10 Sept. 1982, p.1235; and 8 October 1982, p.147.
3. See Legassick (1974), Kaplan (1979), Saul and Gelb (1981), Gelb and Innes (1985), Ginsberg (1985) amongst other numerous works both for the early (1970s) and recent period in which the relationship between apartheid and capital accumulation is discussed.

REFERENCES

ADELMAN, S., 1985. 'Recent events in South Africa', *Capital and Class*, No. 26.

CENTER FOR INTERNATIONAL POLICY, 1982. 'The IMF and South Africa', CIP Publication, International Policy Report, Washington DC.

CENTER FOR INTERNATIONAL POLICY, 1984. 'A victory over apartheid', CIP Publication, International Policy Report, Washington DC.

ECKAUS, R., 1983. Evidence before the US House of Representatives Banking Sub-Committee, pp.639-642, US Congress, Washington DC.

GELB, S. and INNES, D., 1985. 'Economic crisis in South Africa: monetarism's double bind', *Work In Progress*, No. 36.

GINSBERG, D., 1985. 'The crisis of the South African state', paper presented at a seminar on 'Critical perspectives on Southern Africa', University of Natal, Durban.

GIRVAN, N., 1980. 'Swallowing the IMF medicine in the 70s', *Development Dialogue*, No. 2.

GIRVAN, N. and BERNAL, R., 1982. 'The IMF and the foreclosure of development options: the case of Jamaica', *Monthly Review*, No. 33, February.

INTERNATIONAL MONETARY FUND, 1985. *International Financial Statistics Yearbook*, Washington DC.

JOHNSON, R.W., 1977. *How Long Will South Africa Survive?* (London, Macmillan).

KAPLAN, D.E., 1979. 'Towards a Marxist analysis of South Africa, a review of B.M. Magubane's *The Political Economy of Race and Class in South Africa*', *Socialist Review*, No. 48.

LATIN AMERICAN BUREAU (LAB), 1983. *The Poverty Brokers: The IMF and Latin America*, London, Latin American Bureau Publishing.

LEGASSICK, M., 1974. 'Capital accumulation and violence', *Economy and Society*, No. 3.

OMVEDT, G., 1982. 'India, the IMF and imperialism today', *Journal of Contemporary Asia*, Vol. 12, No.2, pp.135-136.

PAYER, C., 1974. *The Debt Trap: The International Monetary Fund and the Third World*, New York and London, Monthly Review Press.

SAUL, J. and GELB, S., 1981. *The Crisis in South Africa: Class Defence, Class Revolution*, New York, Monthly Review Press.

SEIDMAN, A. and SEIDMAN, N., 1978. *South Africa and the US Multinational Corporations*, Westport, Connecticut, Lawrence Hill and Co.

TORRIE, J.C., 1983. *Banking on Poverty: The Global Impact of the IMF and World Bank*, Toronto, Between the Lines Publishers.

UNITED NATIONS GENERAL ASSEMBLY, 'Reports of the Secretary General' (various), 'UN press releases' (various).

VILAS, C.M., 1986. 'Nicaragua: the fifth year — transformations and tensions in the economy', *Capital and Class*, No. 28, pp.108, 124, 120.

The following newspapers and journals were used in the text:

New York Times, Wall Street Journal, Nation, IMF Survey. All these plus the *Financial Times* (London), *Financial Mail* and the *Rand Daily Mail* were studied for the period 1975-1985, except for the *Rand Daily Mail* (1976-1983).

Appendix A

THE FREEDOM CHARTER

We, the People of South Africa, declare for all our country and the world to know:

that South Africa belongs to all who live in it, black and white, and that no government can justly claim authority unless it is based on the will of all the people;

that our people have been robbed of their birthright to land, liberty and peace by a form of government founded on injustice and inequality;

that only a democratic state, based on the will of all the people, can secure to all their birthright without distinction of colour, race, sex or belief;

And therefore, we, the peoples of South Africa, black and white together — equals, countrymen and brothers — adopt this Freedom Charter. And we pledge ourselves to strive together, sparing neither strength nor courage, until the democratic changes here set out have been won.

THE PEOPLE SHALL GOVERN!

Every man and woman shall have the right to vote for and stand as a candidate for all bodies which make laws;

All people shall be entitled to take part in the administration of the country;

The rights of the people shall be the same, regardless of race, colour or sex;

All bodies of minority rule, advisory boards, councils and authorities shall be replaced by democratic organs of self-government.

ALL NATIONAL GROUPS SHALL HAVE EQUAL RIGHTS!

There shall be equal status in the bodies of state, in the courts and in the schools for all national groups and races;

All people shall have equal right to use their own languages, and to develop their own folk culture and customs;

All national groups shall be protected by law against insults to their race and national pride;

The preaching and practice of national, race or colour discrimination and contempt shall be a punishable crime;

All apartheid laws and practices shall be set aside.

THE PEOPLE SHALL SHARE IN THE COUNTRY'S WEALTH!

The national wealth of our country, the heritage of South Africans, shall be restored to the people;
The mineral wealth beneath the soil, the banks and monopoly industry shall be transferred to the ownership of the people as a whole;
All other industry and trade shall be controlled to assist the well-being of the people;
All people shall have equal rights to trade where they choose, to manufacture and to enter all trades, crafts and professions.

THE LAND SHALL BE SHARED AMONG THOSE WHO WORK IT!

Restrictions of land ownership on a racial basis shall be ended, and all the land re-divided amongst those who work it to banish famine and land hunger;
The state shall help the peasants with implements, seed, tractors and dams to save the soil and assist the tillers;
Freedom of movement shall be guaranteed to all who work on the land;
All shall have the right to occupy land wherever they choose;
People shall not be robbed of their cattle, and forced labour and farm prisons shall be abolished.

ALL SHALL BE EQUAL BEFORE THE LAW!

No-one shall be imprisoned, deported or restricted without a fair trial;
No-one shall be condemned by the order of any Government official;
The courts shall be representative of all the people;
Imprisonment shall be only for serious crimes against the people, and shall aim at re-education, not vengeance;
The police force and army shall be open to all on an equal basis and shall be the helpers and protectors of the people;
All laws which discriminate on grounds of race, colour or belief shall be repealed.

ALL SHALL ENJOY EQUAL HUMAN RIGHTS!

The law shall guarantee to all their right to speak, to organise, to meet together, to publish, to preach, to worship and to educate their children;
The privacy of the house from police raids shall be protected by law;
All shall be free to travel without restrictions from countryside to town, from province to province, and from South Africa abroad;
Pass Laws, permits and all other laws restricting these freedoms shall be abolished.

THERE SHALL BE WORK AND SECURITY!

All who work shall be free to form trade unions, to elect their officers and to make wage agreements with their employers;
The state shall recognise the right and duty of all to work, and to draw full unemployment benefits;
Men and women of all races shall receive equal pay for equal work;
There shall be a forty-hour working week, a national minimum wage, paid annual leave, and sick leave for all workers, and maternity leave on full pay for all working mothers;
Miners, domestic workers, farm workers and civil servants shall have the same rights as all others who work;
Child labour, compound labour, the tot system and contract labour shall be abolished.

THE DOORS OF LEARNING AND OF CULTURE SHALL BE OPENED!

The government shall discover, develop and encourage national talent for the enhancement of our cultural life;

All the cultural treasures of mankind shall be open to all, by free exchange of books, ideas and contact with other lands;

The aim of education shall be to teach the youth to love their people and their culture, to honour human brotherhood, liberty and peace;

Education shall be free, compulsory, universal and equal for all children;

Higher education and technical training shall be opened to all by means of state allowances and scholarships awarded on the basis of merit;

Adult illiteracy shall be ended by a mass state education plan;

Teachers shall have all the rights of other citizens;

The colour bar in cultural life, in sport and in education shall be abolished.

THERE SHALL BE HOUSES, SECURITY AND COMFORT!

All people shall have the right to live where they choose, be decently housed, and to bring up their families in comfort and security;

Unused housing space to be made available to the people;

Rent and prices shall be lowered, food plentiful and no-one shall go hungry;

A preventive health scheme shall be run by the state;

Free medical care and hospitalisation shall be provided for all, with special care for mothers and young children;

Slums shall be demolished, and new suburbs built where all have transport, roads, lighting, playing fields, crèches and social centres;

The aged, the orphans, the disabled and the sick shall be cared for by the state;

Rest, leisure and recreation shall be the right of all;

Fenced locations and ghettos shall be abolished, and laws which break up families shall be repealed.

THERE SHALL BE PEACE AND FRIENDSHIP!

South Africa shall be a fully independent state, which respects the rights and sovereignty of all nations;

South Africa shall strive to maintain world peace and the settlement of all international disputes by negotiation — not war;

Peace and friendship amongst all our people shall be secured by upholding the equal rights, opportunities and status of all;

The people of the protectorates — Basutoland, Bechuanaland and Swaziland — shall be free to decide for themselves their own future;

The right of all the peoples of Africa to independence and self-government shall be recognised, and shall be the basis of close co-operation.

Let all who love their people and their country now say,
as we say here:

'THESE FREEDOMS WE WILL FIGHT FOR, SIDE BY SIDE, THROUGHOUT OUR LIVES, UNTIL WE HAVE WON OUR LIBERTY.'

Adopted at the Congress of the People
Kliptown, South Africa, on 26th June, 1955.

Appendix B

This book consists of a selection from the papers tabled at an international conference held at the University of York, United Kingdom, under the title 'The Southern African Economy After Apartheid'. The conference was organised by the university's Centre for Southern African Studies and took place over four days in September/October 1986. One hundred and thirty delegates participated, drawn from the United Kingdom (75 delegates), South Africa (33), the United States (6), Norway and Zimbabwe (3 each), Holland, Mozambique and Sweden (2 each), and Canada, Lesotho, Tanzania and Zambia (1 each).

Most of the delegates were academic economists, political economists and sociologists, but economic consultants and representatives of trade unions and business interests, of churches and charities, and of governmental and quasi-governmental organisations also attended and took part in the discussions. Delegates were invited in strict accordance with the Nassau Declaration of the Commonwealth heads of government of October 1985 (see below). The conference was notable for bringing together for the first time in recent years internal and exiled opponents of the apartheid regime. Members of the African National Congress were present with observer status.

Of forty-five written papers tabled at the conference the present selection includes only those dealing with South (rather than southern) Africa and it has been made with a view to conveying the broad range of economic issues which are likely to arise after a transfer of power.

NASSAU DECLARATION
OF THE COMMONWEALTH HEADS OF GOVERNMENT,
OCTOBER 1985

For our part, we have as an earnest of our opposition to apartheid, reached accord on a programme of common action as follows:

(i) We declare the Commonwealth's support for the strictest enforcement of the mandatory arms embargo against South Africa, in accordance with United Nations Security Council Resolutions 418 and 558, and commit ourselves to prosecute violators to the fullest extent of the law.

(ii) We reaffirm the Gleneagles Declaration of 1977, which called upon Commonwealth members to take every practical step to discourage sporting contacts with South Africa.

(iii) We agree upon, and commend to other governments, the adoption of the following further economic measures against South Africa, which have already been adopted by a number of member countries:

(a) a ban on all new government loans to the Government of South Africa and its agencies;

(b) a readiness to take unilaterally what action may be possible to preclude the import of Krugerrands;

(c) no Government funding for trade missions to South Africa or for participation in exhibitions and trade fairs in South Africa;

(d) a ban on the sale and export of computer equipment capable of use by South African military forces, police or security forces;

(e) a ban on new contracts for the sale and export of nuclear goods, materials and technology to South Africa;

(f) a ban on the sale and export of oil to South Africa;

(g) a strict and rigorously controlled embargo on imports of arms, ammunition, military vehicles and paramilitary equipment from South Africa;

(h) an embargo on all military co-operation with South Africa; and

(i) discouragement of all cultural and scientific events except where these contribute towards the ending of apartheid or have no possible role in promoting it.

Papers presented at the Conference on 'The Southern African Economy After Apartheid'

Adler, David. 'Education and training for and in South Africa beyond apartheid.' 15 pp.

Blumenfeld, Jesmond. 'Investment, savings and the capital market in South Africa.' 35 pp.

Campbell, Horace. 'The dismantling of the apartheid war machine.' 34 pp.

Cassim, Fuad. 'Growth, crisis and change in the South African economy.' 60 pp.

Cobbe, James. 'Economic policy issues in the education sector.' 36 pp.

Cobbett, Matthew. 'The land question in South Africa: a preliminary assessment.' 26 pp.

Cooper, David. 'Ownership and control of agriculture in South Africa.' 46 pp.

Danaher, Kevin. 'Bantustan agriculture in South Africa: obstacles to development under a post-apartheid government.' 44 pp.

Davies, Rob. 'Nationalisation, socialisation and the Freedom Charter.' 32 pp.

Davies, Rob and *Sanders*, David. 'Stabilisation policies and the health and welfare of children in Zimbabwe.' 39 pp.

Freund, Bill. 'South African business ideology: the crisis and the problems of redistribution.' 21 pp.

Glaser, Daryl. 'Regional development in South Africa: past and present patterns and future possibilities.' 39 pp.

Hindson, Doug. 'Alternative urbanisation strategies in South Africa: a critical evaluation.' 30 pp.

Jaffee, Georgina and *Cain*, Colette. 'The incorporation of African women into the industrial workforce: its implications for the women's question in South Africa.' 51 pp.

Knight, J. B. 'A comparative analysis of South Africa as a semi-industrialised developing country.' 34 pp.

Lambert, R. 'Trade unions and national liberation in South Africa: past perspectives and current strategies.' 26 pp.

Le Roux, Peter. 'The state as economic actor: a review of the divergent perceptions of economic issues.' 26 pp.

Mabin, Alan. 'Land ownership and the prospects of land reform in the Transvaal: a preliminary view.' 14 pp.

Machingaidze, Victor E. M. 'Customs and trade relations between South Africa and Zimbabwe: the past and the future.' 21 pp.

Macmillan, Hugh. 'Economists, separate development and the common society.' 41 pp.

Macmillan, Mona. 'South African education after apartheid.' 15 pp.

Makgetla, Neva and *Seidman*, Robert B. 'Ownership of capital and its implications for development in a liberated South Africa.' 22 pp.

Maree, Johann. 'The past, present and potential role of the democratic trade union movement in South Africa.' 25 pp.

McGrath, Michael and *Maasdorp*, Gavin. 'Some limits to redistribution.' 51 pp.

Moll, Terence Clive. ' "The art of the possible": macro-economic policy and income distribution in Latin America and in a future South Africa.' 44 pp.

Moore, John. 'Strategic minerals supply interception scenarios.' 41 pp.

Murray, Colin. 'The dismantling of forced removals.' 17 pp.

Mvelase, Abednego. 'Land use and the community: a case study.' 24 pp.

Nattrass, Jill, with Julian *May*, David *Perkins* and Alan *Peters*. 'The anatomy of black rural poverty: the challenge to a new economic order.' 31 pp.

Niddrie, David and *Barrell*, Howard. 'The South African mass media in a post-apartheid society.' 20 pp.

Padayachee, Vishnu. 'The politics of international economic relations: South Africa and the IMF 1975 and beyond.' 56 pp.

Pangeti, Evelyn. 'Zimbabwean manufacturing industry and its export prospects after apartheid.' 20 pp.

Prah, K. K. 'The laager economy and after: some imponderables.' 25 pp.

Rogerson, C. M. 'Late apartheid and the urban informal sector.' 40 pp.

Robbins, Peter. 'The South African mining industry after apartheid.' 12 pp.

Saul, John. 'Class, race and the future of socialism in South Africa.' 27 pp.

Seidman, Ann. 'The need for an appropriate Southern African strategy.' 55 pp.

Simkins, Charles E. W. 'How much socialism will be needed to end poverty in South Africa?' 21 pp.

Simon, David. 'Noose or lifeline? The role of transport in independent Namibia.' 33 pp.

Simon, David and *Moorsom*, Richard. 'Namibia's political economy: a contemporary perspective.' 13 pp.

Southall, Roger. 'South Africa: constraints on socialism.' 26 pp.

Sutcliffe, Michael O. 'The crisis in South Africa: material conditions and the reformist response.' 43 pp.

Webster, Eddie. 'The goals of management and labour: industrial relations in a post-apartheid South Africa.' 34 pp.

Whiteside, Alan. 'The future of labour migration to South Africa.' 41 pp.

Wright, Carl. 'Trade unions and industrial relations in Southern Africa.' 16 pp.

Index

accumulation, 1, 8, 9, 12, 177, 192, 199, 201, 203
African Exploration Corporation, 163
African National Congress (ANC), x, 19, 32, 33, 164, 173, 180; Women's League (ANCWL), 100
agriculture, 1-2, 10, 16, 25, 44, 113, 174, 175, 177; and community use, 69-75; employment in, 55-9, 60, 63-4; and land ownership, 47-55, 61; in undeveloped areas, 59-62; *see also* land reform
Algeria, 1
Allende, Salvador, 23, 26, 28, 168
ANC, *see* African National Congress
Anglo American Corporation, 4, 54, 55, 60, 163, 175, 176, 177, 178, 185
Anglovaal Corporation, 163, 175, 185, 189
apartheid, 14, 109, 112, 139; and capitalism, 9-13, 191-6, 201; political economy of, 36-46
Argentina, 1, 19, 20, 23, 24, 25, 28
assets, 4, 117, 119, 177; redistribution, 24-5, 26
ASSOCOM, 197
Australia, 58, 164, 165, 166, 200

balance of payments, 1-17 *passim*, 19, 29, 193-5, 199, 203; in Latin America, 20-5
bankruptcies, 3, 8, 11; *see also* debt
banks, 3, 23, 185, 193, 197; credit, 3, 51; debt, 8, 52; and monopoly capital, 175, 176, 177, 178
Bantu Authorities Act, 47, 61
Bantustans, xi, 76, 77, 80, 82, 85, 95-6, 146; agriculture, 47, 50, 57, 58, 59, 60-4, 72, 74; forced removals, 36-46
Barclays Bank, 176
Barlow Rand Corporation, 4, 55, 163, 175, 176, 177, 188
Barolong, 38, 39
Basotho, 39
'Betterment', xi, 61, 67-8

birth rates, 147
black businesses, 12, 139
black councils, 10
'black spots', 36, 61, 64
Bloemfontein, 45
Bolivia, 22
Bophuthatswana, 37-44, 45-6, 62, 82, 95, 96
borrowing, 3, 4, 7, 18, 116, 193, 194, 195; *see also* loans
Botha, P.W., 82, 180
Botshabelo, 36, 37
Botswana, 164
boycotts, 102
Brandfort, 38
Brazil, 1, 24, 195
Brits, 96, 103
budget deficits, *see* balance of payments
building societies, 119
Buthelezi Commission, 82
by-laws, 141

Canada, 164, 166, 195
Cape, the, 48, 53, 54, 59, 93, 101, 102
capital, xi-xii, xiii, 7, 112, 113, 117-20, 185; access to, 109-10; concentration, 4, 8, 175, 177, 187; imports, 2, 6, 8, 9, 116-17, 192, 196; and output, 112-13, 123
capital-labour ratio, 5, 16
capitalism, 20, 25, 84, 85, 110-20, 126, 134, 163, 186, 187-9; in agriculture, 51-9; monopoly, 174-8, 180, 181; and regional development, 77-83; world, 191-203; *see also* economy, South African
Carnegie Commission, ix, x
Catholic Church, 64
Centre of African Studies, 184
Chemical Workers Industrial Union, 97
Chesterville, 101
childcare, 90, 97, 99, 100, 101, 104
children, 26, 32
Chile, 7, 19, 20, 22-8, 30, 31, 32, 168

211

China, 25, 31, 32, 84, 87, 126, 130, 140, 166, 171
Ciskei, 59, 80, 82, 95
city planning, 138-42
Clermont, 135, 137
colonialism, x, 181-2
Commercial, Catering and Allied Workers Union, 98
communism, 84, 86, 87; *see also* socialism
community groups, 68-75, 100-3
companies, 3, 4, 8, 119, 121-2, 175-8; mining, 163-4, 166, 167, 168
Confederation of South African Trade Unions (COSATU), 60, 91, 98, 99-100, 107
Congress of the People, 32, 173, 178
conservation, 53
consumer boycotts, 102
cooperatives, 50-1, 52, 53, 55, 63, 64, 102, 132, 174
copper, 168
cotton, 57, 182
Council of Unions of South Africa (CUSA), 98, 99
credit, 7, 50, 52, 193, 194, 195, 203
crops, 71-4
Crossroads, 136
currency, value of, 6, 8, 52, 164, 177

De Beers Corporation, 168, 169
De Kock Commission, 4, 8
debt, 1, 2, 7, 8, 18, 116, 197; agricultural, 52, 54
decentralisation, 76-83, 85, 88, 92, 95-7
defence, 4, 194
deindustrialisation, 6
demand, 2, 3, 5, 23, 31
deregulation, 8, 141
devaluation, 20, 29, 128
developing countries, *see* Third World
Development Bank, 62
developmentalism, 138, 140, 141
Dewetsdorp, 38
diamonds, 167, 168, 169, 192
divestitures, 4
domestic service, 45
drought, 53, 58, 72
Durban, 101, 137

Eastern Cape Farm Workers Union, 60
ecological damage, 53
economic growth, 2-3, 9, 11, 14, 19, 29, 111-12, 127, 192; in Latin America, 20, 21, 23, 24-5
economic policy, 180-1, 197-203; and decentralisation, 77-83; in Latin America, 19-35; *see also* capital; economy, South African; socialism
economy, South African, 1-2; crisis of, 2-13; reform of, 13-15, 19, 28-32; role of women,
90, 92-7; and world economy, 191-203; *see also* capital
education, x, xi, xii, 12, 19, 30, 101, 109, 146-62; Bantu, 146, 153
emigration, 148, 149
employment, 4, 5, 6, 93-6, 127, 128; in agriculture, 55-60; creation, 27, 30, 32, 118, 126, 185; in mining, 165, 167; and women's rights, 97-100
equal pay, 97-8, 100, 104
examinations, 150, 157-8
exchange control, 7, 176
exchange rates, 4, 8, 22, 29
exports, 1-2, 5, 6, 7, 8, 9, 127, 134, 194, 203; agricultural, 52, 59; in Latin America, 21, 22, 29; of metals, 164, 192, 193

Farm Centre Project, 70-5
farmers, 49-50, 52, 54, 55, 175; *see also* agriculture; farms
farms, 48, 49, 51, 53-4, 64; evictions, 36; prisons, 56; tenancies, 55-6; workers, 55-60; *see also* agriculture
FCI, 197
Federated Foods Ltd., 55
Federated Chamber of Industries, 78
Federation of South African Trade Unions (FOSATU), 100, 103, 107
Federation of Transvaal Women (FEDTRAW), 101, 107
finance, *see* economic policy
financial sector, 4, 6, 10
food, self-sufficiency in, 73
Food and Allied Workers Union, 60
Food and Beverage Workers Union, 60
food industry, 54-5, 176
forced removals, *see* relocation
foreign aid, 129
foreign debt, *see* debt
foreign exchange, xiii, 2, 6, 8, 21, 164, 165
forestry, 59
'free market' policies, 4, 78-81
Freedom Charter, x, xi, xiii, 19, 30-2, 63, 129, 173-4, 178, 179, 181, 185, 205-7
freehold tenure, 48
Frelimo, 181-3
Friedmann, Milton, 80
'front-line' states, xiii

GDP, 1-5, 7, 8, 10, 13, 16, 111, 112, 113, 115, 116, 126, 127; in Latin America, 22, 27
Gencor, 55, 163, 175
General Sales Tax (GST), 90, 114, 115
gold, 16, 168, 169, 192, 200; exports, 8, 164, 170; price of, 6, 193, 195, 200; *see also* gold mining
Gold Fields of South Africa Ltd., 163
gold mining, 10, 37-9, 43, 115, 163, 167, 174, 175; in Mozambique, 182; *see also* mining industry

Good Hope plan, 78, 81-2
government expenditure, 3, 4, 7, 8, 30, 32, 115, 121; in Latin America, 21, 23, 27
graduates, 149, 152-3
Great Britain, *see* United Kingdom
groundnuts, 57
Group Areas Act, 47

Hammarsdale, 78
hawkers, 136, 138-40
headmen, 66-7, 73, 74
health and safety, 99, 100
health care, x, xi, 12, 19, 56, 109
Herschel, 61, 64
higher education, 154; *see also* graduates
History Workshops, 136
Hlubis, 66-8
'Homeland' system, 74, 119, 128
household studies, 37-45
housing, x, xi, 12, 19, 30, 101, 109, 118, 119-20; in Bantustans, 42, 45; for farm workers, 56; and planning, 142
Huletts Ltd., 4, 55

Ibuthwana, 68-9
IMF, *see* International Monetary Fund
import substitution, 5, 6, 8, 20, 29, 181
imports, 2, 5, 7, 127, 172, 192; agricultural, 52, 58; controls, 6; in Latin America, 21, 22, 24
India, 197, 198, 200
Industrial Development Corporation (IDC), 177
industrial production, 1, 2, 4, 5
industrialisation, 1, 5, 8, 11, 20, 23, 29, 36, 112, 139, 141, 191; *see also* decentralisation
industry, role of women in, 92-100
inflation, 1, 2, 3, 4, 7, 19, 28, 29, 30, 114, 177, 193, 194, 201; in agriculture, 52, 57; in Latin America, 20, 21, 22, 23, 25
influx control, 36, 56, 59, 60, 76-7, 84
informal sector, xii, 45, 132-42
Inkatha, 197
interest rates, 3, 4, 7, 8, 52, 57, 114, 117
International Labour Office (ILO), 133, 135, 136, 141
International Monetary Fund (IMF), xii-xiii, 7-8, 22, 191-204
investment, xiii, 22, 23, 28, 110-20, 127, 130; domestic, 3, 4, 5; foreign, 1, 2, 7-9, 176, 192, 193; in mining, 171
Iran, 195

Jamaica, 198, 199-200
Japan, 169
job creation, 27, 30, 32, 126
job reservation, 12
job security, 98

Johannesburg, 43, 45, 136, 137, 139, 140; Stock Exchange, 4, 177-8

Kangwane, 80
Kanhym Estates, 55
Kirsch Group, 176
Kliptown, 32
Kromdraai, 37, 39
Kwa Mashu, 135, 136
KwaNdebele, 36, 61
KwaZulu, 61, 62

labour, 5, 10, 46, 55-60, 95-6, 128, 165, 178; *see also* migrant labour
labour force, 37, 56, 93, 94
land, community use, 66-75; ownership, x, xi, 47-65; tenure, 72; values, 51-2
Land Acts, 36, 55, 60-1, 63
Land Bank, 50, 51, 52, 177
land reform, xi, 19, 25, 30, 32, 129, 130, 174, 197; in Latin America, 21, 26, 27
Latin America, 19-28, 30, 31, 33, 171, 193, 203; *see also* individual countries
Lebowa, 95
Lesotho, 195
Liberty Life, 176, 177, 185, 189
licensing, 141
Limpopo Agro-Industrial Complex (CAIL), 183
livestock industry, 58
loans, 119; foreign, 7, 8, 193-7; 199, 200, 203; to white farmers, 49-50
Lonrho, 163
Luncedo Farm Centre, 64

maize, 57, 71, 74
Mangaung, 45
manufacturing industry, 1, 5-6, 10, 16, 48, 113, 139, 166, 178; concentration of, 2; monopolies, 4; women in, 93-7
Marais/Du Plessis Commission, 49-50
'market socialism', 84, 87-8
marketing, 167, 168-71; boards, 50, 171
markets, 25; *see also* 'free market' policies
Marxism, 80, 133; *see also* socialism
Matanzima, 68
maternity rights, 97, 98, 100, 104
Mdantsane, 136
mechanisation, 178, 185; of agriculture, 50, 54, 57-9; in mining, 165-6
mergers, 4, 176, 177
Metal and Allied Workers Union, 103
metals, 164-72, 192; *see also* mining industry
Mexico, 194
migrant labour, 10, 29, 46, 57, 58, 59, 60, 64, 66, 68; in Mozambique, 182
minerals, *see* metals
minimum wage, 96

mining industry, xii, 6, 10, 16, 23, 54, 113, 115, 164, 174, 175, 178; exports, 1-2; ownership, 163-4; role in post-apartheid economy, 165-72
mixed economy, 198, 199, 201
MNR, 195
monetarism, 3, 4, 12, 20-1, 23, 29
money supply, 194; *see also* monetarism
monopolies, 4, 31, 54, 173-8, 180, 181, 185
Mopeli, Chief Minister of QwaQwa, 39
Moposetola, 37
Moretele-Odi, 36
Morogoro Conference (1969), 173
mortgages, 119
Mozambique, 63, 64, 110, 129, 140, 148, 174, 181-5, 195
multinational companies, 2, 8, 20, 23, 31, 62, 96, 165, 175-6, 189, 196

NAFCOC, 197
Namibia, 50, 164, 168, 194
Nassau Declaration, 208-10
Natal, 53, 54, 55, 58, 64, 66, 93, 101
Natal Women's Organisation (NOW), 101, 108
National Financial Accounts, 118, 119
National Forestry Workers Union, 60
National Housing Fund, 119
National Party, 14, 49, 50, 76, 193; *see also* Nationalist government
nationalisation, xii, xiii, 19, 30, 32, 33, 118, 129, 173-4, 177, 178-86, 197; in Latin America, 21, 23, 24, 25, 26; limits of, 29, 31; of mining, 110, 163, 164, 165, 167, 172
Nationalist government, 4, 10, 13, 61, 175
Native Land and Trust Act (1936), 48
Natives Land Act (1913), 47
Nedbank, 176, 177, 188
Ngoanyana, 42-4
Ngwane, 66
Nicaragua, 24, 197, 198, 199
nickel, 168
Nyanga, 136

oil prices, 193
Onverwacht, xi, 36, 37-42, 44, 45-6
Oppenheimer, Harry, 79
Orange Free State, xi, 37, 39, 49, 53, 54, 66
Orange Vaal General Workers Union, 60
output, 1, 2, 4, 5-6, 7, 16, 22, 111-13
overgrazing, 53
overtime, 98

palladium, 168
parliament, white, 49
part-time farming, 53
pass laws, 42, 45, 100
Peron, 23, 24, 25, 28

Peru, 19, 20, 23, 24, 25, 26, 27, 198
'petty commodity production', 134
Physical Planning Act (1967), 78, 95
Pietermaritzburg, 78
planning, *see* economic policy
platinum, 164, 168, 170, 200
political crises, 1, 2, 8
population, age structure of, 147
Population Registration Act, 47
Port Alfred, 102-3
Portugal, 182, 184, 198
poverty, x, 25, 29, 30, 32, 80, 96, 198; in Latin America, xi, 20, 23, 26-7, 28
Premier Foods Ltd., 55
price controls, 22, 25, 30
privatisation, 118
production, *see* industrial production
profits, 3, 115
Programme for Women, 104-5
property market, 4
public enterprises, 118, 121
public ownership, *see* nationalisation

QwaQwa, 36, 39, 46, 80

racial discrimination, x, 93, 148
rand, value of, 6, 8, 52, 164, 177
rationing, 25
RDO, 69-73
recession, 1, 2-5, 15, 193
redistribution, x, 28-35, 130; in Latin America, xi, 19-28
reform, 13, 14, 30, 46
regional planning, xi, 76-7; and decentralisation, 77-83; and socialism, 83-8
relocation, xi, 36-46
Rembrandt Corporation, 175, 176, 177, 178, 185, 189
Reserve Bank, 52
Reynders Report (1972), 6
Rhodes Fruit Farms, 54
Rhodesia, 182; *see also* Zimbabwe
Rosslyn, 78
RTZ Corporation, 163
Rumania, 31

SA Breweries, 175, 176, 177
SA Mutual, 175, 176, 177, 178, 185, 188
sanctions, ix, 196
Sanlam, 175, 176, 177, 178, 185, 188
Sasol, 177
savings, xi, 110, 111, 114-17, 118; domestic, 3, 4, 7, 9, 114, 115
SAVS, 69
schools, 147, 149-51, 154, 161
segregation, 76, 77, 149, 150
self-management, 25, 87, 130
self-sufficiency, 73-5

sexual discrimination, 91-2, 96, 99, 103
shebeens, 136, 138, 139-40
Sheila project, 62
shipping industry, 176
Sigma Corporation, 176
silver, 168
Small Business Development Corporation, 139
small-scale enterprises, *see* informal sector
Smuts, Jan, 193
social services, 19, 22, 23, 25, 27, 134
socialisation, 30, 174, 177, 178-86; *see also* nationalisation
socialism, 104, 118, 127-30, 174, 180-86, 197-203; and Freedom Charter, 30, 31, 33; in Latin America, 22, 23; and regional planning, 83-9
Soetevelde Farms, 54, 56, 63
soil erosion, 53, 61, 67, 68, 72, 73
sorghum, 71, 74
South African Agricultural Union (SAAU), 50
South African Chamber of Mines, 163, 167, 174
South African Women's Day, 100-1
South America, *see* Latin America
South Sotho, 39
Soviet Union, 84, 129, 197
Soweto, 135, 136, 137, 139-40; uprising, 194
spatial equilibrium, theory of, 80
squatters, 43, 55, 60, 136
state, and economic reform, 21-2, 29, 78-83, 111, 185-6; *see also* socialism
State of Emergency, 8, 74
steel industry, 166, 177
stock exchange, 4, 177-8
street trading, 136, 138-40, 142
strikes, 103
structuralist economic reform, 21-8
subsidiaries, 4, 176-8
subsidies, x, 49-50
suburbanisation, 78, 79
sugar industry, 4, 55, 58-9, 60, 62
Sunduza, 68-9
Surplus People Project, ix, 36, 44
sweat-shops, 139
Switzerland, 169

takeovers, 4, 176, 177
Tambo, Oliver, 180
Tanzania, 110
tariff barriers, 6
taxation, 21, 23, 27, 28, 74, 90, 111, 114-16, 141
teachers, 149, 151, 158, 160
technocrats, 81-3
technology, 2, 5, 8, 116, 126, 192; in agriculture, 57-9
tenure, security of, 42, 64
TEXLOM, 184-5, 186

Thaba'Nchu district, 37, 38, 39, 42, 45-6
Theunissen, 38
Third World, xiii, 84, 85, 86, 96, 97, 133, 134, 141, 142, 170, 194-5, 200, 203
Tiger Foods, 55
Tlokwa, 66
Tomlinson Commission, 61, 62
Tongaat Ltd., 4, 55
townships, 135-6, 139-40
Tracor, 74
tractors, 74
trade, *see* world economy
trade boycotts, 202
trade unions, xi, 10, 25, 60, 64, 90, 91, 96, 185; mining, 165-6, 168; in Mozambique, 182, 184; in small-scale enterprises, 142; and women, 97-100, 103, 104, 105
training, *see* education
Transkei, 59, 61, 66-75, 80, 82, 95
transport, x, 142
Transvaal, 44, 48, 49, 53, 54, 55, 57, 58, 60, 93, 96, 101
Tribal Authorities, 61, 67, 69, 70, 72, 73
tricameral parliament, 10
Trust land, 46, 61, 62
Tweespruit, 42-3

unemployment, xii, xiii, 1, 3, 7, 11, 32, 47, 53, 57, 85, 96, 98, 194, 201; in Bantustans, 36, 44; and economic growth, 112, 126-7, 128; of graduates, 152-3; urban, 132, 133, 135, 140, 141
Unemployment Insurance Act, 57
UNITA, 195
United Democratic Front (UDF), 9, 101
United Kingdom, 194, 195, 200
United Nations, 193
United Party, 193
United States, 3, 4, 8, 24, 164, 176, 177, 191, 192, 193, 195, 196, 199
United Women's Organisation (UWO), 101-2, 107
uranium, 164, 167, 168, 169
Urban Foundation, 19, 139
urban planning, 138-42; *see also* informal sector
urbanisation, 10, 45-6, 47, 61, 76-7, 82, 85, 112, 136, 185

Vaal Triangle, 8, 101
Vaal Women's Organisation (VWO), 101
Venda, 59, 80, 82, 95
vertical integration, 164, 166, 171-2
Verwoerd, H., 78
Virginia, 37-8, 43
Volkskas, 175, 176, 177, 185, 189

wage labour, 55-6, 59
wages, x, 28, 30, 31, 32, 96, 130; of farm

workers, 55, 56, 57, 60; in Latin America, 20-7; value of, 7, 8
Welkom, 37-9, 43
Wesselbron district, 37-8
wheat, 57, 71, 74
white farms, 47-60
Wiehahn Report (1979), 4
Winterveld, 136
Witwatersrand University, 136
women, xi, 26, 32, 60, 70; in community groups, 100-3; employment rights, 97-100; exploitation of, 91-2, 96-7, 99, 103-4; in labour force, 44-5, 135, 136

Women's Charter (1954), 90, 107
wool industry, 58
worker control, 30, 130, 181, 184-5, 197, 202
World Bank, 1, 20, 126, 191, 193
world economy, 1, 7, 8, 127, 192

Zaire, 196
Zambia, 165, 196
Zenzele, 69
Zimbabwe, 63, 64, 110, 127, 128, 129, 130, 141, 142; education, 148, 150, 151-2, 153, 159-61; mining, 164, 165, 166, 169, 171